#26
Angeles Mesa Branch Library
2700 W. 52nd Street
Los Angeles, CA 90043

IOO ESSENTIAL MODERN POEMS
BY WOMEN

#26
ANGELES MESA BRANCH LIBRARY
2700 W. 52nd STREET
LOS ANGELES, CA 90043

MAY 1 4 2016

100 ESSENTIAL MODERN POEMS BY WOMEN

Selected by

JOSEPH PARISI

and

KATHLEEN WELTON

Introductions and Commentary by

JOSEPH PARISI

811.08
0585-3

ROWMAN & LITTLEFIELD

Lanham • Boulder • New York • London

Published by Rowman & Littlefield
A wholly owned subsidiary of
The Rowman & Littlefield Publishing Group, Inc.
4501 Forbes Boulevard, Suite 200, Lanham, Maryland 20706
www.rowman.com

Unit A, Whitacre Mews, 26-34 Stannary Street, London SE11 4AB

Distributed by NATIONAL BOOK NETWORK

Copyright © 2015 by Joseph Parisi and Kathleen Welton

All rights reserved. No part of this book may be reproduced in any form or by any electronic or mechanical means, including information storage and retrieval systems, without written permission from the publisher, except by a reviewer who may quote passages in a review.

British Library Cataloguing in Publication Information Available

The editors and the publisher express their gratitude to the sources listed on pages 279–282 (which form a part of this copyright page) for permission to reprint the works in this book.

Library of Congress Cataloging-in-Publication Data

The hardback edition of this book was previously cataloged by the Library of Congress as follows:

100 essential modern poems by women / edited by Joseph Parisi and
    Kathleen Welton.
        p. cm.
    Includes bibliographical references and index.
    1. English poetry—Women authors. 2. English poetry—20th century.
    3. English poetry—19th century. 4. American poetry—Women authors.
    5. American poetry—20th century. 6. American poetry—19th century.
    I. Parisi, Joseph, 1944- II. Welton, Kathleen, 1956- III. Title: One hundred
    essential modern poems by women.
    PR1177.A14 2008
    821'.9108—dc22   2007038495

ISBN: 978-1-56663-741-1 (cloth : alk. paper)
ISBN: 978-1-4422-6004-7 (pbk. : alk. paper)
ISBN: 978-1-4616-0598-0 (electronic)

∞™ The paper used in this publication meets the minimum requirements of American National Standard for Information Sciences—Permanence of Paper for Printed Library Materials, ANSI/NISO Z39.48-1992.

Printed in the United States of America

For
Susan, Mary,
Margaret, and Marilyn,
with love from
their brother

ACKNOWLEDGMENTS

HAVING committed four already, I had thought myself done with anthologies. So I was hesitant before Kathleen Welton, my eventual collaborator, and Ivan R. Dee, my publisher (and best editor), convinced me of the wisdom of compiling a new collection devoted to modern poems by women, an experience that proved continually fascinating and often surprising. To the authors, their publishers, agents, and heirs, our gratitude for allowing us to represent them here, with special thanks to Mary Oliver and Kay Ryan. Despite several requests to her publisher and executor, work by Elizabeth Bishop could not be reprinted in this book because of restrictions the author placed upon her literary estate; but titles of several recommended poems are included in her biographical-critical essay.

Over several decades, first as a teacher then as editor and director of public programs at *Poetry*, I benefited from the scholarship and criticism of several leading historians of women's literature, among them Sandra M. Gilbert, Alicia Ostriker, and Diane Wood Middlebrook, who also graciously participated in various national projects I organized in the eighties and nineties. Though we may have differed at times in our assessments of individual talents, their research and perceptions, like those of many others whose books are listed in the essays below, continued to help inform the selection process for the poems and the commentaries on the poets. In addition, I wish to give particular thanks to Linda Pastan for her advice during the preliminary stages of this book.

Likewise, I am happily beholden to John Francis Phillimore for his lively discussions and sage recommendations concerning British and Commonwealth poets, as well as for his characteristic generosity in allowing me free rein among the rich verse collections in his extraordinary shop, Old World Books, in Venice. While there completing revisions of the essays, I also enjoyed the warm encouragement of my friend Antonella Mallus, whose hospitality, practical aid, and gift of laughter made my time in that marvelous city very productive and most serene indeed.

To the four women to whom this volume is dedicated, I owe much more than words can say.

J. P.

Chicago
January 2008

CONTENTS

100 ESSENTIAL MODERN POEMS
BY WOMEN

INTRODUCTION

FROM THE belatedly recognized, still provocative musings of that great American original Emily Dickinson, to the many masterworks produced in the constant flux of the eventful last century, to the creations by today's most accomplished younger authors, this anthology traces the development of poetry in English by women over the past 150 years. The four dozen outstanding poets represented here are women of richly varied life experiences and highly diverse points of view. Their work demonstrates the similarly wide spectrum of subjects and styles and the seemingly endless inventiveness in methods that have distinguished modern poetry, the new tradition built by women particularly. Acutely perceptive as artists, among the most articulate voices in the language, these poets have witnessed and reflected on key historic events and central social issues, capturing and vividly expressing the spirit of their times.

In memorable lines they offer as well their insights on perennial questions of existence, love and loss, courage and endurance, gained in their separate searches for meaning amid the challenges of the modern world. And they can be very funny too, exposing the lighter (not to mention absurd) side of life and rendering the foibles of human behavior with rapier wit and ingenious wordplay. Across the decades they speak as authentic individuals—and as one human being to another—in language that is illuminating, accessible (degrees in literature *not* required), and immensely engaging. These are poems to read and reread, to treasure, and above all to enjoy.

Many poems that have achieved the status of classics are presented in the pages that follow, but several other less often reprinted but equally fine pieces by the major authors are included as well, the better to display the range of their interests and accomplishments.

The collection also turns attention again to a number of superior poets once highly celebrated then unjustly neglected—among them Elinor Wylie, Edith Sitwell, Sara Teasdale, and Phyllis McGinley—whose finely crafted lines well deserve revisiting. The pioneering pieces of the daring Mina Loy may prove a revelation while the facts of her free-spirited life may raise some eyebrows, even now as they did almost a century ago. Among the several contemporary writers making appearances are poets whose exceptional talents and unique perspectives should also surprise and stimulate (and amuse) readers meeting them for the first time.

Although many of the authors gathered here are renowned, even the most famous among them, Dickinson included, are not as thoroughly known perhaps as once thought, and may still not be fully appreciated. Thanks to the ongoing investigations of literary researchers, many new facts have been uncovered and old errors corrected, while probing critics have offered fresh interpretations that reveal depths previously unplumbed in the complex art of several of the authors. Some of the more interesting recent scholarship and criticism informs or is listed in the biographical essays preceding the work of the poets.

These prefatory notes place the selections in their literary and larger contexts, tracking movements and trends together with the major historical changes and several cultural transformations that have reshaped society, repeatedly, from the late 1800s to the turn of the present century. In the prefaces I also outline the major facts of the authors' personal lives and professional careers, highlighting, where appropriate, the technical development, aesthetic movement or stylistic school, and so on, that particular poets may have contributed to or been involved in.

Most of the essays offer brief commentaries on individual poems, their backgrounds, structures, and technical elements, or other points of interest. More specific information on unusual terms, historical references, literary allusions, and so forth will be found in the Notes to the Poems at the end of the book. The not-so-hidden agenda of all anthologists is to tempt readers so that, having enjoyed the samples, they will want to become further acquainted with the work of the authors who please them. To that end, titles of the writers' poetry collections and books in other genres are listed, as well as biographies and selected critical studies that will be useful to those who wish to pursue further explorations.

In short, arranged chronologically by birth dates of the authors—and perused in that order, though readers may well prefer to skip to their favorites or pick and choose among the selections as their fancy leads them—the anthology offers a concise Lives of the Poets along with the poems, forming a capsule chronicle of the evolving story of the art of poetry as practiced over fifteen decades by women throughout the English-speaking world.

In the interest of clarity as part of this general overview—and because certain topics are more easily discussed at the start, in one place, rather than repeated throughout the book—a few preliminaries are in order. First among them is the term and definition of "women's poems." Perhaps the best way to approach the matter is to turn to a very wise poet for her views on the subject.

Noted (and notorious) for her irreverent poems on love and sex, Fleur Adcock was asked by an interviewer in 2000 to respond to critics who felt that she had "gone some way to resist the label 'woman poet'" and had "perhaps attenuated the gender question." She replied:

> Well, yes, I'm a human being poet but I do happen to be a woman and I write about a lot of women's concerns. And I think that's the dividing line. I write about things in which women are interested: childbirth, family life, relationships from a woman's view, women's histories, women's health and social questions to do with women. That's what the function of a female poet is. But I don't think you address yourself exclusively to women. That would be to deny half the audience. And I've never felt like that about poetry.

Although she was interrogated in a magazine ominously called *Thumbscrew*, Adcock spoke under no apparent duress, with her usual candor. Most of her peers would probably concur with her analysis of the favorite subject matter and "the function of a female poet," as well as her aim to embrace a wide audience, male and female.

Certainly Adcock's poems—like those by most women, including the authors represented in this anthology—are not for women only. Besides offering their particular takes on the timeless topics of love, marriage, and family relations—which seldom are "women's issues" exclusively, since they ultimately affect everyone—the poets here usually examine larger frames of reference, philosophical questions, or cultural conditions, notably our connections to the community at large and the realm of nature. In well-considered words they also offer wisdom earned while coping with daily practical realities, some of them questions literally of life and death.

Adcock herself sidesteps the name "woman poet," perhaps for the same reasons that this anthology, in its title and its contents, avoids "women's poetry." Besides being misnomers and too restrictive, as noted, the terms today bear unfortunate associations with the sort of old-fashioned versifying that has given poetry a bad name. Very popular in the nineteenth and early twentieth centuries, and even now in some quarters, and identified primarily (if inaccurately) with genteel ladies with three names (several of the sweet songsters were gentlemen), these lyrical effusions were high in lofty sentiment but rather low in genuine thought: short and saccharine, "uplifting" if vaguely abstract, given to cliché emotions and conventional opinions.

Further, and with especially perverse irony for women themselves, the soft-focus portraits of fair damsels in such verse (as in much nineteenth-century fiction) were far from benign, despite their rosy trappings. Retrograde "women's verse" not only reflected but helped reinforce the hoariest, most debilitating stereotypes about the supposedly "weaker sex" and their "place" in society. Fragile, ethereal, angelic—sensitive but unsensual, indeed desexualized— these near-saintly figures were placed on the proverbial pedestal. For middle- and upper-class women this flattering but false image and dubious honor could not quite disguise the less lovely facts, that those so "elevated" felt (as the cliché has it) like birds in a gilded cage. (Females among the working poor enjoyed no such luxuries, of course, and continued to toil exceedingly long hours alongside the men and children in the fields, shops, factories, and even mines of increasingly grim industrialized nations.)

"Protected" but in truth imprisoned within their restricted "sphere" of home and hearth, dominated by patriarchal figures there as in public life, women of the middle and higher social orders had little real power and virtually no control over their own persons, property, or offspring. Only after a struggle of some seventy-five years did the much-derided suffrage movement succeed in gaining the vote for women, and thus by extension their full rights as equal citizens—in 1918 for those over thirty in Britain, in 1920 in the United States as a whole—rather late indeed, and then mainly in response to their huge, unprecedented, and indispensable labors in factories and hospitals and service on battlefields supporting the war effort.

Before this liberation, "women's verse" both in subject matter and style—heavy on feeling, light on serious intellectual content—reflected and underscored the widely held belief in the lower mental capacity of the "female race." (Some still pondered whether the "opposite" sex was fully human or a separate subspecies.) Besides the old legal restrictions, equally effective (and pernicious) in keeping women in their inferior positions was the system of education, or lack thereof. Ensuring that misogynistic presumptions of females' rational deficiencies were not tested or contradicted, women were usually denied the rigorous training that boys received even on the grammar school level, and were not permitted to attend university. In higher education, America led the way for women with the founding, in 1847, of Mount Holyoke Female Seminary (later College), where Emily Dickinson studied for a time, followed by Vassar in 1865 and Smith and Wellesley in 1875. Meanwhile, the opening in London of Queen's College, an elite all-girl "public" school, was marked in 1848, then the establishment of the women-only Girton College (1870) and Newnham College (1871) at Cambridge. (Even so, graduates were denied regular degrees from Cambridge until 1921, and received full membership only in 1948.)

Outside the regular educational establishment, women who were determined and fortunate to have access to books (and the free time to read them) could and did educate themselves, of course. Those without such resources and caught in very limited environments (that is, the vast majority) perhaps could not be blamed for lack of high intellectual achievement. But Emily Dickinson, who did have the opportunities and extraordinary mental resources too, and made the most of them, seems to have had little patience with women of her class who were conventional, complacent, and unaccomplished. She may well have had such souls in mind—both the unthinking ladies in church pews as well as the producers and consumers of insipid "women's verse"—when she wrote in scorn:

> What Soft—Cherubic Creatures—
> These Gentlewomen are—
> One would as soon assault a Plush—
> Or violate a Star—

Her own brainy independence led Dickinson to withdraw from society, while her unorthodox thought and irregular compositional methods rendered her poetry unacceptable by the literary standards of her time. (In 1863, at the height of her powers, she reflected: "Assent—and you are sane— / Demur—you're straightway dangerous— / And handled with a Chain—".) Three decades after her death, other independent-minded, highly original women who followed her in rebellion against the passé propositions and stifling poetic norms that still prevailed in the new century found their own experiments and innovations facing incomprehension and resistance.

Like them, Dickinson had the benefit of a fairly advanced scientific education for the time, and with her native curiosity she came to hold advanced concepts about nature and deeply skeptical, even heretical opinions about religion. But in the late nineteenth century, and well beyond, typical "nature poetry" and "women's verse" (often synonymous) persisted in pre-Darwinian Romantic reveries while ignoring current affairs almost entirely. From their escapist bucolic ruminations, a reader could conclude that these dreamy rhymesters were unaware that the electric lightbulb and the telephone or automobiles and elevators had been invented. Fond of moralizing too, standard practitioners tended to recycle traditional beliefs and received pieties with suitably decorous (that is to say, stilted and archaic) language and hackneyed poetic formulas.

It was precisely these kinds of creaky notions tricked out in threadbare artifices that provided negative inspiration to the aesthetic reformers and innovators who revolutionized art and literature in the early decades of the last century. To a better-educated generation, female and male, coming of age in the early 1900s, both the old-time worldviews and the old-fashioned methods of such anemic verse were tiresome, philosophically untenable, increasingly irrelevant, and inadequate for expressing the complexities of a scientific, rapidly changing, ever more urbanized modern society.

In their separate ways the iconoclasts—several women foremost among them—cleared away hackneyed expressions and empty platitudes, limp phrasing, and equally flaccid rhythms, replacing them with clear images, precise diction, and a more forceful, contemporary tone of voice, the better to represent the New Age with its progressive thought and swift action. For the adventurous younger poets seeking release from moribund ways and a chance to make their mark in fresh art forms, the brave new experiments were exhilarating, and far more accurate in depicting the modern world with its fragmentation, uncertainty, speed, excitement—and freedom.

Mocked when the first sensational examples appeared in avant-garde little magazines around 1912, Modernism was in full sway by 1915 and all the rage by the end of the decade. The novel styles and uninhibited attitudes these radical poems expressed were firmly established during the Jazz Age. This rapid triumph was possible because the core beliefs and cultural values that had supported the old hierarchies (and traditional poetry) had been eroding for years. The intellectual underpinning finally collapsed in the cataclysm of the Great War, during which millions of soldiers and uncounted civilians were slaughtered with ruthless efficiency through mass applications of mechanized arms. The carnage brought an end to much wishful thinking and to most of the dynasties that had ruled the Continent, discrediting the values that had sustained the ancient regimes along with their rigid social structures.

Reflecting and sometimes anticipating the breakdown of the old systems, the challenging methods of what came to be called the New Poetry—especially free verse and the use of ellipses, verbal collages, abrupt juxtapositions, and other disjunctive techniques—were disconcerting to establishment publishers, traditional verse writers, and their readers alike, particularly lovers of comfortable genre pieces and inspirational verse. Leading the avant-garde were Ezra Pound and his "protégé" Hilda Doolittle, forever known as "H.D., *Imagiste*" for her spare, boldly concrete early work; the cerebral and unpredictable Marianne Moore; and the astonishing Mina Loy, a bold visual artist as well as a fearless writer. Long overshadowed by Pound, T. S. Eliot, William Carlos Williams, and other men who have received the major credit for the Modernist revolution, Loy was equally if not more original in her ideas and techniques, and certainly the most audacious in her free-spirited personal affairs. In her spiky lines, jarring jumps in thought, free association, neologisms, and advanced psychology, she pioneered many methods of the more famous male innovators, especially Eliot, who may well have borrowed from her brilliant ideas. (Loy lost interest in literary experiments, and pretentious male experimenters, and voluntarily left the field rather early. H.D. gradually altered her methods but continued to work steadily even though her later poetry, and prose, did not receive careful reading or appreciation until many years after she wrote it.)

When styles changed abruptly through the Modernist revolution, the transformations were not simply a matter of aesthetics: the new forms prefigured then depicted the profound shifts in the fundamental principles and structure of society itself, not least the role of women. But amid the rampant *vers libre* variations of the New Poetry, it should be noted, the old formal verse did not die. (It never has.) Sophisticated young stylists who continued to use traditional forms and techniques, with great panache—notably Edna St. Vincent Millay, Elinor Wylie, and Dorothy Parker—adapted old modes (particularly the sonnet) to new attitudes. If the up-to-date writer could no longer employ stilted, unnatural constructions, obsolete expressions, and archaic diction like "thou," "prithee," "swain," and "forsooth" with a straight face—though Millay persisted, and got away with it—she could still apply these devices with a smirk: for example, to mock old-fashioned mind-sets, especially those about relations between the sexes, which such outmoded terms and methods had long expressed.

We've come a long way, as the old TV ad so blithely put it. Just how far, and by what diverse routes and through what difficulties and setbacks—but with what great delight and exuberance too—many of the poems that follow will demonstrate.

Selecting them was a challenging but inspiriting task. Anyone entering even the mid-sized book store of today cannot help but be impressed, not to say daunted, by the sheer volume of poetry volumes typically on display. Confronted with this embarrassment of riches, even professionals—critics, editors, instructors, poets themselves—must feel overwhelmed at times. Yet even these towering assortments represent but a fraction of recent poetry in English, with only the choicest siftings from decades past. (To keep truly up-to-date with just the new production would require reading three books of poems a day, every day, each year, while trying to track down the thousands of pieces scattered in hundreds of issues of little literary magazines.)

Where to begin, then, particularly if the inquisitive reader isn't a specialist? Out of such profusion, which modern women writers and which of their poems are most important, truly the ones that everybody ought to know? Having been a poetry editor for almost three decades, I discovered, was a mixed blessing in trying to answer those questions. I had a fair notion where to start, but then I found it hard going when it came to the actual picking-and-choosing among authors, especially favorite ones I had printed often. (A number of these women have given me sage advice over the years, including on preliminary long lists for this book, and I remain grateful for their suggestions.) In a former life I was also an English professor, which helped when considering larger literary and cultural contexts.

Even so, settling on a final selection of poems that could reasonably be included on a "100 Essential" list took longer and more effort that I had anticipated. From the outset and throughout the process I enjoyed the good counsel of my astute and always enthusiastic collaborator, Kathleen Welton. From the immense number of excellent poems written by women over the last century and a half, we settled on an initial long list, which was reduced to a more manageable group of semi-finalists. Then, after much deliberation (and with more than a few pangs), we arrived at the poems printed below. In the end, we cheated: I confess, happily without thumbscrews, that besides the one hundred poems enumerated in the table of contents, more than fifty others, in their entirety or in excerpts, have been inserted into the prefaces to the individual authors.

What were the criteria? For inclusion in a compact anthology concentrating on the most *essential* among *modern* poems, the candidates had to demonstrate (as with those in an earlier anthology by this name) certain basic attributes—the three Ms if you will—superbly well. The seven score finalists that emerged share these qualities: First, they are of course modern, in the most pertinent senses of the term. Second, they are meaningful, they have significant things to say—provocative and profound ideas, wise and frequently witty observations—about the human condition. Finally, they are memorable: what the poets state is expressed in extraordinarily well-chosen words, in striking images and arresting metaphors, turns of phrase that stick because of their singular aptness and grace—language one not only keeps in mind but takes to heart, and might wish to learn (as the idiom has it) *by heart*.

To begin, then, all of these poems, while various in subjects and styles, are distinctively modern, though not in the restricted sense of the term as used by literary historians to define works produced in the formative decade of the Modernist movement, 1912–1922, and exhibiting its technical innovations. While this book features several masterpieces written during that revolutionary epoch in the arts, it includes poems composed before and since that period that are modern in the wider, more common sense, as when we say "modern mentality." Created starting in the mid-nineteenth century, the dawn of several of the most fundamental aspects of what became a profoundly different age and outlook, these are works by artists who were attuned to the new as it was emerging and express a consciousness shaped by those particular realities that have formed our complex, often conflicted, and ever-evolving civilization. Because many of the perceptions about this "brave new world" by the earliest contributors to this volume were so original, their poems still have currency. Even ten and more decades after their composition, the verses, the *visions* of Dickinson and H.D. seem startlingly contemporary.

Several others of the women represented in this collection helped alter the course of poetry by their innovative methods. Their bold experiments and subversive attitudes about both art and society often upset the status quo and aroused controversy when they were introduced, but in many cases have now become standard procedures and an integral part of the fabric of modern culture. Some of the inventions changed forever not only the writing of poetry but the very perception of it. "Make it new" was Ezra Pound's command, which H.D. was among the very first to execute, and it became the motto of the other Modernists and all who have followed them in search of fresh ideas and original modes of expression.

Those interested in the course of literary history can trace the principal routes, major side roads, and several scenic byways (as well as some interesting detours) through the selections in this book. They illustrate prevalent trends and topics, from the early experiments in the free verse and Imagism of high Modernism to the brash new rhythms and often cynical attitudes of the Jazz Age following the Great War, then the important aesthetic, artistic, political, and social transformations that followed. The women writers who emerged in the late twenties and thirties were among the most outspoken social critics and forward-thinking commentators on the disasters wrought by the Great Depression, as well as the producers of some of the most elegant, well-wrought forms in the middle decades. They also recorded the harrowing experiences of World War II with its horrific effects on innocent civilian populations.

Both the conservative and the countercultural reactions to the conformist culture of what Robert Lowell called "the tranquillized Fifties" were emphatically stated in poems by women. The surrealistic, Deep Image, and especially the Confessional modes, along with the protest poetry of the sixties and seventies, are well represented among their efforts. The highly influential consciousness-raising, visionary pieces by leaders of the feminist movement became manifestos and inspirations for generations of women during and after its exuberant, transformative Second Wave.

Likewise, generations of African-American women provided moving depictions of the vibrant daily life of their communities, before and following the black liberation movement of the sixties and seventies, reporting and promoting the sea changes that have moved society, at least partially, toward true equality. Further legacies of the civil rights movement and the sexual revolution of that period allowed the voices of other ethnic, sexual, or gendered minorities to be heard—like women generally, they were long denigrated, dismissed as inferior, denied full recognition because of their "differences"—and continue to enrich and expand American poetry into the new century. All these varieties of human and artistic experience, and the extensive range of styles these unfettered poets have fashioned—experimental and formal, mainstream and minority—are represented in the poems that follow.

This collection includes examples (several of them noted ones) of free verse and favorite poetic forms, including the sonnet and sonnet sequence, the ode, as well as lyrics, elegies, satiric stanzas, meditations, and verse narratives. But these poems were not selected only or primarily for their exemplary technique, important as that is. All too often poetry practitioners and scholars place their emphasis heavily on methodology, to the neglect of meaning. The unfortunate impression left by the high Modernist movement, particularly as represented by the esoteric, allusive, "impersonal" style of T. S. Eliot and Ezra Pound, was that the art was "difficult," willfully obscure, contorted, and tricky. The unhappy result of this very partial picture was that *all* poetry acquired the forbidding aura of impenetrability, even though the vast majority of poems written over the decades are fairly straightforward and certainly do not require several academic certificates to appreciate—as the poems here will pleasantly demonstrate.

Inspired and inspirational, intensely felt, worldly wise, and often wickedly funny, these one hundred–plus poems may be justly called *essential* in that they deal with the most fundamental issues everyone eventually faces and express in unforgettable ways the deepest experiences that make us human: love, friendship, family bonds (and frictions), longing and loss, dreams and disappointments, anxiety, suffering, joy, and our relation to nature. It will hardly be surprising, considering the violent history of the past century, that war, death, and disillusionment are frequent topics in these poems—or that the deepest personal and cultural disasters have elicited from poets some of the most moving eloquence in the language.

But beyond fine phrasing, we have come to expect something more from our better poets: wisdom. Although their original positions as prophets and oracles seem to have passed, their ancient roles as mythmakers and sages have not. Thus the great poets have created the images and stories that identify our culture. Occasionally they give us something more personal: ideas and feelings we really did not have, or know we had, until they found words for them and revealed them to us.

Such, then, are the standards upon which this anthology is based. From Dickinson and Amy Lowell to Marianne Moore and Ruth Stone; Dorothy Parker and Louise Bogan to Mary Oliver and Rita Dove; May Swenson to Louise Erdrich; Muriel Rukeyser and Stevie Smith to Maxine Kumin and Anne Sexton; Sylvia Plath to Louise Glück; H.D. to Heather McHugh; Edna St. Vincent Millay to Adrienne Rich—the collection features poets who have best expressed the condition and spirit of modern times. These women and the other poets in the anthology, acclaimed or not as well known (yet), speak compellingly about the perennial concerns of the human heart.

It goes without saying that this anthology, like all anthologies ever assembled, could have included other authors and additional or alternative choices. But after scanning the collection, the candid reader may agree that each of the poems deserves its place among this select company. And if you find the company entertaining and enlightening, or cause for argument, perhaps you will want to revisit your local bookstore or library in search of other companions, perhaps with this short guide by your side.

EMILY DICKINSON

❏ Independent in spirit, unorthodox in thought, and disturbingly original in both the content and form of her art, Emily Dickinson became the most famous unknown American poet of the nineteenth century. Although she was prolific, only ten of her poems appeared in print during her lifetime, in obscure papers, and then anonymously and altered, submitted by friends. Her advanced views and odd techniques proved puzzling or unpalatable to her first readers. Unlike her diversely innovative contemporary, Walt Whitman—the other great godparent of American poetry—Dickinson did not have a talent or inclination for self-promotion. And so her public career did not begin until four years after her death. Even then, her true character remained veiled, when her "irregular" lines were smoothed out by well-meaning editors. No matter: from the first, heavily blue-penciled collection of 1890, her distinctive poems grew in popularity, surprising the publishers by selling out eleven editions in two years.

First reviewers were quick to point out her idiosyncrasies and "errors"; one noted that not one stanza "cannot be objected to upon the score of technical imperfection." Unlike Whitman's expansive, operatic, all-embracing stanzas, Dickinson's short verses, many based on hymn forms, are pithy, elliptical, elusive, their social and philosophical "Circumference" (to use her apt term) ever more finely focused. Many friends to whom she had showed her work criticized it for its deviations from poetical norms of the time, but she was unwilling to "correct" her lines or otherwise mold her verses to fit prevailing tastes. She did ask for "instruction" from one "Master" and even promised "Obedience" to another "Preceptor," but ultimately she refused to dwindle into a typical nineteenth-century poetess. By the early 1860s she was composing as many as three poems a day. She wrote a friend what amounts to a declaration of authorial independence: "My country is Truth . . . I like Truth—it is a free democracy."

Successive editors also felt free, and in each new collection over the decades they continued to "improve" her posthumously, changing words or lineation and modifying punctuation in those less adventurous poems they selected from the several hundred that she left—many neatly sewn into pamphlets (or "fascicles")—to be discovered in her desk drawer after she died. While she was misrepresented in this altered state for some sixty-five years, myths grew around the quirky spinster of Amherst who preferred to dress all in white; some of the distorted image was fostered by her first editor (and her older brother Austin's intimate friend), Mabel Loomis Todd. Dickinson became stereotyped as an ethereal, eccentric soul, neurotic or worse, the proverbial "mad-woman in the attic"—or rather bedroom, where she shrewdly retreated to labor at her art.

Not until 1955 did the authentic author emerge, when her poems were collected in three volumes, and presented at last as she intended, by Thomas H. Johnson: 1,775 poems revealing spiritual depths (and doubts) and stylistic complexities previously unsuspected. Three years later, her correspondence required another three volumes—some one thousand letters, yet only one-tenth of what she probably wrote—which disclose a far more complicated personality than the figure of legend. Forty years later still, R. W. Franklin's definitive edition (also in three volumes), based on some 2,500 surviving manuscripts, further clarified and dated the texts, raising the total number of Dickinson's poems to 1,789.

Emily Dickinson was born in Amherst, Massachusetts, December 10, 1830, to a family prominent in New England since the Puritan landings of the seventeenth century. Her grandfather was a founder of Amherst College. Her father, a respected lawyer, served as treasurer of the school, and sat in the U.S. House of Representatives shortly before the Civil War. High-minded and humorless, he did not approve of his daughter's taste for Victorian novels, but brother Austin smuggled them in. Her other reading ranged from the Romantic poets to the weighty tomes of the physician-philosopher Sir Thomas Browne. After her father's death, she recalled: "His heart was pure and terrible and I think no other like it exists." Of her other parent, Dickinson left the quietly devastating comment: "Mother does not care for thought." Given to illnesses, their mother left the household management to Emily and her younger sister Lavinia ("Vinnie"). Although her siblings shared Emily's sense of humor and love of riddles, they were often bewildered by her gnomic remarks.

Happily, she was allowed to do as she pleased; and as a daughter of an affluent family, she was not forced to find work, or to marry. In her father's house, the Homestead, she entertained their many friends while maintaining her own "domain": the garden, the kitchen, and her bedroom-study. She also received an exceptionally rigorous education for a young woman of her time. From 1840 to 1846 she attended Amherst Academy, where Edward Hitchcock, a scientist as well as minister, had installed an advanced curriculum. Half her courses were in the sciences, including botany, geology, astronomy, and "mental philosophy" (psychology). Dr. Hitchcock found that science and religion were not so much contradictory as complementary: nature too was "God's book" and could be "read" by scientific observation to discover spiritual truths. Dickinson was always precocious, but her own search and strong sense of skepticism may have been inspired during this period. She would later write:

> "Faith" is a fine invention
> For Gentlemen who *see*!
> But Microscopes are prudent
> In an Emergency!

Throughout her poetry, the early scientific training appears not only in her diction (*axiom, distill, experiment, incision*) but in her questioning attitude, above all in her musings on human mortality.

At sixteen, Dickinson entered Mount Holyoke Female Seminary (later College) in South Hadley. When the principal, Mary Lyon, began proselytizing the students and asked those who wished to become Christians to rise, Emily remained seated. She left the school at the end of her first year. Likewise, when popular evangelical revivals came to Amherst, she refused to stand up alongside her family and friends and declare she was "saved." Since such nonconformist behavior from a member of a leading family did not go unnoticed, her independence required some courage. "I am standing alone in rebellion," she noted.

Dickinson never in fact joined the church, and after about age thirty she stopped attending services. She wryly explained in an early poem: "Some keep the Sabbath going to Church / I keep it, staying at Home—." For one thing, she probably was not fond of some she encountered in the congregation, such as the supercilious ladies with "Dimity Convictions" for whom she expresses such contempt in a tart poem, no. 675, from 1863:

> What Soft—Cherubic Creatures—
> These Gentlewomen are—
> One would as soon assault a Plush—
> Or violate a Star—
>
> Such Dimity Convictions—
> A Horror so refined
> Of freckled Human Nature—
> Of Deity—Ashamed—
>
> It's such a common—Glory—
> A Fisherman's—Degree—
> Redemption—Brittle Lady—
> Be so—ashamed of Thee—

More important, she objected to the early coercion of being "Baptized, before, without the choice," and declared:

> I'm ceded—I've stopped being Their's—
> The name They dropped opon my face
> With water, in the country church
> Is finished using, now,
> And They can put it with my Dolls,
> My childhood, and the string of spools,
> I've finished threading—too— . . .

Thereafter, "With Will to choose, / Or to reject," she set her solitary course. With the passing years she withdrew ever further from society, until by 1874 she did not step beyond the boundaries of the family property. At the Homestead the poet did, however, keep a central part of the Protestant church service, the hymnal, but converted its metrics to her own rather dissonant (and dissident) uses. While retaining regular hymn stanzas—the alternating 8- / 6-beat iambic pattern (also called common measure or ballad meter)—she played her phrasing against them. In her poems, Dickinson's uncommon thoughts run on without stopping at line-ends, as expected in hymn lyrics. While her capitalizations indicate emphases, her odd punctuation by incessant dashes is no guide to syntax. These quirks of style can create intriguing ambiguities but also often make the poems challenging to read, since it is not always clear exactly where a pause or logical break should fall.

Within the hymn framework, Dickinson is apt to place bold ideas, as for example in this subversive quatrain from 1870, no. 1181:

> Experiment escorts us last—
> His pungent company
> Will not allow an Axiom
> An Opportunity—

This stanza and many others, it may be noted, can be sung to the tune of "O God, Our Help in Ages Past." It is doubtful an Amherst congregation would have approved of Dickinson's secular hymns.

In a remarkable late poem, no. 1581 from 1881, Dickinson expressed the sense of loss brought on by the crisis of faith following Darwin's theory of evolution. Recalling the certainty offered in the prescientific era by Old Time Religion's promises, the poet observed:

> Those—dying then,
> Knew where they went—
> They went to God's Right Hand—
> That Hand is amputated now
> And God cannot be found—
>
> The abdication of Belief
> Makes the Behavior small—
> Better an ignis fatuus
> Than no illume at all—

Dickinson's expression of the need for a sustaining myth, even one accepted as illusory, anticipates by several decades and in terse form Wallace Stevens's urgent proposal for a "Supreme Fiction" as a necessary compensation for heaven and other comforting traditional beliefs that have been lost in the modern scientific world.

Dickinson might well have yearned for the consolations of religion, especially its promise of an afterlife. Death, the subject of so many of her verses, appears an obsession. The poems frequently are spoken by one on the verge of death; more unnerving, the poet often projects herself imaginatively into the grave. Although her perspective of one entombed is unusual, her preoccupation is not. To live in the nineteenth century, indeed in all the ages before antibiotics, was to be surrounded by death. (In her teens, the poet herself saw five friends die.) But her intellectual integrity did not permit complacent belief; her genius preferred creative speculation to received certainties.

About the time she stopped attending church, Dickinson began to give up assemblies generally. In her youth she had a wide circle of friends, including two cultivated young men who became mentors and encouraged her in her writing. Both died young. She later formed attachments, both platonic and perhaps romantic, with older literary men who were unavailable but served as "Preceptors," mostly notably Thomas Wentworth Higginson, editor of the *Atlantic Monthly*. Starting in 1862, they exchanged letters, and she sent him more than a hundred poems, none of which he published. On meeting her, he found Dickinson's behavior odd. While recognizing her talent, he likewise thought her work peculiar—"spasmodic," "wayward," "uncontrolled"—and advised her to delay "to publish." Ironically, it was Colonel Higginson who, with Mabel Loomis Todd, put together the first, severely edited volumes for the press. Dickinson herself professed not to wish "to print," as she put it, remarking in no. 788 (1863): "Publication—is the Auction / Of the Mind of Man—". She said she "would rather / From Our Garret go / White," and "reduce no Human Spirit / To Disgrace of Price—".

In her twenties Dickinson had made trips to Boston, Philadelphia, and Washington while her father was in Congress. She later returned to the Boston area for several months in 1864 and 1865 to receive treatments for an eye disorder. At thirty she adopted her "white habit," and, rarely leaving home, she restricted her circle to ever smaller groups of visitors. She curtailed her correspondence as well. Once long and chatty, her letters became briefer, their wit more brittle and epigrammatic, as in her verse. In a famous poem, no. 409, she wrote: "The Soul selects her own Society— / Then— shuts the Door— . . . ."

In one of her earliest letters to Higginson, in April 1862, she revealed, "I had a terror—since September—I could tell to none— and so I sing . . . because I am afraid—". What exactly this fear was, is still unknown. In another famous poem from 1862, no. 372, she recalled: "This is the Hour of Lead—". Apparently at or near the nadir of her dark night of the soul in 1863, she penned the particularly bleak lines of no. 581:

> Of Course—I prayed—
> And did God Care?
> He cared as much as on the Air
> A Bird—had stamped her foot—
> And cried "Give Me"—
> My Reason—Life—
> I had not had—but for Yourself—
> 'Twere better Charity
> To leave me in the Atom's Tomb—
> Merry, and nought, and gay, and numb—
> Than this smart Misery.

Yet despite her distress, she produced remarkable work, and at great speed. By R. W. Franklin's reckoning, Dickinson wrote 227 poems in 1862, 295 in 1863, 98 in 1864, and 229 in 1865. She continued to write every year thereafter, but her output fell off drastically, to twenty to forty poems some years, fewer than a dozen in others.

Dickinson's father died in 1874, and from that time she never left the Homestead. Her mother suffered a stroke the following year; she became paralyzed, and the poet nursed her until her death in 1882. Another very close friend and confidant, Judge Otis Lord, died two years later. She never recovered from these losses. By 1884 she had sewn about eight hundred of her poems into fascicles but left many more, fair copies and drafts, in loose sheets. Early in 1886 she was diagnosed with Bright's disease, a kidney disorder, from which she died on May 15. It was then that her sister discovered the hoard of poems, undated and untitled but tidily bundled, in the desk drawer.

Immediately recognized as the extraordinary works they are, the first gathering of *Poems* had great appeal, prompting publication of a *Second Series*, again silently revised by the editors then arranged thematically, which went to five printings by 1893. A *Third Series* appeared in 1896. The poet's niece, Martha Dickinson Bianchi, brought out a new collection in 1914, which was followed by yet more gatherings by Mrs. Bianchi (with Alfred Leete Hampson) in 1929 and 1935. But many other poems still remained. After a falling out between Vinnie and Mabel Todd over payment, Mrs. Todd had held on to more than six hundred unpublished manuscripts. They were finally printed, as *Bolts of Melody*, in 1935.

Even in their adulterated states in the early editions, the poems had great impact, and the ripples continue to spread. It is true that, just as they had no immediate precedents, Dickinson's poems have had no direct descendants. Yet her influence is pervasive; elements of her style may be traced throughout contemporary poetry. Read as she wrote them more than a century ago, the poems sound remarkably modern. In her quizzical attitude toward conventional belief and behavior, frequent irony, satirical wit, and abiding skepticism she was well ahead of her time and more in tune with our own. Her colloquial diction, nonstandard grammar, and offbeat rhythms; her assonance, dissonance, slant- or near-rhymes—these too make her sound more like our contemporary than a typical nineteenth-century voice.

Long before Ezra Pound's stark Imagism tried to modernize poetry by divesting it of empty platitudes, ornate diction, and threadbare formulas, Dickinson emphasized sharp, concrete images in tight lines that create the impression of immediate experience. She likewise anticipated the Modernists of the teens and 1920s in her stylistic innovations, not only in individualistic punctuation but in unpredictable, multivalent syntax, unexpected and highly evocative metaphors, compressed and elliptical phrasing—all conveying meaning obliquely while vividly conjuring psychological states. "Tell all the truth but tell it slant—" she recommended, in 1872, for "Success in Circuit lies . . . ." In 1863, at the peak of her creativity, Dickinson wrote of her own poetry with hopeful stoicism:

> This is my letter to the World
> That never wrote to Me—
> The simple News that Nature told—
> With tender Majesty
>
> Her Message is committed
> To Hands I cannot see—
> For love of Her—Sweet—countrymen—
> Judge tenderly—of Me

R. W. Franklin's single-volume paperback "reading edition" of his three-volume variorum edition was issued in 2005. Thomas H. Johnson's edition of *Emily Dickinson: Selected Letters* was reprinted in 2006. Richard B. Sewell's exhaustively researched two-volume *Life of Emily Dickinson* appeared in 1974, and was reissued as a one-volume paperback in 1980 and remains in print. Cynthia Griffin Wolff's substantial biography *Emily Dickinson* was published in 1986. Particularly useful on the cultural context, *The Cambridge Companion to Emily Dickinson*, edited by Wendy Martin, was issued in 2002. Assessments of recent scholarship and critical studies on the poet's biography, historical background, literary context, manuscripts, letters, aesthetics and experiments, reception and influence are collected in *The Emily Dickinson Handbook* (1998, reissued in paperback 2004), edited by Gudrun Grabher, Roland Hagenbüchle, and Cristanne Miller.

Judith Farr has also gathered useful studies in *Emily Dickinson: A Collection of Critical Essays* (1995) and produced her own extended consideration of the poet with detailed analyses of her work in *The Passion of Emily Dickinson* (1992, reissued 1998). Polly Longworth's *The World of Emily Dickinson* (1990, 1997) offers drawings, maps, photographs, and other visual materials to document the poet's life, family, friends, and environment, with a brief introduction and chronology. Innumerable other biographical and critical essays have appeared in recent decades, some of the best by poets represented in this anthology, who credit Dickinson's pioneering work and example for engendering and sustaining their own often solitary struggles for independence in life as well as art.

[260]—1861

I'm Nobody! Who are you?
Are you—Nobody—too?
Then there's a pair of us!
Dont tell! they'd banish us—you know!

How dreary—to be—Somebody!
How public—like a Frog—
To tell your name—the livelong June—
To an admiring Bog!

[312]—1862

I can wade Grief—
Whole Pools of it—
I'm used to that—
But the least push of Joy

Breaks up my feet—
And I tip—drunken—
Let no Pebble—smile—
'Twas the New Liquor—
That was all!

Power is only Pain—
Stranded—thro' Discipline,
Till Weights—will hang—
Give Balm—to Giants—
And they'll wilt, like Men—
Give Himmaleh—
They'll carry—Him!

[339]—1862

I like a look of Agony,
Because I know it's true—
Men do not sham Convulsion,
Nor simulate, a Throe—

The eyes glaze once—and that is Death—
Impossible to feign
The Beads opon the Forehead
By homely Anguish strung.

[372]—1862

After great pain, a formal feeling comes—
The Nerves sit ceremonious, like Tombs—
The stiff Heart questions 'was it He, that bore,'
And 'Yesterday, or Centuries before'?

The Feet, mechanical, go round—
A Wooden way
Of Ground, or Air, or Ought—
Regardless grown,
A Quartz contentment, like a stone—

This is the Hour of Lead—
Remembered, if outlived,
As Freezing persons, recollect the Snow—
First—Chill—then Stupor—then the letting go—

[448]—1862

I died for Beauty—but was scarce
Adjusted in the Tomb
When One who died for Truth, was lain
In an adjoining Room—

He questioned softly "Why I failed"?
"For Beauty", I replied—
"And I—for Truth—Themself are One—
We Bretheren, are", He said—

And so, as Kinsmen, met a Night—
We talked between the Rooms—
Until the Moss had reached our lips—
And covered up—Our names—

[466]—1862

I dwell in Possibility—
A fairer House than Prose—
More numerous of Windows—
Superior—for Doors—

Of Chambers as the Cedars—
Impregnable of eye—
And for an everlasting Roof
The Gambrels of the Sky—

Of Visitors—the fairest—
For Occupation—This—
The spreading wide my narrow Hands
To gather Paradise—

[479]—1862

Because I could not stop for Death—
He kindly stopped for me—
The Carriage held but just Ourselves—
And Immortality.

We slowly drove—He knew no haste
And I had put away
My labor and my leisure too,
For His Civility—

We passed the School, where Children strove
At Recess—in the Ring—
We passed the Fields of Gazing Grain—
We passed the Setting Sun—

Or rather—He passed Us—
The Dews drew quivering and Chill—
For only Gossamer, my Gown—
My Tippet—only Tulle—

We paused before a House that seemed
A Swelling of the Ground—
The Roof was scarcely visible—
The Cornice—in the Ground—

Since then—'tis Centuries—and yet
Feels shorter than the Day
I first surmised the Horses' Heads
Were toward Eternity—

[591]—1863

I heard a Fly buzz—when I died—
The Stillness in the Room
Was like the Stillness in the Air—
Between the Heaves of Storm—

The Eyes around—had wrung them dry—
And breaths were gathering firm
For that last Onset—when the King
Be witnessed—in the Room—

I willed my Keepsakes—Signed away
What portion of me be
Assignable—and then it was
There interposed a Fly—

With Blue—uncertain—stumbling Buzz—
Between the light—and me—
And then the Windows failed—and then
I could not see to see—

[620]—1863

Much Madness is divinest Sense—
To a discerning Eye—
Much Sense—the starkest Madness—
'Tis the Majority
In this, as all, prevail—
Assent—and you are sane—
Demur—you're straightway dangerous—
And handled with a Chain—

[861]—1864

They say that "Time assuages"—
Time never did assuage—
An actual suffering strengthens
As Sinews do, with Age—

Time is a Test of Trouble—
But not a Remedy—
If such it prove, it prove too
There was no Malady—

CHRISTINA ROSSETTI

▣ Viewed in several portraits by her brother, Christina Rossetti appears pensive, sensitive, and somber: qualities that describe her poetry as well. Both pious and passionate by nature, hers was an often-conflicted personality, which may explain the melancholy strain in her life and work. The youngest child in an intellectual and artistic family, she was born in London on December 5, 1830, five days before Emily Dickinson. Her father Gabriele, a noted poet in Italy, had fled to England in 1824 as a political refugee from Naples, where he had been active in a revolutionary movement. In London he became a professor of Italian at King's College and married Frances Polidori, the sister of Dr. John Polidori, sometime physician and unfortunate friend to Lord Byron.

All four Rossetti children were bilingual, and studious. Like her father, Maria, the oldest, produced a study of Dante; she eventually joined an Anglican order of sisters and worked with the poor. William Michael became a critic and editor. Dante Gabriel, also a poet, gained fame as a painter and founder of the Pre-Raphaelite Brotherhood. This avant-garde group of authors and artists (members included the painters John Ruskin, William Holman Hunt, and John Everett Millais, and Gabriel's business partner, the designer William Morris) sought a return to idealized medieval styles and standards of workmanship, best exemplified in the English Arts and Crafts movement. But their aesthetic principles—realistic and precise but dreamy, sensuous, and often erotic too—influenced much Victorian poetry, as well as the French Symbolist movement, which would inspire T. S. Eliot and other early Modernists.

As children, all four siblings read widely and contributed pieces to the family's commonplace books or journals. In the 1840s the Rossettis fell on hard times, following the physical and mental collapse of the father. Christina herself had a nervous breakdown at age fourteen and thereafter was fragile and suffered from several illnesses, some perhaps imaginary, which saved her from a bleak career as a governess, a fate then common for well-educated but poor young single ladies. When she was seventeen, her grandfather Gaetano Polidori privately printed a book of her verses on his own press. Soon Rossetti was publishing poems in leading magazines. She remained at home to nurse her father and after his death, in 1854, helped run the household with her mother, to whom she was extremely close and to whom she dedicated nearly all her volumes. Both were very devout High Church Anglicans, and during the 1860s Christina volunteered as a social worker at the St. Mary Magdalen Home for Fallen Women. (Earlier she had been turned down for Florence Nightingale's nursing mission in the Crimean War, because of her youth.)

Although not an official member of the "brotherhood," Christina knew all the Pre-Raphaelites well and served as a model for many of their artworks. At age eighteen she fell in love with one of the brethren, the poet-painter James Collinson, but broke off their engagement, perhaps because of his conversion to Roman Catholicism. After Gabriel's wife committed suicide, in 1861, Christina shared hosting duties in his mansion, Tudor House, at a brilliant salon frequented by such literary luminaries as Robert Browning, Lewis Carroll, Algernon Charles Swinburne, and William Meredith. During this period she had a number of romantic attachments, including one with Charles Bagot Cayley, a translator (of Dante and Petrarch among others) whose proposal of marriage she turned down, also perhaps for religious reasons (he was an agnostic). These sacrifices exacted heavy psychic costs. She recorded the tensions of her uneasy relationships, in which she seemed torn between high moral principles and more earthbound sensuality, in several poems discovered after her death.

Rossetti's first book, *Goblin Market, and Other Poems*, published in 1862, was an instant popular and critical success, establishing her reputation at age thirty-one. The long title poem is a complex allegory in the guise of a nursery tale depicting various conflicts between desire and duty, with a theme of redemption from sin through suffering. Modern critics have also interpreted it as a commentary on the role of women in restrictive Victorian society. A second edition came out in 1864, followed by *Prince's Progress, and Other Poems*, in 1866. Both books were illustrated by her brother.

Rossetti became an increasingly well-regarded and versatile writer, publishing a short story collection in 1870 and *Sing-Song*, a book of ingenious nursery rhymes, in 1872. *Speaking Likenesses*, another children's book, appeared in 1874. Later poems were collected in *A Pageant, and Other Poems* (1881) and *Verses* (1893). She also wrote a number of essays on Dante. In 1871 she was afflicted with Graves' disease, an autoimmune disorder of the thyroid that seriously weakened her. She began to write devotional essays and other religious works, in great profusion; these eventually filled six volumes published by the Society for the Propagation of Christian Knowledge. In later life she shared a home with her beloved mother and two aunts; after their passing she lived alone. In 1891 she was diagnosed with cancer and died, after great suffering, on December 29, 1894. She was buried in London's Highgate Cemetery, in the same grave as her mother and father.

Despite her accomplishments and popularity, Rossetti like many another once-esteemed Victorian author unfairly lost standing with the rise of literary Modernism. But a revival of interest begun in the 1970s has grown, particularly as feminist critics and historians have reappraised her work and rediscovered the skilled craftsmanship, subtle sensibility, psychological insight, and genuine originality of her many moving lines.

IN AN ARTIST'S STUDIO

One face looks out from all his canvases,
    One selfsame figure sits or walks or leans:
    We found her hidden just behind those screens,
That mirror gave back all her loveliness.
A queen in opal or in ruby dress,
    A nameless girl in freshest summer-greens,
    A saint, an angel—every canvas means
The same one meaning, neither more nor less.
He feeds upon her face by day and night,
    And she with true kind eyes looks back on him,
Fair as the moon and joyful as the light:
    Not wan with waiting, not with sorrow dim;
Not as she is, but was when hope shone bright;
    Not as she is, but as she fills his dream.

REMEMBER

Remember me when I am gone away,
    Gone far away into the silent land;
    When you can no more hold me by the hand,
Nor I half turn to go yet turning stay.

Remember me when no more day by day
    You tell me of our future that you planned:
    Only remember me; you understand
It will be late to counsel then or pray.

Yet if you should forget me for a while
    And afterwards remember, do not grieve:
    For if the darkness and corruption leave
    A vestige of the thoughts that once I had,
Better by far you should forget and smile
    Than that you should remember and be sad.

EMMA LAZARUS

Along with the National Anthem, "The New Colossus," Emma Lazarus's hymn to the Statue of Liberty, is among all verses, patriotic or otherwise, the most recognizable to Americans. It is doubtless true that, just as the words after "the twilight's last gleaming" begin to fade for singers of "The Star Spangled Banner," the complete text of Lazarus's sonnet may also elude memory. But the cry she voiced for Lady Liberty's "silent lips"—"Give me your tired, your poor, / Your huddled masses yearning to breathe free . . ."—remains indelible, and not without reason. In these few lines the poet crystallized the dream and ideal image of America for generations of immigrants to the Land of the Free. Immortality, attained even through only a single poem or stanza, would be more than sufficient reward for most authors; so it is perhaps unfair to suggest that Lazarus received less than her due. But until recently she was not in fact accorded full recognition for her admirable works—both her writings and her efforts as a social activist.

Emma Lazarus was born, the fourth of seven children, on July 22, 1849, in New York City, to a Sephardic Jewish family whose founders were among the first to immigrate from the Iberian peninsula before the American Revolution. Her family was secular (Emma called them "outlaw" Jews) and thoroughly assimilated, her father Moses a wealthy sugar refiner who moved with ease in Gentile Manhattan Society. Besides their town residence, the family had a summer "cottage" in fashionable Newport, Rhode Island, coincidentally the site of the oldest Jewish place of worship in the United States. In 1867 the teenage poet wrote "In the Jewish Synagogue in Newport," declaring "The sacred shrine is holy yet," in response to Longfellow's assertion in "The Jewish Cemetery at Newport" (1858) that the race of "These Hebrews in their graves" would like other "dead nations never rise again."

Lazarus was educated at home and became proficient in several languages. In 1866 her father underwrote the printing of a volume of poems and translations she produced between the ages of fourteen and sixteen; with some additions, it was brought out by a New York publisher the following year. She sent a copy to Ralph Waldo Emerson, who became an informal mentor through correspondence, though not quite the helper she had hoped for. Lazarus was disappointed when he did not include her in his anthology *Parnassus* (1874), but their friendship continued and the great man invited her to visit him at his Concord home. By then she was publishing poems and essays in *Lippincott's*, *Scribner's*, and other leading magazines. Her second collection, *Admetus and Other Poems*, was published in 1871.

Lazarus also wrote a well-received novel, *Alide: An Episode in Goethe's Life*, in 1874, followed in 1876 by *The Spagnoletto*, a drama that was not performed but won praise from Emily Dickinson's friend Colonel Thomas Wentworth Higginson. Lazarus had made her name and was now associating with the established writers and artists of her time. On trips to Europe she met Robert Browning, Henry James, and William Morris, as well as his fellow Pre-Raphaelites. Her translation of *Poems and Ballads of Heinrich Heine* was published to good reviews in 1881. The German-Jewish poet was her favorite and, like Lazarus, nonpracticing but a defender of their shared Judaic heritage.

Beyond this intellectual respect, a deeper attachment to her religious and cultural roots was awakened in Lazarus in the early 1880s when she met Jewish refugees from Eastern Europe, particularly exiles fleeing the pogroms and repressions in Russia that followed the assassination of Tsar Alexander II. Working on Ward's Island with these and other immigrant groups then pouring into New York, Lazarus (who had seldom experienced prejudice herself) became aware of the rising anti-Semitism abroad, and feared its spread in the New World. She began writing articles against it, warning of the dangers of stereotypes.

She declared her own Jewish identity in *Songs of a Semite: The Dance to Death and Other Poems*, published in 1882. In the *American Hebrew* newspaper she presented a series of fifteen "letters" in 1882–1883 entitled "An Epistle to the Hebrews," arguing that assimilated Jewish Americans should be more aware of their potential vulnerability. By that time Jewish exiles from Russia were arriving at the rate of about two thousand a month. While organizing refugee relief for the Hebrew Emigrant Aid Society, she suggested that Eastern European Jews settle in Palestine. In "The Jewish Problem," an essay printed in the *Century* in 1883, she noted the perennial "antagonism" toward the Jews and proposed further that a solution might be the founding of a Jewish state in Palestine—an idea offered more than a dozen years before the founder of the Zionist movement, Theodor Herzl, was to advocate the creation there of a Jewish homeland.

Such was her background (and unwitting preparation) when in 1883 Lazarus received a request to aid in a fund-raising effort for the pedestal for *La liberté éclairant le monde*—Liberty Enlightening the World. Originally intended as a gift from the French to commemorate the centennial of the Declaration of Independence, the monument was designed by the sculptor Frédéric Auguste Bartholdi, with engineering for the interior structure by Gustave Eiffel, creator of the famous Tower. Work on the 151-foot statue was completed in Paris in July 1884, and it was shipped over in pieces a year later. Construction of the base (designed by Richard Morris Hunt) was to be paid for by the American side, but funds were embarrassingly slow in arriving. Finished first, the head had been exhibited in Paris and the torch-bearing arm in New York, to help raise money. Then civic-minded individuals and groups across the country sponsored events—theater benefits, auctions, art exhibits, even boxing matches—to attract donations and complete the project.

In New York City the socialite author Constance Cary Harrison organized a major art exhibit and auction for the Pedestal Fund, which included an elaborate catalogue. (The exhibit became a precursor of the famous Armory Show of dissident art in 1913.) When she asked her friend Emma for a poem to include in her "Portfolio," Lazarus had nothing "suitable" to contribute. In her *Recollections, Grave and Gay* (1912), Mrs. Harrison wrote that she reminded the poet "of her visits to . . . the newly arrived immigrants whose sad lot had so often excited her sympathy." Lazarus soon sent her "The New Colossus," and it was first printed in the catalogue.

Realizing the statue's newer, greater symbolic potential, in her poem Lazarus refocused the perspective of Liberty, from the revolutionary past to the contemporary reality and future prospects of the United States. Instead of looking back to the Declaration of Independence ("JULY IV MDCCLXXVI" is engraved on the tablet in Liberty's arm), Lazarus shifted emphasis to the New Country's more recent, unparalleled position as *the* land of freedom and opportunity to downtrodden masses throughout the world. The seven spikes in the crown, representing the seven seas and seven continents, now radiated heightened significance for immigrants in the 1880s. Similarly, the torch that until 1903 made the monument a lighthouse—like that "brazen giant," the original Colossus of Rhodes—became figuratively a beacon of hope to the "storm-tost" and dispossessed streaming to America. Officialdom apparently did not appreciate Lazarus's new slant: "The New Colossus" was not read at the dedication ceremony, October 28, 1886.

James Russell Lowell did, however, recognize her achievement when he told Lazarus: "your sonnet gives its subject a raison d'etre." But it was only in 1903, sixteen years after her death, that the poem that made Lazarus's name forever known was cast as a brass plaque and erected in the hall inside the pedestal. (Only the final lines are embossed outside on the base.) In her final few years, Lazarus continued to publish poems and essays on literary and social topics in the *Century* and other journals. She returned to Europe for a long tour beginning in the spring of 1885 but grew ill and returned to the States in the fall of 1887. She died of Hodgkin's disease on November 19, at age thirty-eight.

Her sisters Mary and Annie brought out *The Poems of Emma Lazarus*, including her translations of medieval Hebrew poets, in two volumes in 1888, with an introduction by her sister Josephine. *The Letters of Emma Lazarus, 1868–1885*, edited by Morris U. Schappes, appeared in 1949. Recent biographical studies include Bette Roth Young's *Emma Lazarus in the World: Life and Letters* (1995) and Esther Schor's *Emma Lazarus* (2006). *Emma Lazarus: Selected Poems*, edited with an introduction by John Hollander, was printed in the Library of America's American Poets Project Series in 2005.

THE NEW COLOSSUS

Not like the brazen giant of Greek fame,
With conquering limbs astride from land to land;
Here at our sea-washed, sunset gates shall stand
A mighty woman with a torch, whose flame
Is the imprisoned lightning, and her name
Mother of Exiles. From her beacon-hand
Glows world-wide welcome; her mild eyes command
The air-bridged harbor that twin cities frame.
"Keep, ancient lands, your storied pomp!" cries she
With silent lips. "Give me your tired, your poor,
Your huddled masses yearning to breathe free,
The wretched refuse of your teeming shore.
Send these, the homeless, tempest-tost to me,
I lift my lamp beside the golden door!"

AMY LOWELL

Amy Lowell was a large woman with large ambitions. During her relatively short professional career, she created an imposing profile with her abundant output and an outsized personality that made her compelling at the podium. Her success on the lecture circuit prompted T. S. Eliot to call her "the demon saleswoman of poetry." Unkinder still, Edgar Lee Masters referred to her as "the tremendous Amazon who for the time being is rampaging through the flower gardens of America," after she slighted him in one of her books. Masters proved correct in his belief (and fond hope) that her moment in the limelight would be brief, for without her commanding presence and shrewd promotion, her artifices declined in estimation after her premature death. Yet amid her prolific productions there remain several fine poems that still reward attention, though perhaps they are not the ones she considered major works.

Amy Lowell was born in Brookline, Massachusetts, February 9, 1874, at Sevenels, her father's ten-acre estate, which she acquired after his death. In her impressive library—she was an avid collector of rare books—she held court before literary friends and labored through the night while smoking thin cigars. Like others of her class, she was active on committees and had a sense of noblesse oblige that, with her domineering air, often came off as patronizing or pushy. The Lowell wealth she so generously shared, particularly in support of poets, stemmed from the textile mills of her forefathers. Other prominent family members included generals and judges, the poet James Russell Lowell, and Amy's brothers Percival Lowell, the astronomer and founder of the Lowell Observatory, and Abbott Lawrence Lowell, the president of Harvard.

She was first taught at home by a governess, then attended private schools. Her formal education ended at age seventeen, when she came out to Society. Although she was a very popular debutante, she did not attract a husband. Her mother had a volume of Amy's juvenilia printed when she was thirteen, but Lowell decided to devote her life to Art rather late, in 1902, when she was inspired to write verse, she said, after seeing performances of the celebrated Italian actress Eleanora Duse. She then very deliberately set about training herself in poetry. In 1912 she met the actress Ada Dwyer Russell, a divorcee a dozen years her senior, who became her devoted companion and helpmeet, and the subject of her most touching love poems.

Following her long and diligent preparations, in 1912 also Lowell published her first collection, *A Dome of Many-Coloured Glass*, a lackluster effort in the Romantic mode. (Her lifelong idol was John Keats.) Then, in the January 1913 issue of the newly founded *Poetry*, she came upon the spare, bracing lines of Ezra Pound's young protégée, "H.D., *Imagiste*," and had an epiphany: "Why, I too am an Imagiste!" She decided to go directly to the source, and carrying a letter of introduction to Pound from Harriet Monroe, the editor of the magazine, she sailed for England, retinue (and limousine) in tow. At first Pound found Lowell "pleasingly intelligent" and agreed to "modernize" her by instructing her in Imagist doctrine: no unnecessary words; natural rhythms, not "the metronome"; concrete images instead of abstractions. He also introduced her to his friends, including W. B. Yeats, Ford Madox Ford, H.D. herself, and John Gould Fletcher, who became Lowell's close confidant. Soon she was composing in the new Imagistic style, though Pound later complained that she had badly diluted his strict and astringent standards.

When she returned to London the following year, Lowell found that Pound had alienated almost every one of "his" Imagists by his high-handedness. Lowell, who could be quite imperious herself but possessed excellent political skills, had little trouble convincing H.D., D. H. Lawrence, and others of the group to participate in a collection called *Some Imagist Poets* in 1915. Thanks to her extensive reading tours, it became a best-seller, prompting new editions in 1916 and 1917. (Pound's own earlier anthology, *Des Imagistes* of 1914, was a flop, on both sides of the Atlantic; some disgruntled buyers even demanded their money back.) A disgusted Pound dubbed and dismissed Lowell's imprecise, watered-down versions of his principles as "Amygisme."

Lowell was seldom spontaneous or truly "new" in her poetry, but what she lacked in originality she made up for by indefatigable industry. In 1914 she published *Sword Blades and Poppy Seed*, followed by *Men, Women, and Ghosts* (1916), *Con Grande's Castle* (1918), *Pictures of a Floating World* (1919), and *Legends* (1921). With substantial aid from her collaborator Florence Ayscough, she brought out a book of Chinese translations, *Fir-Flower Tablets*, also in 1921. Lowell wanted always to be up-to-date and experimented constantly. She wrote in many forms—free verse, narratives, monologues in dialects—but was most proud of an innovation she called "polyphonic prose," a mixture of verse and prose elements, with repetitions, internal rhymes, and other devices. In these constructs as elsewhere, Lowell tried assiduously to be inventive and fresh—perhaps too much so, for the results can seem merely artificial and forced. But when she relaxed her determined drive for literary stature and wrote directly and unaffectedly, an authentic lyric voice could emerge in lines that are genuinely moving and memorable. Among these are such brief but quietly assured and perfectly realized pieces as "Venus Transiens," "Katydids," "The Taxi," and "The Letter."

Beyond the creative realm, Lowell also sought fame as a literary critic and historian. In 1917 she brought out *Tendencies in Modern American Poetry*, a highly selective and inaccurate study that was panned by several poets besides Masters. In a tart letter to Harriet Monroe, Alice Corbin Henderson, her associate editor at *Poetry*, opined, "Good in spots, the whole tone of it is unspeakably banal." Reviewing Lowell's career up to 1918, Alfred Kreymborg, editor of the pioneering journal *Others*, concluded: "[S]he is facile, prolific, a reader of good books, a genius as a propagandist, and a scintillating lady; but she has contributed absolutely nothing which is new to poetry."

Chronically overweight and overworked, Lowell began to fail in health, and in 1918 she had the first of several operations that further sapped her strength. Yet she maintained her usual hectic schedule, to which she added a big new project, a biography of Keats. The huge study was finally completed in 1925 and published in two volumes. Critical reception was decidedly mixed, and Lowell was crushed. Following a massive stroke, she died on May 12, 1925, at age fifty-one. Ada Russell saw through the press her final books, *What's O'Clock* (1925, winner of the Pulitzer Prize), *East Wind* (1926), and *Ballads for Sale* (1927). In her eulogy in *Poetry*, Harriet Monroe, who admired Lowell's energy and printed her often, declared: "She was a great woman," but as a poet, "she had everything but genius."

Ten years after her death, S. Foster Damon published a lengthy study, *Amy Lowell: A Chronicle with Extracts from Her Correspondence*. Forty years later, in 1975, two new reassessments appeared, *Amy: The World of Amy Lowell and the Imagist Movement*, by Jean Gould, and *The Thorn of a Rose: Amy Lowell Reconsidered*, by Glenn Richard Ruihley. In 1980, C. David Heymann provided an astute analysis in *American Aristocracy: The Lives and Times of James Russell, Amy, and Robert Lowell*. Richard Benvenuto's critical biography, *Amy Lowell*, followed in 1985. A new *Selected Poems*, edited by Honor Moore, was issued by the Library of America in 2004.

THE LETTER

Little cramped words scrawling all over the paper
Like draggled fly's legs,
What can you tell of the flaring moon
Through the oak leaves?
Or of my uncurtained window and the bare floor
Spattered with moonlight?
Your silly quirks and twists have nothing in them
Of blossoming hawthorns,
And this paper is dull, crisp, smooth, virgin of loveliness
Beneath my hand.

I am tired, Beloved, of chafing my heart against
The want of you;
Of squeezing it into little inkdrops,

And posting it.
And I scald alone, here, under the fire
Of the great moon.

KATYDIDS

Shore of Lake Michigan

Katydids scraped in the dim trees,
And I thought they were little white skeletons
Playing the fiddle with a pair of finger-bones.

How long is it since Indians walked here,
Stealing along the sands with smooth feet?
How long is it since Indians died here
And the creeping sands scraped them bone from bone?
Dead Indians under the sands, playing their bones against
    strings of wampum.
The roots of new, young trees have torn their graves asunder,
But in the branches sit little white skeletons
Rasping a bitter death-dirge through the August night.

MINA LOY

◧ Fearless and free-spirited in her provocative writing and art-
works, and especially in her unconventional lifestyle, Mina Loy cut
a glamorous figure amid innovative art circles in the first decades of
the twentieth century. Born in the repressive Victorian era, she
eluded a staid middle-class existence, imaginatively reinvented her-
self, and came to personify the daring, and dangerous, New Woman.
At the very center of the principal avant-gardes on both sides of the
Atlantic, the beautiful and multitalented Loy became friends with
virtually all of the most important artists and authors of her time—
and had affairs with several—and won the admiration of such di-
verse individualists as Gertrude Stein, Constantin Brancusi, James
Joyce, Marcel Duchamp, and Ezra Pound. In truth, Loy was not
only *in* the vanguard but frequently *ahead* of it, and so even now her
poetry makes arresting reading.

Loy started out as and remained foremost a visual artist. She
was also a genuine if eclectic thinker, conversant in the latest ad-
vanced theories in Europe (of Nietzsche, Bergson, and Freud par-
ticularly) as well as the arcane teachings of the East. A combination
of cutting-edge ideas and even sharper images gives her poetry its
distinctive piquancy. Pound declared Loy an author of intellect (for
him the highest compliment), an artist who avoided the sentimen-
tality he felt typically weakened "women's poetry." (In fact he coined
the term "logopoeia" for the unique "dance of intelligence among
words and ideas" in Loy's work.) On a more personal level, it was
her sense of adventure and zest for life that endeared the thoroughly
modern Mina to so many fractious egotists in those early decades of
creative ferment.

She was born Mina Gertrude Löwry in London on December
27, 1882, to a Jewish father and Protestant mother, and grew up in
a conventionally straitlaced bourgeois household. At seventeen she
left school and went to Munich, where she studied art for two years.
She returned to England and continued to study painting, for a time
with Augustus John, and met Stephen Haweis, a fellow art student.
They went to Paris, where they married at the end of 1903 and Mina
chose her new name. Their first child, Oda, was born in 1904; she
died on her first birthday. During their three years in Paris, Loy
formed what became lifelong friendships with Gertrude Stein and
Djuna Barnes. At Gertrude and Leo Stein's salon she met Guillaume
Apollinaire, Pablo Picasso, Henri Rousseau, and other upstarts. Loy
later summarized her friend's achievement in the pithy comparisons
of "Gertrude Stein":

> Curie
> of the laboratory
> of vocabulary
>   she crushed
> the tonnage
> of consciousness
> congealed to phrases
>   to extract
> a radium of the word

In 1906, Loy and Haweis moved to Florence. Although they
were already drifting apart, the couple had two more children, Joella
in 1907 and Giles in 1909; the boy died in 1923. Loy had passionate

affairs with Filippo Marinetti and then Giovanni Papini, the founders of the Futurist art movement. She also formed friendships with several expatriates from Manhattan who gathered at the millionaire art patron Mabel Dodge's Medici villa, including the *Masses* journalist and Communist activist John Reed and the novelist and critic Carl Van Vechten, who eventually became her agent. She began to publish extremely original poems and articles in irreverent little magazines such as *Rogue*, attracting the attention of the New York avant-garde. *Trend* printed "Parturition," her graphic poetic description of childbirth, and Alfred Stieglitz's influential *Camera Work* presented her "Aphorisms on Futurism," both in 1914.

Eventually Loy became repelled by the macho elements in Futurism and its drift toward fascism. She recorded her disillusionment with its doctrines and the dissolution of her relationship with Papini in "Songs to Joannes," one of the truly remarkable early Modernist poems. Originally printed as "Love Songs" in July 1915 in the inaugural issue of *Others*, edited by Alfred Kreymborg and William Carlos Williams, the opening sections created a sensation. First readers were shocked by Loy's risqué expressions of human sensuality, particularly her uncensored depictions of erotic desire and the body, including its fluids and functions. Fragmentary, collagelike, largely unpunctuated, the sequence was unsettling in its techniques, prefiguring much later Modernist poetry. (T. S. Eliot appears to have picked up several points from her.) But beyond their sensational surfaces, Loy's complex, ambiguous, and witty constructs here and elsewhere exposed the inequities and pious hypocrisies of male-dominated society, and the resulting physical and psychological damage suffered by women. Further, Loy was not afraid to criticize the supposedly superior theories (and self-satisfied pretensions) of her fellow iconoclasts as well.

Early in World War I she served in an army hospital. In the fall of 1916, leaving her children with a nurse, she went to New York. She was welcomed into bohemian circles and the *Others* group, becoming friends with Dr. Williams, Man Ray, Marcel Duchamp, and Marianne Moore. Like Edna St. Vincent Millay, she joined the Provincetown Players as both a playwright and actress. In Greenwich Village in 1917, Loy met the "boxer-poet" Arthur Cravan. (Born Fabien Avernarius Lloyd, he was a nephew of Constance Lloyd, the wife of Oscar Wilde. The resemblance between their names, real and adopted, did not escape Loy.) When he fled to Mexico to avoid the draft, Loy followed. They were married in Mexico City after her divorce from Haweis became final, then lived in poverty as Cravan fought (literally) to support them. When Loy became pregnant, they decided to move to Buenos Aires. Sailing separately, Cravan disappeared and was never seen again. Their daughter Fabienne was born in April 1919.

Loy returned to Florence and her other children, but in 1920, hoping to find Cravan, she sailed to New York where again she was active in several art scenes. In 1923 she moved to Paris, renewed her friendships in the Stein circle, and became a star in the large expatriate community of the "Lost Generation." Years later in her autobiography, *Poetry*'s Harriet Monroe held vivid memories of "the quite irresistible Mina Loy" and her grand entrance at an artists' café with Tristan Tzara ("the original dada-ist"), Ezra Pound, and Jane Heap, who was trying to restart her *Little Review* in Paris. With backing from the noted arts patron Peggy Guggenheim, Loy designed and was quite successful selling unusual lampshades, paper cutouts and flower arrangements, and other decorative items.

She continued to write as well, and grew close to H.D. and her lover Bryher, the novelist and heiress Winifred Ellerman. In 1923 Loy's first book, *Lunar Baedecker* [sic], was issued by Robert McAlmon's Contact Editions (the press was funded by his wife Bryher). Also in 1923, sections of Loy's heavily satiric, lightly veiled autobiographical poem *Anglo-Mongrels and the Rose* were printed in Heap's *Little Review*. But by the end of the twenties, Loy's literary profile began to fade. She also gave up her business and became a representative for important Surrealists such as Max Ernst, Salvador Dali, and René Magritte, acting for her son-in-law Julien Levy's noted New York gallery.

With the rise of the Nazis and the growing threats of war, Loy left Paris in 1936 and returned to New York—not to her former sophisticated bohemian haunts, however, but to the slum district of the Bowery. Living among the derelicts on Skid Row, she painted and began to assemble art pieces from junk and other "found objects." She became a close friend of Joseph Cornell, the creator of evocative box sculptures also assembled from found materials. In 1958, Loy the radical Modernist was "rediscovered," and thirty-five years after the first edition the enlarged *Lunar Baedeker & Time-Tables* was published by the Jargon Society Press. She had moved to

Aspen in 1951, to be with her daughters, and died there in 1966, at age eighty-three.

In recent years Loy has been the subject of numerous scholarly articles and critical studies, including reassessments in *Mina Loy: Woman and Poet*, edited by Maeera Shreiber and Keith Tuma (1998), and *Writing for Their Lives: The Modernist Women, 1910–1940*, edited by Gillian Hanscombe and Virginia L. Smyers (1987, reprinted 1999). The first full biography, Virginia M. Kouidis's *Mina Loy: American Modernist Poet*, was issued in 1980. Carolyn Burke's thorough and very well-written *Becoming Modern: The Life of Mina Loy* appeared in 1996. A new edition of *The Lost Lunar Baedeker: Poems by Mina Loy*, prepared and introduced by Roger L. Conover, was also published in 1996.

From SONGS TO JOANNES

I

Spawn   of   Fantasies
Silting the appraisable
Pig Cupid   his rosy snout
Rooting erotic garbage
"Once upon a time"
Pulls a weed   white star-topped
Among wild oats   sown in mucous-membrance

I would   an   eye in a Bengal light
Eternity in a sky-rocket
Constellations in an ocean
Whose rivers run no fresher
Than a trickle of saliva

These are suspect places

I must live in my lantern
Trimming subliminal flicker
Virginal   to the bellows
Of Experience
                    Coloured   glass

II

The skin-sack
In which a wanton duality
Packed
All the completion of my infructuous impulses
Something the shape of a man
To the casual vulgarity of the merely observant
More of a clock-work mechanism
Running down against time
To which I am not paced
       My finger-tips are numb from fretting your hair
A God's door-mat
                    On the threshold of your mind

III

We might have coupled
In the bed-ridden monopoly of a moment
Or broken flesh with one another
At the profane communion table
Where wine is spill'd on promiscuous lips

We might have given birth to a butterfly
With the daily news
Printed in blood on its wings

IV

Once in a mezzanino
The starry ceiling
Vaulted an unimaginable family
Bird-like abortions
With human throats
And Wisdom's eyes
Who wore lamp-shade red dresses
And woolen hair

One bore a baby
In a padded porte-enfant
Tied with a sarsenet ribbon
To her goose's wings

But for the abominable shadows
I would have lived
Among their fearful furniture
To teach them to tell me their secrets
Before I guess
—Sweeping the brood clean out

V

Midnight empties the street
Of all but us
Three
I am undecided which way back
                    To the left a boy
—One wing has been washed in the rain
   The other will never be clean any more—
Pulling door-bells to remind
Those that are snug
                    To the right a haloed ascetic
                    Threading houses
Probes wounds for souls
—The poor can't wash in hot water—
And I don't know which turning to take
Since you got home to yourself—first

VI

I know the Wire-Puller intimately
And if it were not for the people
On whom you keep one eye
You could look straight at me
And Time would be set back

VII

My pair of feet
Smack the flag-stones
That are something left over from your walking
The wind stuffs the scum of the white street
Into my lungs and my nostrils
Exhilarated birds
Prolonging flight into the night
Never reaching— — — — — —

VIII

I am the jealous store-house of the candle-ends
That lit your adolescent learning
— — — — — — — — — —

Behind God's eyes
There might
Be other lights

IX

When we lifted
Our eye-lids on Love
A cosmos
Of coloured voices
And laughing honey

And spermatozoa
At the core of Nothing
In the milk of the Moon

X

Shuttle-cock and battle-door
A little pink-love
And feathers are strewn

XI

Dear one   at your mercy
Our Universe
Is only
A colorless onion
You derobe
Sheath by sheath
            Remaining
A disheartening odour
About your nervy hands

XII

Voices break on the confines of passion
Desire   Suspicion   Man   Woman
Solve in the humid carnage

Flesh from flesh
Draws the inseparable delight
Kissing at gasps   to catch it

Is it true
That I have set you apart
Inviolate in an utter crystallization
Of all   the jolting of the crowd
Taught me willingly to live to share

Or are you
Only the other half
Of an ego's necessity
Scourging pride with compassion
To the shallow sound of dissonance
And boom of escaping breath

XIII

Come to me   There is something
I have got to tell you   and I can't tell
Something taking shape
Something that has a new name
A new dimension
A new use
A new illusion

It is ambient   And it is in your eyes
Something shiny   Something only for you
                       Something that I must not see

It is in my ears   Something very resonant
Something that you must not hear
                       Something only for me

Let us be very jealous
Very suspicious
Very conservative
Very cruel
Or we might make an end of the jostling of aspirations
Disorb inviolate egos

Where two or three are welded together
They shall become god
— — — — — — —

Oh that's right
Keep away from me   Please give me a push
Don't let me understand you   Don't realise me
Or we might tumble together
Depersonalized
Identical
Into the terrific Nirvana
Me you — you — me

XIV

Today
Everlasting   passing   apparent   imperceptible
To you
I bring the nascent virginity of
—Myself   for the moment

No love   or the other thing
Only the impact of lighted bodies
Knocking sparks off each other
In chaos

XV

Seldom   Trying for Love
Fantasy dealt them out as gods
Two or three men   looked   only human

But you alone
Superhuman   apparently
I had to be caught in the weak eddy
Of your drivelling humanity
                To love you most

. . . .

XXVI

Shedding our petty pruderies
From slit eyes

We sidle up
To Nature
— — — that irate pornographist

XXVII

Nucleus   Nothing
Inconceivable concept
Insentient repose
The hands of races
Drop off from
Immodifiable plastic

The contents
Of our ephemeral conjunction
In aloofness from Much
Flowed to approachment of — — — —
NOTHING
There was a man and a woman
In the way
While the Irresolvable
Rubbed with our daily deaths
Impossible eyes

. . . .

XXIX

Evolution   fall foul of
Sexual equality
Prettily miscalculate
Similitude

Unnatural selection
Breed such sons and daughters
As shall jibber at each other
Uninterpretable cryptonyms
Under the moon

Give them some way of braying brassily
For caressive calling
Or to homophonous hiccoughs

Transpose the laugh
Let them suppose that tears
Are snowdrops or molasses
Or anything
Than human insufficiencies
Begging dorsal vertebrae

Let meeting be the turning
To the antipodean
And Form   a blurr
Anything
Than seduce them
To the one
As simple satisfaction
For the other

Let them clash together
From their incognitoes
In seismic orgasm

For far further
Differentiation
Rather than watch
Own-self distortion
Wince in the alien ego

XXX

In some
Prenatal plagiarism
Foetal buffoons
Caught tricks
— — — — —

From archetypal pantomime
Stringing emotions
Looped aloft
— — — —

For the blind eyes
That Nature knows us with

And the most of Nature   is green

— — — —- — — — — — —

What guaranty
For the proto-form
We fumble
Our souvenir ethics to

— — — — — — —

                              XXXI

Crucifixion
Of a busy-body
Longing to interfere so
With the intimacies
Of your insolent isolation

Crucifixion
Of an illegal ego's
Eclosion
On your equilibrium
Caryatid   of an idea

Crucifixion
Wracked arms
Index extremities
In vacuum
To the unbroken fall

                              XXXII

The moon is cold
Joannes
Where the Mediterranean — — — — —

                              XXXIII

The prig of passion — — — —
To your professorial paucity

Proto-plasm was raving mad
Evolving us — — —

XXXIV
Love — — — the preeminent litterateur

SARA TEASDALE

□ Sara Teasdale was, after her chief rival, Edna St. Vincent Millay, the most popular woman writing poetry in America in the twenties and early thirties. Both concentrated on love themes and chose to compose in forms. But where Millay often cast an ironic eye on romance, Teasdale viewed the pangs and disappointments of human attachments with somber stoicism. Both were superb technicians who exploited the resources of traditional verse with seemingly effortless grace; but the flamboyant, liberated Millay appeared the more sophisticated and contemporary, whether in an archly exuberant or in a wittily hard-edged mood. Narrower in range and restricted in her methods, the demure, "ladylike" Teasdale could seem old-fashioned, not unlike the "genteel" poetesses of the preceding age. But she was in fact just as up-to-date (and undeluded) as Millay in her attitudes. Although Teasdale definitely did not burn *her* candle at both ends, in her poems very strong emotions are held in check by well-wrought forms. Her verses express a cool modern psychology, and beneath their placid surfaces are contained depths of understanding in matters of the heart.

Sara Teasdale was born in St. Louis, August 8, 1884, to a prosperous family. Her middle-aged parents were self-conscious about her late birth and overprotected their shy and hypersensitive child. She was first educated at home, then attended private schools. As a girl she was sickly, and throughout her life she suffered from a variety of real or psychosomatic illnesses that required frequent rest cures. After employing private tutors, maids, and nurses to tend to the invalid she created, her mother was able to keep the fragile child under her control until she was thirty.

Writing provided Teasdale an emotional and artistic outlet. It was also her only way of making money and thus of escaping total dependence upon her family. Her early work appeared in *Reedy's Mirror*, and her parents underwrote publication of her first, rather conventional book, *Sonnets to Duse*, in 1907. *Helen of Troy* came out in 1911. On visits to New York City in the early teens, Teasdale attended meetings of the Poetry Society of America, making friends particularly with older women helpful to her career, including PSA president Jessie Rittenhouse, who later arranged that she receive the Columbia Poetry Prize (precursor of the Pulitzer) in 1917 for her *Love Songs*. In New York she also met the editor Harriet Monroe, who presented her often in *Poetry*. Teasdale did not wholly approve of the magazine, which she felt was overly committed to Ezra Pound and printed too much material reflecting his difficult Modernist tastes. She did like the fact that *Poetry* paid. Indeed, she never contributed to a journal that did not pay.

Besides publication fees and prizes, Monroe offered Teasdale advice, and in 1913 even tried to play matchmaker. As her ideal candidate she proposed Vachel Lindsay, the self-described "literary tramp" whose huge popular success Monroe had been highly effective in promoting. At the time Teasdale was already in love with the poet and editor John Hall Wheelock, who was cultivated, tall, dark, and handsome: all that Lindsay was not. She knew instantly that the improvident Lindsay was unsuitable as a spouse. In fact, in terms of social background, temperament, and artistic ambitions, they could hardly have been more incompatible. Teasdale gently reminded Monroe that Vachel was "a perfect child about money" and could never provide adequately for her, let alone children. But not wanting to hurt the feelings of either, she permitted a courtship of several months. At one point Lindsay visited St. Louis and thrilled Teasdale's family and friends with one of his famously theatrical poetry performances. Ultimately Wheelock did not reciprocate her affection and proved not the ideal man she had imagined. But Sara also felt Vachel's protestations of love were not entirely genuine, and turned him down.

Meanwhile, Monroe's assistant Eunice Tietjens had offered a solid alternative, her friend the St. Louis businessman Ernst Filsinger, who Sara discovered was a secret admirer. Indeed, he had many of Teasdale's poems by heart and had fallen in love with her through her work. After a whirlwind courtship, they married in December 1914. The marriage was not a success, perhaps because of Sara's unaddressed or unresolved issues of sexual identity. (They never shared a bedroom, even when traveling by ship.) Yet Ernst remained utterly devoted. Teasdale was often alone in their fine Manhattan apartment on Central Park West, because Filsinger's successful shoe business took him abroad for extended periods. But even when he was back in

New York, they were much apart, as Sara frequently found herself unwell and sought respite at health resorts. Finally, in 1929, she obtained a Reno divorce and received a generous settlement.

Whatever the personal costs of her unhappiness, as an artist Teasdale turned her depressions and losses into ever more subtly crafted and evocative verses. With the passing years, her poems became more taut and spare in their means, more direct in their emotional impact. Besides *Love Songs*, her other well-received later volumes include *Rivers to the Sea* (1915), *Flame and Shadow* (1920), and *Dark of the Moon* (1926). She also assembled an anthology of children's verse, *Rainbow Gold* (1921), and worked on an edition of Christina Rossetti's poems. *Stars Tonight: Verses for Boys and Girls* appeared in 1930. But with age Teasdale's illnesses and groundless financial fears increased. As William Drake records in his sympathetic biography, *Sara Teasdale: Woman & Poet* (1979), she became increasingly isolated, even as her popularity grew.

In the early twenties, while Teasdale's career was on the ascendant, Lindsay's declined drastically. In 1923 he suffered a nervous breakdown and was often in precarious health, and in dire financial straits, thereafter. He married in 1925, and to support his wife and two children he resumed giving dramatic readings (which he now abhorred), usually of "The Congo" and other pieces that first brought him fame. By the late twenties he was having trouble placing poems or freelance articles and was forced to go on the road again, despite the dangers to mind and body. In December 1931 he committed suicide by swallowing a bottle of Lysol. He and Teasdale had remained good friends, and she was profoundly affected by his death.

In her last years she was befriended by a college student, Margaret Conklin, who looked after her (no easy task, given the poet's gloomy self-absorption) and eventually became her literary executor. Death, which looms as an obsession in much of Teasdale's work, came through an overdose of sleeping pills on January 29, 1933. Her final poems were collected later that year in *Strange Victory*.

AFTER LOVE

> There is no magic when we meet,
>   We speak as other people do,
> You work no miracle for me
>   Nor I for you.

You were the wind and I the sea—
    There is no splendor any more,
I have grown listless as the pool
    Beside the shore.

But tho' the pool is safe from storm
    And from the tide has found surcease
It grows more bitter than the sea,
    For all its peace.

ELINOR WYLIE

▣ Movie-star glamorous, captivating in conversation and elegant in attire, the thrice-married Elinor Wylie scandalized Society on both sides of the Atlantic before finding fame and social rehabilitation through her likewise exceptionally engaging and perfectly fashioned verses. Wylie's striking appearance and personal charm mesmerized both women and men, but it was her genuine talent that earned her the regard of the literary world, including such demanding critics as Edmund Wilson and Carl Van Vechten and fellow artists like Elizabeth Bishop and Louise Bogan. She even won the affectionate respect of the equally glamorous Edna St. Vincent Millay, with whom she shared "star" billing among the highly popular women poets of the twenties and thirties. Eighty years after her untimely death, Wylie's well-wrought poems have lost little of their freshness or power to delight by their subtle use of language, original angle of vision, emotional resonance, and arresting wit.

    Wylie was born Elinor Hoyt on September 7, 1885, in Somerville, New Jersey, a fact she did not like repeated (the place, not the date), into a socially prominent family. Her grandfather Henry Martyn Hoyt had been governor of Pennsylvania. Her similarly named father served under Presidents Theodore Roosevelt and William Howard Taft, eventually rising to solicitor general of the United States. She attended Miss Baldwin's School near Bryn Mawr, Pennsylvania, then finished high school and her formal education at the Holton-Arms School in Washington, D.C. In 1906 she married Philip Hichborn, the son of a rear admiral; their son was born a year later. Hichborn proved highly neurotic, deeply depressive, and often abusive. When Elinor told her mother she wanted out of the marriage, Mrs. Hoyt was not sympathetic: such things simply were not done. (Mr. Hoyt, meanwhile, continued a longtime affair with his mistress.) In 1910 she was persuaded to run off to Canada by Horace Wylie, a socialite attorney almost twenty years her senior and the father of four, who was smitten with and indeed had stalked Elinor for years. (Her own three-year-old Philip III was left with her parents, who raised the boy.) Both elopers were ostracized by their families and friends, so they fled to England, hoping to find a quiet life. Under an assumed name, they settled in the village of Bournemouth. In due course their notoriety caught up with them, and once again they became social outcasts.

In 1915, with the onset of World War I, they returned to the States, after Hichborn had shot himself dead and Wylie's wife at last gave him a divorce. They married the following year, and settled finally in Washington, despite their darkened reputations there. While in England in 1912, Elinor had privately printed a collection called *Incidental Numbers*, which she later rejected as immature. In the habit of writing a poem a day, she was now determined to become a serious author. In 1919 she left Wylie and moved to New York. She created a brilliant impression and made many literary friends, including Wilson, John Dos Passos, and John Peale Bishop, who encouraged her endeavor.

She said she hesitated to send work to *Poetry*, thinking her verse insufficiently "modern," but upon her first submission in 1919 Harriet Monroe accepted four poems—and asked for more. Wylie first appeared in Monroe's monthly in April 1920 and frequently thereafter, while also contributing verse, essays, reviews, and short fiction to the *Woman's Home Companion*, *The New Republic*, *Scribner's*, and diverse other leading magazines. She was asked to be literary editor of *Vanity Fair* in 1922. Amid this work and her active social life, she managed to complete four poetry books and four novels in just eight years.

With the aid of William Rose Benét, a poet and later editor of the *Saturday Review of Literature* (and older brother of the more famous Stephen Vincent Benét), Wylie's first mature collection, *Nets to Catch the Wind*, was published in 1921, to glowing reviews. It remained her favorite book and included arguably her best poems, though equally fine were several in her second collection, *Black Armour*, issued two years later. In 1923 she divorced Horace Wylie and married William Rose Benét, but kept the now-famous Wylie name.

She was invited to the MacDowell Colony, the artists' retreat in New Hampshire, where she worked on her first novel, *Jennifer Lorn*, a romance set in eighteenth-century India, also published in the eventful year 1923, and again to wide praise. Three other historical novels followed at regular intervals, along with two more verse collections, *Trivial Breath* (1928) and *Angels and Earthly Creatures* (1929). Although not as spirited or original as her first two books of poems, in their superb technique, particularly with sonnets, the collections demonstrated Wylie's undiminished mastery of her craft.

By the late twenties, the romance had long gone out of her third marriage, and she and Benét separated, though they reunited at various times and always remained good friends and supportive literary colleagues. In 1928 Wylie had an affair with the husband of a friend in England; the liaison elicited the sonnet sequence that became her last book. In hopes of marrying her new love, she planned to divorce Benét and returned to New York to inform him. She had long suffered from high blood pressure, and shortly after making final corrections to *Angels and Earthly Creatures*, she suffered a massive stroke and died on December 16, 1928. Ever devoted, Benét saw the volume through the press.

Mary Hoyt composed a memoir of her sister, *Elinor Wylie: The Portrait of an Unknown Lady*, in 1935. Alfred A. Knopf issued her *Collected Poems* in 1932 (with many reprintings thereafter) and the almost eight hundred pages of her *Collected Prose* in 1933. Both were edited by Benét, who also printed his lectures on *The Prose and Poetry of Elinor Wylie* in 1934. *The Last Poems of Elinor Wylie*, edited by Jane D. Wise with an introduction by Benét, appeared in 1943. Stanley Olson's full-length study, *Elinor Wylie: A Life Apart: A Biography*, was published in 1979 and Judith Farr's *The Life and Art of Elinor Wylie* in 1983. An analysis of Wylie (along with Amy Lowell, Teasdale, Millay, Bogan, and H.D.) is included in Cheryl Walker's *Outrageous and Obscure: Culture, Psyche, and Persona in Modern Women Poets*, 1991.

THE EAGLE AND THE MOLE

Avoid the reeking herd,
Shun the polluted flock,
Live like that stoic bird,
The eagle of the rock.

The huddled warmth of crowds
Begets and fosters hate;
He keeps, above the clouds,
His cliff inviolate.

When flocks are folded warm,
And herds to shelter run,
He sails above the storm,
He stares into the sun.

If in the eagle's track
Your sinews cannot leap,
Avoid the lathered pack,
Turn from the steaming sheep.

If you would keep your soul
From spotted sight or sound,
Live like the velvet mole;
Go burrow underground.

And there hold intercourse
With roots of trees and stones,
With rivers at their source,
And disembodied bones.

PARTING GIFT

I cannot give you the Metropolitan Tower;
I cannot give you heaven;
Nor the nine Visigoth crowns in the Cluny Museum;
Nor happiness, even.
But I can give you a very small purse
Made out of field-mouse skin,
With a painted picture of the universe
And seven blue tears therein.

I cannot give you the island of Capri;
I cannot give you beauty;
Nor bake you marvellous crusty cherry pies

With love and duty.
But I can give you a very little locket
Made out of wildcat hide:
Put it into your left-hand pocket
And never look inside.

H.D.

◧ Hilda Doolittle became identified by her initials after Ezra
Pound blue-penciled her early poems, scrawled "H.D., *Imagiste*" be-
low them, and attached a cover letter to Harriet Monroe at *Poetry*
magazine declaring the work was "Objective—no slither; direct . . .
It's straight talk—straight as the greek!" (The scene of this Major
Moment in literary history was the tea room of the British Mu-
seum.) Four of the poems were printed in *Poetry* in January 1913 and
created much speculation about the mysterious author. Within
months Doolittle asked Monroe to drop the "affected" *Imagiste* tag.
But thus she was known ever after—to her frustration when her
writing changed and broadened in scope, to longer sequences and
narratives, but editors kept asking for poems in her terse early style.
    Doolittle was born in Bethlehem, Pennsylvania, on September
10, 1886, the only girl among five brothers. Her father Charles
taught mathematics and astronomy, subjects that the poet invested
with mystical significance. Dr. Doolittle eventually became a pro-
fessor at the University of Pennsylvania and the director of the
Flower Observatory. Her mother Helen was a member of the Mora-
vian brotherhood, a dissident Protestant sect originally from Ger-
many that believed in direct contact with and enlightenment from
God. This numinous connection with the deity was passed down
family to family, they taught, and the writer herself thought part of
her gifts as a poet stemmed from this visionary tradition.
    After attending a Quaker school, Hilda entered Bryn Mawr
College, where she met Marianne Moore and developed a close
bond with an art student, Frances Gregg. She also had a romance
with Pound—she inspired several of his early poems, and they were
engaged for a time—then became friends with William Carlos
Williams while the men were students at Penn. Doolittle stayed in
college only briefly. She failed English (her spelling and punctuation

always remained shaky) and had a nervous breakdown, precipitated by her conflicted feelings about Pound and Gregg, as she later revealed in her autobiographical novel *HERmione* (written in 1923 but not published until twenty years after her death).

In 1911, with Frances Gregg and Gregg's mother, she traveled to Europe (as Pound had strongly recommended), intending only a short visit, but stayed the rest of her life. In London Pound introduced her to important literary friends as well as to several emerging authors he herded under the Imagist banner: the nineteen-year-old poet and translator Richard Aldington, the still unknown James Joyce, and the likewise obscure D. H. Lawrence, to whom she became attracted despite her ambivalent feelings about him. (Aldington wrote of their friendship with Lawrence in *Portrait of a Genius, But . . .* [1950].) Pound later admitted to Harriet Monroe that he had hastily made up the Imagist "movement" mainly to get H.D. into print. But gradually she, like his other "protégés," became weary of Pound's high-handed ways and began to distance herself and take her instruction from Aldington, who encouraged her reading, particularly of the French Symbolists. Later the two also accepted the invitation of Pound's by-then archrival Amy Lowell to contribute to her *Some Imagist Poets* anthologies (1915, 1916, 1917).

In 1913 Doolittle married Aldington, who with Pound's help had acquired an editorial position at *The Egoist*, the important early little magazine. (She also worked there for a time.) In 1917, after Aldington went off to fight in the Great War, H.D. had a brief liaison with the composer (and future noted music critic) Cecil Gray and became pregnant. She also became seriously ill with pneumonia and feared she would lose the child. (She had suffered the stillbirth of her first child, by Aldington, in 1915.) But she was cared for through the safe delivery of her daughter Perdita by her new friend, the novelist and shipping heiress Winifred Ellerman—known by her adopted name Bryher—eight years her junior, and the two became loving companions to the end. H.D. and Aldington separated after the war, and Bryher eventually adopted the child. In 1919 Bryher took H.D. on her first visit to Greece, where the poet had the first of a number of "visions," and also brought her to Egypt and the United States (twice) in the twenties.

When Bryher entered into a marriage of convenience with the gay novelist Robert McAlmon in 1921, H.D. accompanied them to Paris, where Bryher underwrote McAlmon's adventurous Contact

Press, publisher of the earliest books of Ernest Hemingway, Djuna Barnes, Mina Loy, and Gertrude Stein. Retaining her deep interest in classical mythology—which she recast from a feministic viewpoint or revised to present strong matriarchal figures—H.D. published the poetry volumes *Hymen* (1921), *Heliodora and Other Poems* (1924), *Collected Poems* (1925), *Hippolytus Temporizes* (1927), and *Red Roses for Bronze* (1931), as well as the experimental prose of *Palimpsest* (1926), which fictionalizes her early relationship with Bryher, and *Hedylus* (1928).

Meanwhile, Bryher divorced McAlmon and in 1927 married Kenneth Macpherson, an avant-garde filmmaker, and together they started the cinema journal *Close Up* and a production company. H.D. appeared in three movies (she had movie-star looks but limited acting ability) and became acquainted with the great Russian film pioneer Sergei Eisenstein and other movie directors. She began to have trouble writing and feared the loss of her talent. An early supporter of psychoanalysis, Bryher arranged for H.D. to meet Sigmund Freud in Vienna, and the poet became his analysand in 1933 and 1934. (*Tribute to Freud*, her memoir of the experience, which was not entirely satisfactory—Doolittle considered his diagnosis incorrect— was printed in 1956.) In the thirties Bryher's house in Switzerland, at Territet near Montreux, became their primary residence. One of the first to relay news of the brutality and terror tactics behind the rise of the Nazis, Bryher frequently crossed the border into Germany and helped many Jews, leftist intellectuals, and other political refugees escape.

During World War II, despite the dangers of the frequent bombings and ensuing fires, the couple moved to London (they lived in the heart of the city, near Hyde Park), where Bryher published the magazine *Life and Letters Today* while H.D. worked on new prose and poetry, including *The Walls Do Not Fall* (1944), her evocative reflections on existence in the ravaged London of the war years. It became the first volume of *Trilogy*, completed with *Tribute to the Angels* (1945) and the *Flowering of the Rod* (1946). Always interested in spiritualism and Moravian doctrine and ritual, she became ever more involved in the forties with the occult, astrology, Tarot cards, and other esoteric arts.

After the war H.D. had a severe nervous breakdown and returned to Switzerland for treatment. Still, she continued to write. Her *Selected Poems* appeared in 1957, the novel *Bid Me to Live* in

1960, and *Helen in Egypt* in 1961. She made her last trip to the United States in 1960, to accept the Award of Merit Medal from the American Academy of Arts and Letters. In July 1961 she suffered a stroke and died two months later in Zurich. Other books waiting to be published posthumously were *Hermetic Definition* (1972), *End to Torment: A Memoir of Ezra Pound* (1979), and *The Gift* (1982).

In recent decades Doolittle's life and works have attracted increasing attention from literary historians, scholarly critics, and feminist theorists. Susan Stanford Friedman's *Psyche Reborn: The Emergence of H.D.* appeared in 1981, Barbara Guest's biography *Herself Defined: The Poet H.D. and Her World* was published in 1984, and Rachel Blau DuPlessis's *H.D.: The Career of That Struggle* in 1986. Friedman and DuPlessis also edited *Signets: Reading H.D.* (1990). Other, more specialized studies include Gary Burnett, *H.D. Between Image and Epic: The Mysteries of Her Poetics* (1990), and Dianne Chisholm, *H.D.'s Freudian Poetics: Psychoanalysis in Translation* (1992).

BIRDS IN SNOW

See,
how they trace
across the very-marble
of this place,
bright sevens and printed fours,
elevens and careful eights,
abracadabra
of a mystic's lore
or symbol
outlined
on a wizard's gate;

like plaques of ancient writ
our garden flags now name
the great and very-great;
our garden flags acclaim
in carven hieroglyph,
here king and kinglet lie,
here prince and lady rest,
mystical queens sleep here
and heroes that are slain

in holy righteous war;
hieratic, slim and fair,
the tracery written here,
proclaims what's left unsaid
in Egypt of her dead.

From THE WALLS DO NOT FALL

I

An incident here and there,
and rails gone (for guns)
from your (and my) old town square:

mist and mist-grey, no colour,
still the Luxor bee, chick and hare
pursue unalterable purpose

in green, rose-red, lapis;
they continue to prophesy
from the stone papyrus:

there, as here, ruin opens
the tomb, the temple; enter,
there as here, there are no doors:

the shrine lies open to the sky,
the rain falls, here, there
sand drifts; eternity endures:

ruin everywhere, yet as the fallen roof
leaves the sealed room
open to the air,

so, through our desolation,
thoughts stir, inspiration stalks us
through gloom:

unaware, Spirit announces the Presence;
shivering overtakes us,
as of old, Samuel:

trembling at a known street-corner,
we know not nor are known;
the Pythian pronounces—we pass on

to another cellar, to another sliced wall
where poor utensils show
like rare objects in a museum;

Pompeii has nothing to teach us,
we know crack of volcanic fissure,
slow flow of terrible lava,

pressure on heart, lungs, the brain
about to burst its brittle case
(what the skull can endure!):

over us, Apocryphal fire,
under us, the earth sway, dip of a floor,
slope of a pavement

where men roll, drunk
with a new bewilderment,
sorcery, bedevilment:

the bone-frame was made for
no such shock knit within terror,
yet the skeleton stood up to it:

the flesh? it was melted away,
the heart burnt out, dead ember,
tendons, muscles shattered, outer husk dismembered,

yet the frame held:
we passed the flame: we wonder
what saved us? what for?

VI

In me (the worm) clearly
is no righteousness, but this—

persistence; I escaped spider-snare,
bird-claw, scavenger bird-beak,

clung to grass-blade,
the back of a leaf

when storm-wind
tore it from its stem;

I escaped, I explored
rose-thorn forest,

was rain-swept
down the valley of a leaf;

was deposited on grass,
where mast by jewelled mast

bore separate ravellings
of encrusted gem-stuff

of the mist
from each banner-staff:

unintimidated by multiplicity
of magnified beauty,

such as your gorgon-great
dull eye can not focus

nor compass, I profit
by every calamity;

I eat my way out of it;
gorged on vine-leaf and mulberry,

parasite, I find nourishment:
when you cry in disgust,

a worm on a leaf,
a worm in the dust,

a worm on the ear-of-wheat,
I am yet unrepentant,

for I know how the Lord God
is about to manifest, when I,

the industrious worm,
spin my own shroud.

EDITH SITWELL

Although in her aesthetics she was vigorously forward-looking, in her appearance Edith Sitwell seemed a throwback to a much earlier era. Six feet tall, gaunt, and with a sharply angular face and aquiline nose, she bore a striking resemblance to Queen Elizabeth I, a likeness accentuated by age and the poet's artifices: starkly pale makeup, elaborate brocaded gowns and headdresses, and heavy jewelry, some now on display in London's Victoria and Albert Museum. The total effect was arresting, and irresistible to painters and photographers, notably her friend Cecil Beaton, whose dramatic portraits helped attract attention to her work. Less happily, her exotic looks and avant-garde experiments also made her the object of derision—a later generation would call her "campy"—though much of the mockery was *ad feminam* and grossly unfair.

Taking their cue from the title of her most famous work, *Façade*, Sitwell's critics considered her pieces (and their author) put-ons: superficial, pretentious, or worse. But like Ezra Pound, her friend T. S. Eliot, and other Modernist insurgents, she was in dead earnest in her efforts to reform poetry. Like them, she wanted to clear away trite, outmoded conventions—"the rhythmical flaccidity, the verbal deadness, the dead and expected patterns"—particularly as represented by the genteel traditional verse of the Georgians, the Establishment authors named after the then-reigning monarch.

In "Some Notes" that preface her *Collected Poems*, the poet offered an apology for her methods. While Pound and the Imagists emphasized sight and word pictures to express contemporary reality, Sitwell ingeniously manipulated sounds and rhythms in an attempt, she explained, to represent in verse the motion—the *speed*—of the modern world. In her early work, verbal music, not meaning, became her primary interest: assonance, dissonance, intricate metrical patterns, jazz syncopations, witty nonsense with clever end- and internal-rhymes, all inventively deployed to often hypnotic effect. Early listeners remarked on the stylization of her pieces and their percussive qualities, not unlike performances on a xylophone.

Many of these technical marvels, above all *Façade* (1922), remain entertaining, or at least intriguing in their elaborate mechanics. But following this initial period of witty, irreverent virtuoso display, Sitwell became more conservative in attitude and accessible in method, like Eliot. (Both also got religion and converted, first Eliot to Anglicanism, then Sitwell eventually to Catholicism.) With the years, she took herself ever more seriously. Indeed, she solemnly declared in her introduction to "The Canticle of the Rose" (1949) that she considered her poems "hymns of praise to the glory of life." Such statements merely encouraged her detractors to pitch more darts to deflate the high-mindedness.

Edith Louisa Sitwell was born at Scarborough, Derbyshire, in 1887, on September 7 (coincidentally Elizabeth I's birthday), the first child of the eccentric Sir George Sitwell, 4th Baronet, and his very young wife Lady Ida, a granddaughter of the Duke of Beaufort. Both sides of the aristocratic family had ancient roots, and Edith could claim descent from the Plantagenet dynasty. She and her siblings grew up amid stately-home splendor at Renishaw Hall and Scarborough, but her parents' marriage was not happy. Both treated their daughter badly. In her autobiography, *Taken Care Of* (1965), the poet remembered: "My parents were strangers to me from the moment of my birth."

Sir George was partial only to her younger brothers, Osbert and Sacheverell, also talented writers, and spent most of his time restoring his villa near Florence until he died, bankrupt, in 1943. The free-spending Lady Ida had money problems too, which eventually led to blackmail and her imprisonment for fraud. Beautiful and elegant herself, she was repelled by Edith's gawky height and unlovely features. When her mother died, in 1937, the uncomely but now-famous author did not attend the funeral.

True good fortune arrived in 1903, however, in the person of Helen Rootham, who was first hired as Sitwell's governess then became her devoted, lifelong friend. Rootham introduced her charge to modern music and the poetry of the French Symbolists, and encouraged her to break free of her unloving home and assert her individuality. In 1914 they moved together to London and rented a small flat in Bayswater, where Sitwell embarked on her literary career. She published her first poem in 1915 and her first book, *Clowns' Houses*, in 1918. From 1916 to 1921 she edited *Wheels*, an annual, aggressively avant-garde anthology that featured herself, her brothers (always her staunchest allies), the novelist and essayist Aldous Huxley, and Wilfred Owen, whose collected poetry she helped get printed after his death in the Great War.

Meanwhile, up at Oxford, her brothers met and virtually adopted William Walton, a very young, precocious, impoverished composer, who in a few weeks in 1922 brilliantly set the several sections of *Façade* to music. His jazzy score and Sitwell's declamations of her texts from backstage—through a megaphone inserted in the curtain, which was painted with a huge mouth—created a sensation at its Aeolian Hall premiere in 1923. Poetry volumes as well as several prose books followed at regular intervals thereafter, as did controversy. Her verse collections chronicle the ever-shifting course of her experiments. *Rustic Elegies* was published in 1927 and *Gold Coast Customs* in 1929. At the same time she championed the work of Gertrude Stein, who introduced her to the Russian painter Pavel Tchelitchew. Sitwell fell in love with him, and remained so, though he was homosexual and never fully reciprocated her affection. She also befriended the young Dylan Thomas. When he made his debut with *18 Poems* in 1934, she gave the book a glowing review that immediately placed him, at age twenty, in the front rank of the younger generation.

In 1928, Helen Rootham was operated on for cancer, and Sitwell cared for her as Rootham declined to an invalid. They moved to Paris in 1932, where Rootham died in 1938. The thirties were distressing to Sitwell also for lack of money, and the poet turned to prose to generate income. With the outbreak of the war, she returned to England where she moved in with Osbert and his lover at Renishaw Hall and began to write poems in more traditional styles. *Street Songs*, her collection of 1942, included the elegiac but defiant "Still Falls the Rain," composed in response to the horrific bombings in London during the Blitz. It became extremely popular, particularly as set to music by Benjamin Britten. *The Song of the Cold* (1945) and *The Shadow of Cain* (1947) were also very well received, by the public if not always by the critics.

In 1948 all three Sitwells went on a highly publicized and extremely successful tour of the United States, during which Edith not only intoned her poems but gave dramatic readings of Lady Macbeth's Act V sleepwalking soliloquy. In 1950 she published *Façade and Other Poems*. From its debut, attention to the theater piece was ensured by Sitwell's mesmerizing recordings, first with the composer Constant Lambert, then with Peter Pears, the noted tenor (and Britten's lover), as co-narrators. *Gardeners and Astronomers* appeared in 1953, and finally *The Outcasts* in 1962. In 1954, Queen Elizabeth II made her a Dame Commander of the British Empire. She also received honorary doctorates from both Oxford and Cambridge, among other universities.

Sitwell's several lively prose books were no less successful (and usually far more lucrative) than her poetry collections. Her biography *Alexander Pope* came out in 1930 and in 1933 the extremely popular *English Eccentrics*, a subject on which she was well informed. She also wrote *two* biographies of Elizabeth I, *Fanfare for Elizabeth* (1946) and *The Queens and the Hive* (1962), as well as *Victoria of England* (1963). By that time she had become an invalid herself, confined to a wheelchair. She gave her last public reading in 1962. Sitwell suffered a cerebral hemorrhage and died at St. Thomas's Hospital in London on December 9, 1964. Always noted for her witty remarks, on her deathbed she was heard to say (according to Elizabeth Salter's memoir, *The Last Years of a Rebel*, 1967): "I'm afraid I'm being an awful nuisance."

Sitwell's *Collected Poems* first appeared in 1930, was enlarged with its informative preface and new poems in 1954 and later, and has been reprinted several times, most recently in 2006. Victoria Glendinning's study *Edith Sitwell: A Unicorn Among Lions* first appeared in 1981 and was reissued in a new edition in 1993.

From FAÇADE

37. Sir Beelzebub

When
Sir
Beelzebub called for his syllabub in the hotel in Hell
    Where Proserpine first fell,

Blue as the gendarmerie were the waves of the sea,
　　　　　(Rocking and shocking the barmaid).

Nobody comes to give him his rum but the
Rim of the sky hippopotamus-glum
Enhances the chances to bless with a benison
Alfred Lord Tennyson crossing the bar laid
With cold vegetation from pale deputations
Of temperance workers (all signed In Memoriam)
Hoping with glory to trip up the Laureate's feet,
　　　　　(Moving in classical metres) . . .

Like Balaclava, the lava came down from the
Roof, and the sea's blue wooden gendarmerie
Took them in charge while Beelzebub roared for his rum.
　　　　　. . . None of them come!

STILL FALLS THE RAIN

The Raids, 1940. Night and Dawn

Still falls the Rain—
Dark as the world of man, black as our loss—
Blind as the nineteen hundred and forty nails
Upon the Cross.

Still falls the Rain
With a sound like the pulse of the heart that is changed to
　　　　the hammer-beat
In the Potter's Field, and the sound of the impious feet

On the Tomb:
　　　　　Still falls the Rain
In the Field of Blood where the small hopes breed and
　　　　the human brain
Nurtures its greed, that worm with the brow of Cain.

Still falls the Rain
At the feet of the Starved Man hung upon the Cross.
Christ that each day, each night, nails there, have mercy
　　　on us—

MARIANNE MOORE · 71

On Dives and on Lazarus:
Under the Rain the sore and the gold are as one.

Still falls the Rain—
Still falls the Blood from the Starved Man's wounded Side:
He bears in His Heart all wounds, —those of the light
        that died,
The last faint spark
In the self-murdered heart, the wounds of the sad un-
        comprehending dark,
The wounds of the baited bear, —
The blind and weeping bear whom the keepers beat
On his helpless flesh . . . the tears of the hunted hare.

Still falls the Rain—
Then—O Ile leape up to my God: who pulles me
        doune—
See, see where Christ's blood streames in the firmament:
It flows from the Brow we nailed upon the tree
Deep to the dying, to the thirsting heart
That holds the fires of the world, —dark-smirched with
        pain
As Caesar's laurel crown.

Then sounds the voice of One who like the heart of man
Was once a child who among beasts has lain—
'Still do I love, still shed my innocent light, my Blood,
        for thee.'

[All ellipses in the originals.]

MARIANNE MOORE

▣ When she accepted the National Book Award in 1952, Mari-
anne Moore remarked that her work was called poetry only for lack
of any other category in which to put it. Her style is indeed idio-
syncratic: meticulously detailed yet concise, suggesting much by
means of well-chosen natural images; replete with wry observations
and quotations (always carefully identified) from diverse texts, often

nonliterary and esoteric; and formed of long sentences broken into intricate, quirky patterns. Moore was fond of animals, particularly the armored kinds, and liked to draw ironic analogies between their behavior and that of supposedly superior humans. In her later years she became something of a pet herself. Photographed by *Life* and *Look* in her signature tricorne hat and cape, she became a kind of mascot to the non-poetry-reading public, an enthusiastic if eccentric baseball fan so beloved she was given the honor of throwing out the first ball of the 1968 season at Yankee Stadium.

Marianne Moore was born in Kirkwood, Missouri, November 15, 1887. Her father had a nervous breakdown and was institutionalized before she was born, and she lived with her mother and year-older brother, John Warner Moore, in her grandfather's house until his death in 1894. The three then moved to Carlisle, Pennsylvania, where they lived briefly with relatives as her mother took a job teaching. This precarious early life of genteel poverty made the little family particularly close. (In their affectionate and lively correspondence, Warner is nicknamed, among many other things, "Pidge," "Bullfrog," and "Bible"—he became a Presbyterian minister and navy chaplain—and she is addressed as "Sissy," "Gater," "Fang," and eventually "Rat," after the character in *The Wind in the Willows*, which appeared in 1913; Warner then became "Badger" and their mother "Mole.") Moore entered Bryn Mawr College in 1905, made friends with her schoolmate Hilda Doolittle, and studied history and biology, which honed her skills at precise description. After graduation in 1909 she took secretarial courses at a commercial college, then taught typing and bookkeeping for more than four years at the United States Industrial Indian School in Carlisle. One of her students was the formidable future baseball and football player and Olympic decathlon champion Jim Thorpe.

In April 1915, Moore had her first professional publication in the *Egoist*, edited in London by H.D. In May she made her American debut in *Poetry*. Alfred Kreymborg presented her in his newly founded *Others* soon after. In 1918 she moved with her mother to New York City, to St. Luke's Place in Greenwich Village, where Moore made friends with the authors and artists associated with *Others*, including William Carlos Williams, Man Ray, Alfred Stieglitz, and particularly Wallace Stevens, with whom she maintained a life-long correspondence. She took a part-time job in a branch of the public library, continued publishing, and won the admiration of Eliot and Pound. In 1921 in London, H.D. and her lover Bryher (Winifred Ellerman) took the liberty of compiling and printing Moore's early work in *Poems*. An expanded, authorized edition entitled *Observations* appeared in 1924 and won a $2,000 prize from the *Dial*, the most prominent arts journal in America at that time.

In 1925, Moore was asked to take over the *Dial* and edited it with great distinction until it folded in 1929. With her mother she then moved from Manhattan to Brooklyn, supporting herself as a freelance writer. She remained there until 1965, when she relocated to West Ninth Street in Greenwich Village. In 1932, when it appeared that *Poetry* too would collapse, she contributed "The Steeple-Jack," "The Student," "The Hero," and "No Swan So Fine," which were awarded the magazine's Levinson Prize, boosting her career. In 1935 her *Collected Poems* appeared with a preface by Eliot, who declared that her work formed "part of the small body of durable poetry written in our time"; even so, the book was remaindered. *The Pangolin and Other Verse* followed in 1936, then *What Are Years* (1941) and *Nevertheless* (1944). Although she produced several other volumes, the later work seldom surpassed her earlier poems, many of which she revised (sometimes drastically and usually unwisely). In the most notorious example, from the so-called *Complete Poems* of 1967 (which in fact contained less than half of her work), she reduced the original five stanzas of "Poetry," perhaps her most famous piece, to:

I, too, dislike it.
Reading it, however, with a perfect contempt for it, one discovers in it, after all, a place for the genuine.

In July 1947, Moore's mother died, a devastating loss the poet may have tried to assuage by completing her translation of Jean de la Fontaine's *Fables*, a project she had begun some time before. After years of labor, and four revisions, it was rejected by the first house she offered it to, but finally was published in 1954, to mixed reviews. The French government awarded her the Croix de Chevalier des Arts et Lettres, and in following years she won nearly all the major American awards for poetry.

In 1951 Moore's *Collected Poems* won the literary Triple Crown: the Pulitzer Prize, the National Book Award, and the Bollingen Prize. So high became her profile that in 1955 a Ford Motor Company executive asked her to propose names for their new car. She offered several, including the Turcotingo, the Mongoose Civique, and the Utopian Turtletop. Ford thanked her for the suggestions but decided to christen it the Edsel, after the son of the company's founder. Besides the later poetry collections *Like a Bulwark* (1956), *O to Be a Dragon* (1959), and *Tell Me, Tell Me* (1966), she gathered her prose pieces in *Predilections* (1955), *Idiosyncrasy and Technique* (1959), and *Poetry and Criticism* (1965). Moore always was partial to athletes, and the most unusual prose she ever penned was the liner notes she composed to accompany a work by a boxer-poet she greatly admired, Muhammad Ali, for his spoken-word album, *I Am the Greatest!*

After suffering a series of strokes, Marianne Moore died in her apartment on February 5, 1972. Her manuscripts, diaries, books, letters, and other papers were acquired by the Rosenbach Museum and Library in Philadelphia, to which she bequeathed her furniture and other personal items, which are now displayed there, on the third floor, in a recreation of her living room–study. A revised but still incomplete *Collected Poems* was published in 1981. *The Complete Prose*, edited and introduced by Patricia C. Willis, appeared in 1986, and Charles Molesworth's biography, *Marianne Moore: A Literary Life*, in 1990. In 1997 a *Selected Letters* appeared, with an introduction and notes by Bonnie Costello, who edited the collection with Celeste Goodrich and Cristanne Miller.

Documenting in detail the poet's habit of frequent revision, Robin G. Schulze's *Becoming Marianne Moore: Early Poems, 1907–1924* (2002) presents the pieces in their multiple variants, in facsimiles as they first appeared in little magazines and as altered, often substantially, in subsequent book publication (*Observations* of 1924 is also reprinted in facsimile), along with an introduction, variorum table, and bibliographical notes. Schulze also produced a biographical study, *The Web of Friendship: Marianne Moore and Wallace Stevens* (1996), based on their correspondence. A new, truly complete collection of *The Poems of Marianne Moore*, including many previously unpublished and uncollected pieces, edited and annotated by Grace Schulman, was at last issued in 2003.

NO SWAN SO FINE

"No water so still as the
  dead fountains of Versailles." No swan,

with swart blind look askance
and gondoliering legs, so fine
   as the chintz china one with fawn-
brown eyes and toothed gold
collar on to show whose bird it was.

Lodged in the Louis Fifteenth
   candelabrum-tree of cockscomb-
tinted buttons, dahlias,
sea-urchins, and everlastings,
   it perches on the branching foam
of polished sculptured
flowers—at ease and tall. The king is dead.

THE PAST IS THE PRESENT

If external action is effete
   and rhyme is outmoded,
     I shall revert to you,
   Habakkuk, as when in a Bible class
     the teacher was speaking of unrhymed verse.
He said—and I think I repeat his exact words,
     "Hebrew poetry is prose
   with a sort of heightened consciousness." Ecstasy affords
     the occasion and expediency determines the form.

SILENCE

My father used to say
"Superior people never make long visits,
have to be shown Longfellow's grave
or the glass flowers at Harvard.
Self-reliant like the cat—
that takes its prey to privacy,
the mouse's limp tail hanging like a shoelace from its mouth—
they sometimes enjoy solitude,
and can be robbed of speech

by speech which has delighted them.
The deepest feeling always shows itself in silence;
not in silence, but restraint."
Nor was he insincere in saying, "Make my house your inn."
Inns are not residences.

EDNA ST. VINCENT MILLAY

Brilliant and bold, Edna St. Vincent Millay became noted as much for her uninhibited lifestyle as for her gift for creating memorable lines. With virtuosic technique applied with apparent ease, almost nonchalance, she preferred to compose in traditional verse forms—sonnets were her forte—but filled their strict confines with unfettered sentiments shaped by attitudes of the emancipated modern woman. She was born in Rockland, Maine, February 22, 1892. When her mother gave her father his walking papers, she moved Edna and her sisters Norma and Kathleen to a poor section of Camden, supporting them with a nursing job. Cora Millay encouraged her girls to pursue their artistic ambitions, and Edna had her first publication when she was fourteen.

She became famous in 1912, at age twenty, for *losing* a contest. When her poem "Renascence" was awarded only fourth prize in an annual competition sponsored by *The Lyric Year*, the public and critics alike protested. In particular, Harriet Monroe's stinging editorial in the January 1913 issue of *Poetry* brought the precocious author much attention. A wealthy woman, Caroline Dow, heard Edna recite the poem and was so impressed she encouraged her to apply for a scholarship to Vassar, and offered to cover her remaining expenses.

At Vassar Millay was flamboyant, had affairs with schoolmates, and provoked the administration while she continued to write poems and began acting in school productions. In her senior year she took the lead in her own play, "The Princess Marries the Page." Immensely popular, Vincent (as she was known to her friends) did not take kindly to the strictures of college, particularly when they impinged on her social life, and her infractions of the rules brought her often to President Henry Noble MacCracken's office. He gave her reprimands but recognized her talents (she took his drama course), and though she persisted in flouting regulations, he declined to expel her. As he told her, he did not want another "banished Shelley" (who had been thrown out of Oxford) to be held against him. Millay replied: "On those terms, I think I will continue to live in this hell-hole."

She graduated in 1917, the year she published her first book, *Renascence and Other Poems*. She moved to Greenwich Village, joined the Provincetown Players (for whom she wrote the anti-war play *Aria da Capo* in 1919), and led a bohemian life with many artist and writer friends—Eugene O'Neill, Hart Crane, and Wallace Stevens among them—and lovers, female and male, including the well-known critic and lecher Edmund Wilson, the editor Floyd Dell of the revolutionary the *Masses*, and the poet and essayist John Peale Bishop. In 1920 she published *A Few Figs from Thistles*, of which the famous "First Fig" became an anthem for the liberated Roaring Twenties:

> My candle burns at both ends;
>   It will not last the night;
> But ah, my foes, and oh, my friends—
>   It gives a lovely light!

In 1921, Millay wrote a verse play, *The Lamp and the Bell*, and later the libretto for Deems Taylor's opera *The King's Henchman* (1927), which was produced at the Metropolitan Opera in New York then toured the country to tremendous applause. In 1922, she became the first woman to win the Pulitzer Prize, for *The Harp-Weaver*. She was now without question the most popular (and richest) poet in America, and considered by many critics the best as well, often compared with Keats and even Donne.

Millay entered into an "open" marriage with the wealthy Dutch coffee importer Eugen Boissevain in 1923. Twelve years her senior (and the widower of Inez Milholland, the noted early feminist activist), he was an exceedingly tolerant partner who looked after the poet with selfless devotion, catered to her every whim, and astutely managed her career. The couple moved to Steepletop, a large farm in upstate New York, in 1925 and made it a showplace. With her magnetic personality and seductively low voice, Millay became highly successful as a reader, on tour and especially on the radio, and her growing royalties supplemented Eugen's income to sustain their luxurious lifestyle.

One of her last serious romantic liaisons was with the young poet George Dillon, whom she met in Chicago while promoting

The Buck in the Snow (1928). A recent college graduate when she first met him and later an editor of *Poetry*, Dillon was handsome and intelligent but reticent, gay, and rather overwhelmed by her attentions. (Totally smitten, she continued their *amour* in Paris when he won a Guggenheim fellowship in 1932. Ever indulgent, Boissevain sailed home to give them free rein.) The affair, however ambivalent on Dillon's part, inspired Millay's sonnet-sequence *Fatal Interview* (1931), which quickly sold some fifty thousand copies. The two collaborated on a very fine translation of Baudelaire's *Flowers of Evil*, printed in 1936.

As Millay's beauty began to fade, so did her self-confidence, and she began to reduce her public appearances. Her once-glowing reviews were becoming fewer too, and critics voiced disappointment at the diminished quality of her later work. To compound her problems, in 1936 she was injured in a car accident, had to take painkillers, and became addicted to the drugs. The manuscript of her *Conversation at Midnight* went up in flames when the hotel where she was vacationing caught fire. (She later rewrote the book from memory, and it was printed in 1937.) During World War II, at the behest of the Writers' War Board, she produced some deliberately political poetry, which she later dismissed as not very good. (One piece, "The Murder of Lidice," commemorating the annihilation of the small Czech village by the Nazis, was broadcast nationally in 1942.) Boissevain attended her faithfully during her later years, which were plagued by alcoholism as well as her drug abuse, until his death, from lung cancer, in 1949. Millay died at home the following year, alone; a caretaker discovered the body. The newspapers attributed her demise to a heart attack. The truth was more appalling: after an apparent bout of drinking, she fell down a flight of steps and broke her neck.

After her death Millay's work was gathered by her sister Norma in the *Collected Poems*, filling more than seven hundred pages (published in 1956 and frequently reprinted). In 2001 two biographies appeared: Daniel Mark Epstein's *What Lips My Lips Have Kissed: The Loves and Love Poems of Edna St. Vincent Millay* and, after many years of anticipation, Nancy Milford's *Savage Beauty*, an exhaustive study of the poet and her times. Milford also edited and introduced *The Selected Poetry* for the Modern Library (2001). J. D. McClatchy has provided an excellent assessment of her life and work in his own edition of *Selected Poems* for the Library of America, published in 2003.

[WHAT LIPS MY LIPS HAVE KISSED]

What lips my lips have kissed, and where, and why,
I have forgotten, and what arms have lain
Under my head till morning; but the rain
Is full of ghosts tonight, that tap and sigh
Upon the glass and listen for reply,
And in my heart there stirs a quiet pain
For unremembered lads that not again
Will turn to me at midnight with a cry.
Thus in the winter stands the lonely tree,
Nor knows what birds have vanished one by one,
Yet knows its boughs more silent than before:
I cannot say what loves have come and gone,
I only know that summer sang in me
A little while, that in me sings no more.

[I, BEING BORN A WOMAN AND DISTRESSED]

I, being born a woman and distressed
By all the needs and notions of my kind,
Am urged by your propinquity to find
Your person fair, and feel a certain zest
To bear your body's weight upon my breast:
So subtly is the fume of life designed,
To clarify the pulse and cloud the mind,
And leave me once again undone, possessed.
Think not for this, however, the poor treason
Of my stout blood against my staggering brain,
I shall remember you with love, or season
My scorn with pity,—let me make it plain:
I find this frenzy insufficient reason
For conversation when we meet again.

DOROTHY PARKER

In an era abounding with exceedingly clever verbal inventors, Dorothy Parker proved a standout from the very start of her career, an exceptional talent in print and especially in person, when her gifts for brilliant impromptu wordplay and devastating repartee established her as a prime mover among her acid-tongued peers. In the 1920s and '30s she was an almost iconic figure, both admired and feared for the shrewd observations she expressed with often cruel wit. At the high points and the later, more frequent low points of her professional and personal life, she also unfortunately became representative of many other dazzling but distressed and self-destructive artists of her generation. Despite bad behavior and more than her share of bad breaks, Parker was, however, a survivor. And though satire generally has the shortest shelf life of all literary forms, her own productions in the genre have also endured. Her comic and not-so-light verses, short stories, and reviews have continued, decade after decade, to delight and instruct through the acerbic vision and bittersweet wisdom of their funny, finely crafted lines.

Parker was born Dorothy Rothschild on August 22, 1893, in Long Branch, New Jersey, where her well-to-do family had a summer home, and grew up on Manhattan's Upper West Side. Her mother died when she was not yet five. Her father, a garment manufacturer, soon remarried. Her stepmother, whom she disliked, died only three years into the marriage, and her father passed away a decade later, in 1913. Although nominally Jewish, she attended a private Catholic grammar school, then ended her formal education at Miss Dana's, a finishing school in Morristown, New Jersey. Already an accomplished writer of verse, she became a skilled pianist as well. By her late teens she was well known for her biting humor.

In the mid-teens she had no trouble getting poems accepted at *Vogue* and *Vanity Fair*, and was offered editorial positions at both journals. She was a staff writer, then became the drama critic at *Vanity Fair*, until she got fired for penning caustic reviews of plays backed by the magazine's sponsors. In 1917 she married a stockbroker, Edwin Pond Parker II, who soon went off to the Great War. He was wounded in action and, already an alcoholic, returned addicted to morphine. They divorced, but, ambivalent about her Jewish heritage in an age of blatant anti-Semitism, the author found it an asset to retain his Waspy name.

In 1919, with the dramatist Robert Sherwood and the humorist Robert Benchley, she formed the notorious Round Table at the Algonquin Hotel on West Forty-fourth Street in New York, near their offices. The "Vicious Circle" grew to include the journalist and screenwriter Ring Lardner, the comic author and artist James Thurber, the novelist Edna Ferber, the newspaper critic and columnist Alexander Woollcott, the Broadway playwright and producer George S. Kaufmann, and other wits, including occasionally Harpo Marx. Parker also became friends with Ernest Hemingway and had a romantic interlude with F. Scott Fitzgerald in Paris in the twenties. She joined *The New Yorker* at its founding in 1925, and over three decades she contributed many sharp poems, stories, and reviews as Constant Reader. (In 1928 she tartly ended a swift pan of A. A. ["Whimsy-the-Pooh"] Milne's saccharine *The House at Pooh Corner*: "Tonstant Weader fwowed up.")

Parker's first poetry volume, *Enough Rope* (1927), became a best-seller and was followed by *Sunset Gun* (1928) and *Death and Taxes* (1931), also well received. Her highly popular fiction was collected in *Laments for the Living* (1930), *After Such Pleasures* (1933), and *Here Lies* (1939). (*The New Yorker* writer Brendan Gill later remarked that the titles "amounted to a capsule autobiography.") Amid her critical and financial successes, Parker suffered bouts of depression and, like so many other authors of her era, she drank to excess. The dark side is apparent in her crisp and usually comic compositions in both fiction and poetry, where emotions are however kept firmly in check. (Overt sentimentality, for Parker and her cerebral set, was considered bad form.) Her sophisticated light verses are cunningly constructed, concise, and acutely perceptive, treating with irony and a cynical air the heartaches and other hard realities just beneath their elegant surfaces. Among the most famous of her pieces in this vein is "Résumé":

> Razors pain you;
> Rivers are damp;
> Acids stain you;
> And drugs cause cramp.
> Guns aren't lawful;
> Nooses give;
> Gas smells awful;
> You might as well live.

Parker joined the flock of New York writers who went to Hollywood in the thirties, and worked on several pictures, often without credit. She married the actor Alan Campbell, and they collaborated on several scripts, including the original version of *A Star Is Born*

(1937), which won them an Academy Award nomination. Their marriage was rocky, and they divorced in 1947 but reunited in 1950. With scores of others in show business, in 1955 Parker was called before the House Un-American Activities Committee and pleaded the Fifth Amendment. (She had reported on the Spanish Civil War for the *New Masses* and had protested the Sacco and Vanzetti trial in 1927 and became a socialist, like many writers at the time, but was never a member of the Communist party.) She was also investigated by the FBI and then blacklisted from the movie industry—a bitter turn, since she had helped organize the Screenwriters Guild, with Lillian Hellman and Dashiell Hammett, in 1937. At one point she went to the unemployment office and was soon surrounded by female fans who applauded the author of the immortal couplet: "Men seldom make passes / At girls who wear glasses" ("News Item," *Not So Deep as a Well*, 1936).

As a screenwriter, Parker had made (and squandered) enormous sums, and she was now reduced to freelance journalism, including writing movie reviews for *Esquire*. Meanwhile her alcoholism worsened, and with it the quarrels with her husband. She produced literary pieces only sporadically but did return to script work with Campbell. One of the few encouraging moments during the long decline occurred when Parker was inducted into the American Academy of Arts and Letters in 1959. Her husband died in 1963, of an overdose, and she moved back to New York City. Alone in her hotel apartment, Parker succumbed to a heart attack on June 6, 1967. As her epitaph, she had suggested, "Excuse my dust"—an ironically apt injunction, as it turned out, since her ashes lay unclaimed in her lawyer's filing cabinet for several years. She willed her literary estate to Dr. Martin Luther King, Jr. When he was assassinated ten months after her death, it was turned over to the NAACP.

Brendan Gill introduced *The Portable Dorothy Parker*, first published in 1973 and often reprinted. *Not Much Fun: The Lost Poems of Dorothy Parker*, edited by Stuart Y. Silverstein, was published in 1996. The *Complete Stories*, edited by Colleen Breese and introduced by Regina Barreca, was issued in 1999. She has been the subject of several biographies, including John Keats's *You Might As Well Live: The Life and Times of Dorothy Parker* (1970), Marion Meade's *Dorothy Parker: What Fresh Hell Is This?* (1988), and Kevin C. Fitzpatrick's *A Journey into Dorothy Parker's New York* (2005). Since her earliest publications, many of her *bons mots* have entered popular culture. Parker has been quoted, alluded to, and represented in many songs, plays, and television programs, and was portrayed in the 1995 film *Mrs. Parker and the Vicious Circle*, with Jennifer Jason Leigh in the title role.

ONE PERFECT ROSE

A single flow'r he sent me, since we met.
    All tenderly his messenger he chose;
Deep-hearted, pure, with scented dew still wet—
    One perfect rose.

I knew the language of the floweret;
    "My fragile leaves," it said, "his heart enclose."
Love long has taken for his amulet
    One perfect rose.

Why is it no one ever sent me yet
    One perfect limousine, do you suppose?
Ah no, it's always just my luck to get
    One perfect rose.

SYMPTOM RECITAL

I do not like my state of mind;
I'm bitter, querulous, unkind.
I hate my legs, I hate my hands,
I do not yearn for lovelier lands.
I dread the dawn's recurrent light;
I hate to go to bed at night.
I snoot at simple, earnest folk.
I cannot take the gentlest joke.
I find no peace in paint or type.
My world is but a lot of tripe.
I'm disillusioned, empty-breasted.
For what I think, I'd be arrested.
I am not sick, I am not well.
My quondam dreams are shot to hell.
My soul is crushed, my spirit sore;

I do not like me any more.
I cavil, quarrel, grumble, grouse.
I ponder on the narrow house.
I shudder at the thought of men. . . .
I'm due to fall in love again.

LOUISE BOGAN

🔲 For almost forty years Louise Bogan was one of the most power-
ful if self-effacing figures in American poetry, serving with distinc-
tion as the poetry editor and principal reviewer of verse for *The New
Yorker*. During her tenure from 1931 to 1969, American poetry un-
derwent several sea changes in styles and aesthetics, and with sure
judgment and broad taste she identified and promoted several of the
strongest writers from the pre– through the post–World War II pe-
riods. She herself did not alter course from traditional forms and
techniques. Her lyrics were understated and very finely crafted, elic-
iting the praise of many fellow artists, notably W. H. Auden, who also
thought her the best American critic. Her poetry production was rel-
atively small—she published only five collections—but like that of
the similarly unprolific Elizabeth Bishop (who contributed almost
exclusively to her magazine), Bogan's work was constructed to last.

Louise Marie Bogan was born August 11, 1897, in Livermore
Falls, Maine. Her father was a supervisor in paper mills, and the
family moved several times to different but uniformly bleak factory
towns in New England. Her parents' marriage was stormy, largely
because of her mother's infidelities, and grim memories from child-
hood shadowed Bogan's own adult relationships. Looking back, she
said she could not bear to describe "the horrors of the pre-1914
lower-middle-class life, in which [her parents] found themselves."
The family eventually moved to Boston in 1909 where, thanks to
support from a generous woman, Bogan was able to attend the pres-
tigious Girls' Latin School. She then enrolled in Boston University,
and after her first year was offered a scholarship to Radcliffe.

Instead of taking the opportunity, she married an army corpo-
ral, mainly to escape her unpleasant family. The young couple were
stationed in the Panama Canal Zone, where in 1917 Bogan gave
birth to a daughter. She left her husband in 1919, he died the fol-

lowing year, and she received a meager military pension. With the money she managed to travel in 1922 to Vienna and study the piano. (She left her child in the care of her parents.) She returned in 1923 and settled in New York City, where she met Raymond Holden, a minor novelist, and they married in 1925. In the meantime she published freelance articles and film reviews to support herself while composing poetry. Her serious interest had begun in high school when, as she recalled, she "tracked down" *Poetry* in the Boston Public Library and studied its pages, starting with its inaugural issue in 1912. In the early depression years the magazine's editor Harriet Monroe, an early booster who also sat on the literary panel of the Guggenheim Foundation, saw to it that she received a fellowship, which allowed Bogan to return to Europe.

Her first collection, *Body of This Death*, appeared in 1923. *Dark Summer* followed in 1929. Both volumes were artfully composed of spare verses on love, loneliness, and loss that balance strong feeling with cool reason, a style she always maintained. Her work won the respect of her peers, and she became friends with the key members of the advanced New York poetry set, including William Carlos Williams, Marianne Moore, Lola Ridge, and the critic Edmund Wilson. She began to print outstanding critical pieces herself in the leading journals, primarily *The New Yorker*, and in 1931 she was asked to become the magazine's poetry editor.

Throughout the twenties she suffered frequent bouts of depression and sought help from a therapist. By the early thirties the spells became so severe she required treatment in psychiatric hospitals, first in 1931 and again in 1933. In 1935 she had a brief affair with the young, and equally troubled, Theodore Roethke. (She did not think much of his apprentice poems, but she became a champion of his mature work.) Her marriage was unhappy and quarrel-filled, as Bogan's jealousy exacerbated her paranoid tendencies. She finally divorced Holden in 1937. Her lonely turmoil was transmuted into her lyrics, though never explicitly as in the so-called confessional poetry that became a vogue in the sixties. Bogan always remained a private, guarded poet and person. (Few of her friends knew she had a daughter.) Her third book, *The Sleeping Fury*, came out the year of her divorce. Her later volumes consisted mainly of previously published work with handfuls of recent pieces. *Poems and New Poems* appeared in 1941; her second gathering, *Collected Poems, 1923–1953*, was co-winner of the Bollingen Prize in 1955.

Like Elizabeth Bishop, Bogan was a very slow and meticulous writer given to painstaking revision. She alludes to the process in "The Daemon," where the muse becomes relentlessly demanding, even sadistic. Since her themes centered on love and its disappointments, poetry writing must have exacted great psychic costs for one of such fragile sensibility. But writing criticism was not always easy for her, either, especially if the work under consideration was by a woman. Bogan noted, from long experience, that "one woman poet is at a disadvantage in reviewing another, if the review be not laudatory."

Starting in the forties she occasionally taught at the University of Chicago, Brandeis, the University of Washington, and other schools. She served as Consultant in Poetry at the Library of Congress in 1945–1946. Asked to write a history of American verse in 1951, she produced *Achievement in American Poetry, 1900–1950*; she did not mention her own work in the book. She also translated poetry by Ernst Jünger, Goethe, and Jules Renard. In 1959 she won an award from the Academy of American Poets, and received recognition from the National Endowment for the Arts in 1967. Many of her poetry reviews and literary essays were collected in *A Poet's Alphabet: Reflections on the Literary Art and Vocation* in 1970.

In the preceding year she had given up her post at *The New Yorker* with relief, saying: "No more pronouncements on lousy verse. No more hidden competition. No more struggling not to be a square." Bogan's collected works, *The Blue Estuaries: Poems 1923–1968*, was published in 1968. It contains 103 poems, slightly fewer than Elizabeth Bishop allowed to be printed in her lifetime. Among Bogan's last poems are such exceptionally fine lyrics as "The Dream" and "Women," her stark psychological profile of women in their "traditional" roles. Alone in her Manhattan apartment, she died of a heart attack on February 4, 1970.

Various of her autobiographical pieces were collected and published posthumously in *Journey Around My Room* (1980). Elizabeth Frank's biography, *Louise Bogan: A Portrait*, won a Pulitzer Prize in 1986. Ruth Limmer edited Bogan's correspondence in *What the Woman Lived: Selected Letters of Louise Bogan, 1920–1970* (1973). Martha Collins's collection of reviews and articles, *Critical Essays on Louise Bogan*, was published in 1984, as was Jacqueline Ridgeway's more systematic study, *Louise Bogan*. Gloria Bowles's assessment from a feminist perspective, *Louise Bogan's Aesthetic of Limitation*, appeared in 1987.

WOMEN

Women have no wilderness in them,
They are provident instead,
Content in the tight hot cell of their hearts
To eat dusty bread.

They do not see cattle cropping red winter grass,
They do not hear
Snow water going down under culverts
Shallow and clear.

They wait, when they should turn to journeys,
They stiffen, when they should bend.
They use against themselves that benevolence
To which no man is friend.

They cannot think of so many crops to a field
Or of clean wood cleft by an axe.
Their love is an eager meaninglessness
Too tense, or too lax.

They hear in every whisper that speaks to them
A shout and a cry.
As like as not, when they take life over their door-sills
They should let it go by.

STEVIE SMITH

◩ Odgen Nash once described Stevie Smith's poems as "Songs of deadly innocence." The allusion to William Blake is appropriate, and there is more than a touch of Edward Lear in her lines as well. At first sight Smith's verses seem slight, humorous, whimsical, an impression reinforced by the wry drawings she inserted among the texts. Her deceptively naive tone and nursery-rhyme formulas can create a fairy-tale atmosphere. But on closer inspection there are dark corners in the nursery, as the poet reveals the quandaries, losses, and longings of the heart and, in her sardonic way, critiques middle-class conventions. Smith's dry but curiously upbeat tone amid dreary circumstances and even disaster is unmistakable. Reviewing her *Collected Poems* with relish, another appreciative peer, Robert Lowell, lauded her "unique and cheerfully gruesome voice."

Stevie Smith was born Florence Margaret Smith in Hull, Yorkshire, on September 20, 1902. She acquired her new name as a young woman when a friend said the diminutive author reminded him of Steve Donaghue, the champion jockey. When she was three, Smith's father virtually abandoned the family, shipping out for the North Sea Patrol—a dereliction she never forgave—and she, her mother, older sister Molly, and two aunts moved together into a house in Palmers Green, then on the outskirts of London. Smith grew very close to her mother's sister, unflappable Aunt Madge, who was indifferent to her work but devoted to her, and whom she affectionately dubbed "the lion of Hull." Their long life together was dramatized in the film *Stevie* (1978), starring Glenda Jackson and Mona Washbourne.

When she was five, Smith developed tuberculosis and was sent to a sanatorium, where she felt so lonely without her mother, she said she wished to die. When she did not, she came to believe death would come when required. Like her family, Smith attended church in her youth but became an agnostic. Yet there was always the danger, she admitted, that she might have a relapse into religious faith. Death and doubt became recurring topics, indeed obsessions, in her work.

Smith went to a local girls' school but was dissuaded from going to university. After attending secretarial college, she took a clerical job at a publishing firm and eventually became personal secretary to the directors. She remained there from 1923 until 1953, when she suffered a breakdown, attempted suicide, and was retired from the company with a small pension, which she supplemented by writing reviews. Smith never married, but after publication of her first poetry book, *A Good Time Was Had by All* (1937), she made many friends in the literary world. Her subsequent collections include, among others, *Tender Only to One* (1938), *Mother, What Is Man?* (1942), *Harold's Leap* (1950), and *Not Waving but Drowning* (1957). The title poem of the last volume is probably Smith's finest and certainly her best-known work:

NOT WAVING BUT DROWNING

Nobody heard him, the dead man,
But still he lay moaning:
I was much further out than you thought
And not waving but drowning.

Poor chap, he always loved larking
And now he's dead
It must have been too cold for him his heart gave way,
They said.

Oh, no no no, it was too cold always
(Still the dead one lay moaning)
I was much too far out all my life
And not waving but drowning.

Beginning with *Novel on Yellow Paper; or, Work It Out for Yourself* (1936), she also wrote three novels, all drawn from her life—to the chagrin of certain friends who found themselves depicted in them. (The others are *Over the Frontier*, 1938, and *The Holiday*, 1949.) In 1958 she published a book of her sketches, *Some Are More Human Than Others*. In the 1960s, Smith gave many poetry readings, including programs on the BBC, gaining wide popularity especially with young audiences. In 1962 the first edition of her *Selected Poems* appeared, and in 1966 she received the Cholmondeley Award for Poets. That year she also published *The Frog Prince and Other Poems*.

As her elderly "Auntie Lion" grew disabled, Smith cared for her (and for the first time ran the house) until she suffered a stroke and died in 1968, at the age of ninety-six. In 1969 Smith was presented the Queen's Gold Medal for Poetry. A year later she became ill and was diagnosed with a brain tumor. She died on March 7, 1971. Her *Collected Poems*, edited by her longtime friend James MacGibbon, came out in 1975 and has been reprinted in numerous editions. Her uncollected pieces—poems, reviews, stories, essays, drawings, letters—were published, with a preface by MacGibbon, in *Me Again*, in 1981. *A Very Pleasant Evening with Stevie Smith: Selected Short Prose*, eight stories and four essays, appeared in 1995.

THE QUEEN AND THE YOUNG PRINCESS ✕

Mother, mother, let me go
There are so many things I wish to do.
My child, the time is not yet ripe
You are not yet ready for life.
But what is my life that is to come to be?
Much the same, child, as it has been for me.
But Mother you often say you have a headache
Because of the crown you wear for duty's sake.
So it is, so it is, a headache I have
And that is what you must grow up to carry to the grave.
But in between Mother do you not enjoy the pleasant weather
And to see the bluebottle and the soft feather?
Ah my child, that joy you speak of must be a pleasure
Of human stature, not the measure
Of animals', who have no glorious duty
To perform, no headache and so cannot see beauty.
Up, child, up, embrace the headache and the crown
Married pleasure's best, shadow makes the sun strong.

PHYLLIS McGINLEY

For more than forty years Phyllis McGinley and Ogden Nash were the most popular writers of light verse in America. From the decade before World War II through the three decades after, more people read their poetry than that of probably any other contemporaries (Frost, Auden, and Eliot excepted: but they were mandatory in schools). McGinley and Nash (1902–1971) were almost exact contemporaries, and published their humorous pieces (both verse and prose) in the same major periodicals, principally *The New Yorker* and the *Saturday Evening Post*. Few if any poets today can claim the huge, truly broad, and enthusiastic audiences they enjoyed.

Nash, the more puckish of the two, penned his witty observations on American life, history, and human behavior using clever rhymes, sly literary and cultural allusions, dreadful puns, and genial nonsense. The equally well-read McGinley examined mores and manners, mainly of the middle class and, after the war, particularly as exhibited by the denizens of the suburbs, using ingenious rhymes and intricate forms, educated references, and assorted drollery too. But her humor was less whimsical than Nash's, alternating between jocular or wary statements on The Way Things Are and sardonic stanzas that betrayed the ethical underpinnings of her worldview. (Inside every satirist resides a frustrated or disillusioned idealist.)

Phyllis McGinley was born March 21, 1905, in Ontario, Oregon. Her father speculated in land, unprofitably, so the family moved frequently before settling on a farm in tiny Iliff, Colorado, a lonely place for Phyllis and her brother. She wrote her first verses when she was six, and from that time knew she would be a poet. Her father died when she was twelve, so her mother moved the family to Odgen, Utah, to live with relatives. McGinley later remarked, "[W]e never had a home, and to have a real home, after I got married, was just marvelous." A "cradle Catholic," she attended Sacred Heart Academy, then Ogden High School.

While at the University of Utah, she later admitted, she "didn't learn very much," deliberately, to void the negative stereotypes of "brainy women." But she did enter school literary competitions, under pseudonyms, and won cash prizes in all categories—poetry, short stories, and essays—twice. She also began to submit poetry to major magazines. Katharine White, the legendary New Yorker editor, accepted a serious piece, with a helpful query: "[B]ut why do you sing the same sad songs all lady poets sing?" McGinley got the message and switched to light verse.

She moved to New York in 1929 and continued publishing. But as a backup she took a teaching job at a junior high school in New Rochelle. When the principal discovered McGinley's sideline in humor, he was not amused; she resigned at the end of the year. In Manhattan she took jobs as an advertising copywriter, then as a staff writer at Town and Country. In 1934 she was introduced to Charles Hayden. He worked in public relations at Bell Telephone by day and played jazz piano by night. Sharing an old prejudice about musicians' wandering ways, the poet was initially skeptical about Hayden's suitability for marriage, but they wed a few years later. Their daughters were born in 1939 and 1941. Recalling the first blessed event, she exclaimed: "I have never felt so divine in my life as the time before she was born."

Fulfilling McGinley's dream of having a "real home," the family moved to Larchmont, the upscale suburb north of New York

City, where the devoted wife and mother ran the household, raised the children, and entertained often (aided by full-time "help"), while the prolific professional writer produced a steady stream of poems, articles, and children's books. During the depression years, McGinley's shrewd and witty observations on the rigors, rewards, and absurdities of everyday life proved welcome diversions while they reaffirmed basic beliefs and hopes about family bonds, endurance, common sense, and other verities. Her first verse collection, *On the Contrary* (1934), was a success, as were *One More Manhattan* (1937), *A Pocketful of Wry* (1940), and *Husbands Are Difficult* (1941).

While she excelled on topics of home and hearth and child-rearing, the Domestic Muse (as she was inevitably dubbed) could be equally incisive on other issues that interested her, as in "Public Journal," a good example of McGinley's gift for satire, here directed at the topical and formal clichés in then-prominent poetry. Writing on the eve of World War II, she further excoriated the famously "socially engaged" W. H. Auden and his poet friends, and by extension all "bright young," well-educated but ignorant and self-righteous intellectual do-gooders (and poseurs), who presumed to comprehend the grave political and social issues of the day and to pronounce upon them—with theories, slogans, and fashionably unpoetic (if poorly understood "proletarian") slang—from the safety of their privileged positions.

After the war McGinley published *Stones from a Glass House* (1946) and *Love Letters* (1954), provided lyrics for the musical revue *Small Wonder* (1948), was elected to the National Academy of Arts and Letters (1955), and became the first woman to win the Pulitzer Prize for light verse, with *Times Three: Selected Verse from Three Decades with Seventy New Poems* (1960). She also produced more than a dozen children's books and contributed many articles to such journals as *America*, the *American Scholar*, *Commonweal*, *Good Housekeeping*, *Harper's*, *Ladies' Home Journal*, *Mademoiselle*, *Reader's Digest*, *Saturday Review*, and *Woman's Day*. She conducted a wide correspondence with high-profile clergy (Francis Cardinal Spellman, Daniel Berrigan, Richard Cardinal Cushing), writers (Marianne Moore, Anne Sexton, John Updike), politicians (Senator Jacob Javits, presidential candidate Eugene McCarthy, Governor Nelson Rockefeller, who asked her to serve on a panel reviewing New York's abortion laws in 1968), and theater people (Richard Rodgers, Oscar Hammerstein, Helen Hayes, Groucho Marx).

McGinley appeared on the cover of *Time* on June 18, 1965, not only for her long fame as a light versifier but for her recent notoriety in a feminist controversy. In 1963 another suburban mother, Betty Friedan, argued in *The Feminine Mystique* that the idealized (and restricting) image of femininity was a source of deep unhappiness for modern, educated women, who would be more fulfilled using their talents in the workplace rather than languishing in the confines of home. Friedan asserted that American women were "kept from growing to their full human capacities," so much so that it was "taking a far greater toll on the physical and mental health of our country than any known disease."

Given her lifelong extolling of traditional domestic roles, McGinley's publisher persuaded her to offer a rebuttal to Friedan and others who downgraded them. Her answer was *Sixpence in Her Shoe* (1964), in which she reiterated that happiness was entirely possible in the home, even for the highly schooled. In fact, she added, staying at home was not only advisable for women themselves but for the good of society: the educated mother and homemaker would "be able to judge a newspaper item more sensibly, understand a politician's speech more sagely, talk over her husband's business problems more helpfully, and entertain her children more amusingly."

Noting that women were already the greatest consumers of cultural goods (books, music, theater performances, art gallery shows) and most involved with schooling and charity fund-raising, McGinley concluded that "we who belong to the profession of housewife hold the fate of the world in our hands. It is our influence that will determine the culture of coming generations." She conceded that working outside the home could be commendable, if the family wasn't "stinted," but insisted: "By and large, though, the world runs better when men and women keep to their own spheres." In its first six months, *Sixpence* sold more than 100,000 copies.

McGinley's other prose books include *The Province of the Heart* (1959), *Wonderful Time* (1966), and *Saint-Watching* (1969). Her last poetry collections were *A Wreath of Christmas Legends* (1967) and *Confessions of a Reluctant Optimist* (1973). After her husband died in 1972, McGinley moved from her treasured house in the suburbs to an apartment in Manhattan. She died February 22, 1978. In the *Time* profile she had reflected: "I do think I have been a useful person. At a time when poetry has become the property of the universities and not the common people, I have a vast number of people who have become my readers. I have kept the door open and perhaps led them into greater poetry."

PUBLIC JOURNAL

Verses inspired by a day spent in
communion with the bright young
men of English verse

CHRISTOPHER ISHERWOOD, STEPHEN SPENDER,
    AUDEN AND L. MACNEICE—
I CAN'T COME ALONG ON AN ALL-NIGHT BENDER,
    BUT I'LL HAVE A QUICK ONE WITH YOU.

It is four in the afternoon. Time still for a poem,
A poem not topical, wholly, or romantic, or metaphysic,
But fetched from the grab-bag of my mind and gaudy with
Symbol, slogan, quotation, and even music.
And many a Marxian maxim and many allusions
To a daft system and a world-disorder.
I will mention machines and the eight-hour day and
Czecho-Slovakia and the invaded border.

I will speak of love and I will do it slyly,
Unloosing the sacred girdle with a tired air,
Taking particular pains to notice the elastic garters
And the literal underwear.

I will put learning into my poem, for I acquired learning
At Cambridge or Oxford, it does not matter which.
But I'll freshen it up with slang which I got by ear,
Though it may sound a little off pitch.
And I'll be casual with rhymes for that is the trend,
Fashionable as the black hat of Anthony Eden.
I may put them at the middle of the stanza instead of the end,
For really amazing effect.
Or perhaps I'll find that assonance heightens the meaning better.
Yes, definitely, I prefer the latter.

Well, it will be sport, writing my private hates
And my personal credo.
I must bring in how I went to Spain on a holiday.
And how cold it was in Toledo.
There was a bootblack, too, in Madrid,
Who gave my shoes a burnish.
He told me something important which I cannot repeat,
For though I understand Spain, I do not understand Spanish.

I'll recall autumn weather in Birmingham,
Drearier than Boston.
And the pump-attendant there who sold me stormy petrol
For my thirsting Austin.

I will put tarts into my poem, and tenement people,
The poor but not the meek;
And pieces of popular songs for a hint of nostalgia,
And a bit of Greek.

I shall be tough and ardent and angry-eyed,
Aware that the world is dying, gasping, its face grown pallid;
But quick to embalm it in language as an aspic
Enfolds the chicken salad.

Now it is five o'clock. The poem is finished
Like Poland, like the upper classes, like Sunday's roast.
I must straighten my waistcoat and see that it goes straight out
By the evening post.

For what is left for us? Only
The stanza a day,
And the American royalties, and an inherited income,
To keep the wolf at bay.

ELIZABETH BISHOP

Elizabeth Bishop, James Merrill once remarked, was "a genius who impersonated a normal woman." Accessible and engaging, her work appears quite straightforward. But within the meticulously observed details and below the carefully controlled surfaces of her poems lie depths of meaning and emotion. Bishop's artistic output was small but as perfect as she could make it. (She worked twenty years on one poem, "The Moose," before she allowed it to see print.) In her craftsmanship she is reminiscent of her early mentor, Marianne Moore; but unlike Moore, Bishop refrains from drawing overt lessons. And in contrast to her lionized friend Robert Lowell, the reticent author is loath to make revelations of private pains and losses in her work. Uprooted and insecure early in her life, a world traveler as an adult, Bishop made geography and dislocation dominant themes in her poems, and many readers can empathize with her restlessness, indecision, and continual search for identity. Ironically, while Lowell's gaudy reputation has dimmed since his death, Bishop's understated achievement has grown steadily in appreciation, making her one of the most acclaimed of twentieth-century poets.

Elizabeth Bishop was born in Worcester, Massachusetts, February 8, 1911. Her father died when she was a baby. After several breakdowns, her mother was sent to a mental institution in 1916. Bishop never saw her again, though she lived until 1934. In her long story "In the Village," printed at Lowell's prompting in *Questions of Travel* (1965), she relates her reactions to her mother's descent into madness. The little girl stayed briefly with her grandparents in Nova Scotia, a happy interlude that ended abruptly when she was sent to live with her father's wealthy but emotionally cold family in Worcester. A lonely child, she suffered from asthma, bronchitis, and eczema. She eventually was taken in by her aunt and uncle.

After Walnut Hill boarding school in Natick, Massachusetts, in the fall of 1929 she entered Vassar, where she became friends with the future novelists Mary McCarthy and Eleanor Clark and the poet Muriel Rukeyser. She helped found a literary magazine, *Con Spirito*, edited the yearbook, and had her first poems printed in respected journals. In college Bishop also began drinking, a habit that would prove increasingly destructive with the years. The college librarian introduced her to Marianne Moore, who encouraged her and helped arrange other publications. Moore's assistance was gratefully received by the young writer, who already had her own ideas and distinctive style but always treated the older author with due deference. Gradually their relationship evolved into friendship, and they remained in contact until Moore's death in 1972. Their first meeting and later history is recounted in "Efforts of Affection: A Memoir of Marianne Moore," in Bishop's *Collected Prose*.

After graduation in June 1934, Bishop moved to New York City. A group of her poems, with an introduction by Moore, appeared in an anthology, *Trial Balances*, in 1936. Others were soon appearing in important magazines. In 1935 Bishop traveled to Europe for the first time, and in following years she lived in Paris and visited London, Spain, Italy, and North Africa. After a trip to Florida in 1937, she decided to settle in Key West, where she shared a house for many years with the paper-mill heiress Louise Crane. She worked briefly for the Navy Department in 1942, then visited Mexico and became friends with the Chilean poet Pablo Neruda.

In 1946, with the aid of Marianne Moore, Bishop won a major prize from the publisher Houghton Mifflin for her first book manuscript, which contained the often-reprinted "The Fish" and "Roosters." Issued as *North & South* the following year, the collection was lavishly praised by the demanding poet-critic Randall Jarrell and by Robert Lowell, who became one of her closest friends. Bishop later dedicated "The Armadillo" to Lowell, who used it as a model for "Skunk Hour," and returned the compliment. In 1947 she also met the young James Merrill, another ardent admirer and in time a devoted friend. Further professional recognition also arrived in abundance, including a Guggenheim Fellowship in 1947, appointment as Consultant in Poetry at the Library of Congress in 1949, and an award from the American Academy of Arts and Letters in 1950.

In November 1951, with a traveling fellowship from Bryn Mawr College, Bishop went to South America for the first time. She had planned to visit Brazil for only a few weeks, but an allergic reaction detained her for several more. While recuperating she again encountered the aristocratic Lota de Macedo Soares, a member of a prominent family whom she had met years before, and they became lovers. Bishop remained with Soares, living in the mountains near Petrópolis north of Rio and later in Ouro Prêto, for the next seventeen years. During this unusually settled and happy period, she wrote slowly, as always, and translated from the Portuguese, notably *The Diary of "Helena Morley"* (1957). She later edited, with Emanuel Brasil, *An Anthology of Twentieth-Century Brazilian Poetry* (1972). Never prolific, in 1955 she published *Poems: North & South—A Cold Spring*, which combined her first book with new poems. It won the

Pulitzer Prize. A decade later, *Questions of Travel* collected new poems along with the autobiographical "In the Village." Her *Complete Poems* of 1969 received the National Book Award.

By the mid-sixties Bishop's personal life had become less satisfactory, however, as tensions arose in her relationship with Lota Soares, who had taken on an urban development project in Rio de Janeiro. The creation of a "people's park" on reclaimed land along the Copacabana beach consumed ever more of Lota's time and energy, and so Elizabeth frequently found herself alone and feeling neglected. She sought solace in alcohol, to the highly stressed Lota's great irritation. Bishop began to spend more time away from Brazil and eventually formed other romantic attachments. In 1966 she accepted her first teaching position, at the University of Washington. In the summer of 1967, Soares joined her in New York. The reunion was not a success, and the first night Soares overdosed on tranquilizers, went into a coma, and died five days later. This trauma—and other losses over many years—eventually found expression in the strict framework of the bitterly ironic villanelle that has become one of Bishop's most often quoted and well-beloved poems, "One Art."

Over the next years, Bishop traveled widely and held visiting professorships at various universities, then taught poetry-writing seminars for several years at Harvard, in the beginning as a substitute for Robert Lowell. Her last collection, *Geography III*, was published in 1976 and won the National Book Critics Circle Award. The book included such major poems as "Crusoe in England," "One Art," and "In the Waiting Room," her poetic reconstruction of a pivotal experience from childhood. Accompanying her aunt to the dentist's, the seven-year-old leafs through a *National Geographic* and is struck by the unusual appearance of people in the magazine. Hearing her "foolish, timid" aunt's cry of pain, she has a sudden, startling realization of her own identity, and says that she knew that "nothing / stranger could ever happen." This unnerving sense of the peculiar—the uncanny—particularly amid the ordinary, appears often in Bishop's poems, along with the motifs of displacement and homelessness.

By the seventies Bishop was probably the most esteemed woman writing poetry in the United States. But her later years were marked by the unpleasant consequences of substance abuse, and her behavior became both distressing and problematic for the friends who observed and had to contend with it. Fortunately, she met and fell in love with Alice Methfessel, who became a stalwart helpmeet and eventually her literary executor. Bishop suffered a cerebral aneurysm and died in her Boston apartment on October 6, 1979. Robert Giroux, her longtime publisher and friend, edited *The Complete Poems 1927–1979* (1983), *The Collected Prose* (1984), and *One Art: Selected Letters* (1993). Britt C. Millier's full-scale, unvarnished biography, *Elizabeth Bishop: Life and the Memory of It*, appeared in 1995.

Regrettably, because of restrictions imposed by the author, Bishop's poems cannot be presented in this anthology. But "One Art" and "Manners" may be found in *100 Essential Modern Poems* (Ivan R. Dee, 2005). Besides the other poems just mentioned, readers are also particularly directed to "Sestina," "The Fish," "Roosters," "The Man-Moth," "At the Fishhouses," "Pink Dog," "Sandpiper," and "The Burglar of Babylon."

MAY SWENSON

▣ "I have spent my life having fun," May Swenson reflected two years before her death. "To make poetry is pleasure. When you write a poem it has surprises in it. It tells you things you never knew and there is no obligation in it." She explained, "I don't feel I have to follow certain rules or write a certain way. Poetry lets you lead a very selfish life."

Because of her persistent, usually successful pursuit of happiness and creative freedom, Swenson was among the most joyful of American poets. She was always open to new ideas and experimented continually, most obviously in her shaped poems, where typography is cleverly arranged to demonstrate what the texts describe. Of more lasting interest, her vivid poems on nature view the world attentively in its own complex otherness rather than using it merely to project states of mind or to symbolize human attributes. But Swenson excelled particularly in her love lyrics, where emotion and mind, sensuality and wit, pungently combine.

She was born Anna Thilda May Swenson on May 28, 1913, in Logan, Utah, the first of twelve children. In their Mormon home Swedish was spoken, and May did not use English until she entered first grade. When not helping her mother with cleaning and cooking, she looked after her many siblings, entertaining them with her storytelling. By fifth grade she was reading serious books on her own. Her father encouraged her writing and made up little blank books for her diaries. A cousin, reading passages aloud, noticed her entries scanned like verse, though May did not consider herself a poet then.

Swenson entered Utah State Agricultural College (now University) in 1930 and became involved in theater her freshman year. She also wrote a humor column for the college paper and contributed poetry to the literary magazine. She had already drifted from the Mormon faith, though she accompanied her family to services when at home, and never formally left the church. Her mother had hoped that all five daughters would lead "normal lives" in the faith. But a classmate recalled May saying, "It's not for me—religion. It seems like a redundancy for a poet."

After graduation in 1934, Swenson moved to Salt Lake City where she got a job in the advertising department of a newspaper. By 1936 she had decided to go east and set out for New York City. She tried to get work as a reporter, without success, but eked out a living doing freelance editing and ghostwriting. She moved frequently since often she could not make the rent. Not wanting to ask her family for help, she landed a position on the Federal Writers' Project of the WPA, interviewing workers for oral histories in the Living Lore Unit. After a year, the government discovered she was ineligible (since she had relatives who could support her), so she returned to her precarious existence.

Swenson eventually got a job editing trade journals for the wholesale drug industry (1942–1949), and found a tiny third-story walk-up apartment (actually a bedroom with shared kitchen and bath) in Greenwich Village, her home for almost twenty years. Always frugal, she saved enough to take a year off simply to write. To meet expenses at various intervals in later years too, she deliberately took boring clerical jobs, thus leaving her mind undistracted for poetry. (Later, Mary Oliver would use the same approach.)

She also tried to get to know people in the literary world and began submitting work. Swenson made her first appearance in the *Saturday Review of Literature*. Then James Laughlin, the founding editor of New Directions, took a group for his annual anthology. His press was famous for promoting controversial avant-garde authors, so Swenson, an experimentalist herself, was pleased when a few years later Laughlin asked her to help part-time as a first reader of manuscripts; she held the job until 1966. On the basis of her first publications, in 1950 she won a residency at Yaddo, the artists' colony in Saratoga Springs, New York, where she met Elizabeth Bishop. They maintained a lifelong friendship through letters.

After several rejections, Swenson received word from Howard Moss in 1951 that he would take a poem for *The New Yorker*, the first of some sixty she contributed over almost forty years. She entered her first book for the Yale Younger Poets award, but W. H. Auden named it a finalist, not the winner. Two other collections went out to several publishers, again without success. At last, a new book, *Another Animal*, was taken by Scribner's for its Poets of Today series and published in 1954. The acceptance letter, from Sara Teasdale's old friend John Hall Wheelock, arrived on her birthday.

Swenson continued to take temporary clerical jobs through the sixties. Of her nine-to-five chores, she once wrote, "I must turn myself into a mechanism outwardly but can live free inside." She saved and was able to piece together fellowships and further residences at Yaddo and the MacDowell Colony to gain time for her writing. The poet and translator John Ciardi named her a Robert Frost Fellow at the Bread Loaf Writers' Conference, and she received grants from the Rockefeller Foundation, the Poetry Society of America, the Academy of American Poets, and other groups. In 1958 she published her second book, *A Cage of Spines*, and began to give readings.

In 1960 she won both a Guggenheim and an Amy Lowell Traveling Fellowship, which enabled her to go to Europe. To save expenses she bought a tent, sleeping bag, and cooking equipment and camped through Spain, France, and Italy. She kept writing and produced her third collection, *To Mix with Time*, in 1963. The following year she received a grant from the Ford Foundation to return to the theater work she had loved in college. In 1966 she published a collection of "riddle poems" for children, *Poems to Solve*. (*More Poems to Solve* appeared in 1971, and *The Guess and Spell Coloring Book* in 1976.) She accepted a position as writer in residence at Purdue for 1966–1967, though with some fear. She had no advanced degrees, never in fact took a poetry class or workshop, and had turned down other teaching jobs; but the pay was good and allowed her to provide for the future. From the outset she admitted to the students, "I don't consider myself a teacher." But she made detailed lesson plans, discussed with the students poems *they* wanted to talk about, and encouraged individuality in their own work.

At Purdue she met an English faculty member, R. Rozanne (Zan) Knudson, also an author of children's books, and they became lifelong companions. In 1967 they bought a cottage in Sea Cliff, on the North Shore of Long Island, which became their home for the next twenty-two years. As a diversion, Swenson began more experiments with typography, creating the intriguing shaped poems in *Iconographs* (1970); the book was recognized by the American Institute of Graphic Arts. With support from the Bollingen Foundation, she had already begun making translations from Swedish poets, some of which appeared in her collection *Half Sun Half Sleep* (1967). In 1970 the University of Pittsburgh Press commissioned a collection of translations of Tomas Tranströmer (b. 1931), then collaborated with Leif Sjöberg to produce *Windows and Stones: Selected Poems of Tomas Tranströmer* (1972), which helped spread his name far beyond Stockholm.

In the seventies she and her partner began spending summers in Arizona and Los Angeles, and fitted camping trips between readings and the poetry classes Swenson taught occasionally, in Canada, in the New York public schools, and at the University of California–Riverside and the University of North Carolina–Greensboro. In 1978 she brought out *New and Selected Things Taking Place* (1978), reprinting some of her best work from earlier volumes.

In the eighties Swenson published fewer poems, but the awards multiplied, including the major recognition of her election as a chancellor of the Academy of American Poets in 1980, the Bollingen Prize (shared with Howard Nemerov) in 1981, presentation of the Phi Beta Kappa Poem at Harvard in 1982, and a MacArthur Foundation fellowship in 1987. She was also named a "Literary Lion" of the New York Public Library in 1988.

By this time her health problems, especially chronic asthma and high blood pressure, had become debilitating. In 1987 she assembled *In Other Words*. In 1989 she managed to give the Theodore Roethke memorial reading at the University of Washington, then attended her last Swenson family reunion in Utah. She died, of a heart attack, on December 4, 1989, while working on her twelfth book. *Nature: Poems Old and New* was published posthumously in 1994.

In 1993, R. Rozanne Knudson published a biography for children, *The Wonderful Pen of May Swenson*, with letters, extracts from her diaries, and photographs, and in 1996 *May Swenson: A Poet's Life in Pictures*. Her alma mater, Utah State University, has established a

May Swenson website, from which several biographical details and quotations here are taken. Since 1997 its press has sponsored the annual May Swenson Poetry Award, which includes book publication. *The Complete Love Poems of May Swenson*, with a foreword by Maxine Kumin, was issued in paperback in 2003.

NEITHER WANTING MORE

To lie with you
in a field of grass
to lie there forever
and let time pass

Touching lightly
shoulder and thigh
Neither wanting more
Neither asking why

To have your whole
cool body's length
along my own
to know the strength
of a secret tide
of longing seep
into our veins
go deep . . . deep

Dissolving flesh
and melting bone
Oh to lie with you
alone

To feel your breast
rise with my sigh
To hold you mirrored
in my eye

Neither wanting more
Neither asking why

Unconscious
came a beauty to my
wrist
and stopped my pencil,
merged its shadow profile with
my hand's ghost
on the page:
Red Spotted Purple or else Mourning
Cloak,
paired thin-as-paper wings, near black,
were edged on the seam side poppy orange.
as were its spots.

UNCONSCIOUS

CAME A BEAUTY

I sat arrested, for its soot-haired
body's worm
shone in the sun.
It bent its tongue long as
a leg
black on my skin
and clung without my
feeling,
while its tomb-stained
duplicate parts of
a window opened.
And then I
moved.

STARING AT THE SEA ON THE DAY OF THE DEATH OF ANOTHER

The long body of the water fills its hollow,
slowly rolls upon its side,
and in the swaddlings of the waves,
their shadowed hollows falling forward with the tide,

like folds of Grecian garments molded to cling
around some classic immemorial marble thing,
I see the vanished bodies of friends who have died.

Each form is furled into its hollow,
white in the dark curl,
the sea a mausoleum, with countless shelves,
cradling the prone effigies of our unearthly selves,

some of the hollows empty, long niches in the tide.
One of them is mine
and gliding forward, gaping wide.

MURIEL RUKEYSER

◨ Muriel Rukeyser was an energetic, inelegant poet. To fulfill her roles of engagement both as a poet and as a person, she neglected certain artistic graces and broke the stereotypes of the gentle Lady Author. As an independent writer and political activist, engaged teacher and mentor, bisexual and single mother in the preliberation era, she was a pioneer whose long career became an inspiration for the generations of women poets coming of age in the late fifties and after. Anne Sexton called her, simply, "Muriel, mother of everyone."

Rukeyser was prolific, overly so, for her uneven output shows signs of haste and is marked by awkward rhythms and phrasing (a roughness appropriate, though, for certain of her subjects) as well as by imprecision and, for some critics, confusion. With them, David Perkins in his *History of Modern Poetry* finds: "Her poems are difficult if one seeks intelligibility, but not at all for readers satisfied with vague, intense, idealistic emotion." Such summary judgment is somewhat unfair to both the poet and the public, for at her considerable best Rukeyser sees and speaks with bracing clarity, fusing perception, feeling, and form into memorable lines, most notably in her shorter late pieces.

Reviewers during the poet's lifetime and literary historians since have oscillated in their opinions. Even those who admire her ambition and idealism are not always enthusiastic about her methods. Noting the "pendulum swings" in Rukeyser's reputation, Adrienne Rich in introducing her edition of *Selected Poems* (2005) speaks for the many who find her a bold role model. Her interests, issues, and techniques are extremely varied, Rich observes, and "she refused to compartmentalize herself or her work, claiming her right to intellect and sexuality, poetry and science, Marxism and myth, activism and motherhood, theory and vision."

Muriel Rukeyser was born December 15, 1913, in New York City. Her mother had been a bookkeeper, her father a salesman who became wealthy as a partner in a sand and gravel company that prospered during the Manhattan skyscraper boom in the teens and twenties. As a girl she attended Ethical Culture schools, first in Manhattan and then in the Bronx (Fieldstone), driven there by the family chauffeur. In 1930 she entered Vassar College, where she became friends and started a literary magazine with Elizabeth Bishop, Eleanor Taylor, and Mary McCarthy, the future author of *The Group,* the noted novel based on their lives during and after college. In 1931 and 1932, Rukeyser also took summer courses in psychology and anthropology at Columbia. In the aftermath of the 1929 stock market crash, her family fell on hard times, and she was forced to quit school after her sophomore year. In 1935, two years after leaving Vassar without a degree, Rukeyser won the Yale Younger Poet Award for her first collection, *Theory of Flight,* which drew on the flying lessons she had taken in 1933.

Attracted to liberal causes from her teens, Rukeyser participated in leftist political and literary groups and started writing for socialist and Communist journals, including *The New Republic,* the *Daily Worker,* and the *New Masses.* Although she later fell victim to the anti-Communist witch-hunts, she never did join the party, as she found its doctrinaire policies too confining. In 1933 she traveled to Alabama to witness the notorious trial of the Scottsboro Boys, nine black youths accused of raping two white women. Rukeyser was herself arrested, for fraternizing and discussing the case with black journalists, and contracted typhoid fever while in custody. She then worked for International Labor Defense, which handled the appeals.

She went to Spain to report on the Olimpiada Popular (People's Olympiad), organized in opposition to the official 1936 Olympic Games hosted by the Nazis in Berlin, but was soon forced to leave Barcelona with the outbreak of the Spanish Civil War. She later supported the anti-fascists who opposed the ultimately victorious Generalissimo Francisco Franco. The experience formed the basis for her fourth book, *Mediterranean* (1938). In 1937 she traveled to Gauley Bridge, West Virginia, the construction site of a tunnel for a hydroelectric plant, to investigate the deaths from silicosis by thousands of workers left unprotected from the danger by callous managers. The disaster inspired the long sequence "The Book of the Dead" in her second collection, *U.S. 1* (1938).

During and after World War II, Rukeyser gave a series of public lectures, later collected in *The Life of Poetry* (1949, reissued 1996). In 1945 she went to San Francisco and taught at the International Labor School. She married, had the brief union annulled, and in 1947 gave birth to a son by another man; she chose to raise the child by herself. Her family did not approve and in fact disinherited her. She returned to New York City where until 1960 she served as an executive at the House of Photography. In 1964 she suffered several strokes—she later recounted her efforts of recovery in "The Resurrection of the Right Hand" (1976)—then not only continued to write but kept up her strenuous activities in response to current political problems.

Chief among them, she organized and openly protested against the Vietnam War and was arrested at a demonstration on the steps of the Capitol. In 1972 she also traveled to Hanoi with Denise Levertov. Because of her strong social stands, she was frequently attacked by literary critics and partisans of both the right and the left. But these activities brought her to the attention of the new generation of readers and aspiring women poets. In 1975, while president of the American Center of P.E.N., she went to Seoul in an attempt to argue on behalf of the imprisoned Korean poet Kim Chi-Ha, who had been condemned to death on charges of a Communist "conspiracy" against the state. The episode formed the basis of "The Gates," the title poem of her last separate volume (1976). Following a heart attack, she died on February 12, 1980.

Rukeyser never held a permanent academic post, but over the decades she taught and gave poetry workshops in several institutions, including Vassar, Sarah Lawrence, and Rutgers. Others of her individual poetry books are *Beast in View* (1944), *The Green Wave* (1948), *Elegies* (1949), *Body of Waking* (1958), *The Speed of Darkness* (1968), and *Breaking Open* (1973). Her novel/memoir *The Orgy* (1965) was reissued in 1997 with a preface by Sharon Olds. Rukeyser also collaborated on translations of work by the Swedish poet Gunnar Ekelöf (1967) and the Mexican poet Octavio Paz (1973). Besides children's book and plays, she also wrote biographies of the first American physicist, Willard Gibbs (1942); the early English astronomer Thomas Hariot (1971); and Wendell Willkie, the 1940 presidential candidate (1957).

Since her death she has been the subject of numerous studies. Louise Kertesz's *The Poetic Vision of Muriel Rukeyser* appeared in 1980, with a foreword by Kenneth Rexroth, who long championed her work. Jan Heller Levi edited *A Muriel Rukeyser Reader* in 1994, with an introduction by Adrienne Rich. Suzanne Gardinier's *A World That Will Hold All the People* was published in 1996. A new *Collected Poems of Muriel Rukeyser*, edited by Janet E. Kaufman and Anne R. Herzog, was published in 2005. Kaufman and Jan Heller Levi also edited *How Shall We Tell Each Other of the Poet? The Life and Writings of Muriel Rukeyser* (1999, reissued 2001).

MORE OF A CORPSE THAN A WOMAN

Give them my regards when you go to the school reunion;
and at the marriage-supper, say that I'm thinking about them.
They'll remember my name; I went to the movies with that one,
feeling the weight of their death where she sat at my elbow;
        she never said a word,
        but all of them were heard.

All of them alike, expensive girls, the leaden friends:
one used to play the piano, one of them once wrote a sonnet,
one even seemed awakened enough to photograph wheatfields—
the dull girls with the educated minds and technical passions—
        pure love was their employment,
        they tried it for enjoyment.

Meet them at the boat : they've brought the souvenirs of boredom,
a seashell from the faltering monarchy;
the nose of a marble saint; and from the battlefield,
an empty shell divulged from a flower-bed.
        The lady's wealthy breath
        perfumes the air with death.

The leaden lady faces the fine, voluptuous woman,
faces a rising world bearing its gifts in its hands.
Kisses her casual dreams upon the lips she kisses,
risen, she moves away; takes others; moves away.
        Inadequate to love,
        supposes she's enough.

Give my regards to the well-protected woman,
I knew the ice-cream girl, we went to school together.
There's something to bury, people, when you begin to bury.
When your women are ready and rich in their wish for the world,
                  destroy the leaden heart,
               we've a new race to start.

WHAT THEY SAID

  : After I am dead, darling,
        my seventeen senses gone,
  I shall love you as you wish,
        no sex, no mouth, but bone—
        in the way you long for now,
  with my soul alone.

  : When we are neither woman nor man
        but bleached to skeleton—
  when you have changed, my darling,
        and all your senses gone,
        it is not me that you will love:
  you will love everyone.

WAITING FOR ICARUS

He said he would be back and we'd drink wine together
He said that everything would be better than before
He said we were on the edge of a new relation
He said he would never again cringe before his father
He said that he was going to invent full-time
He said he loved me that going into me
He said was going into the world and the sky
He said all the buckles were very firm
He said the wax was the best wax
He said Wait for me here on the beach
He said Just don't cry

I remember the gulls and the waves
I remember the islands going dark on the sea

I remember the girls laughing
I remember they said he only wanted to get away from me
I remember mother saying : Inventors are like poets, a trashy lot
I remember she told me those who try out inventions are worse
I remember she added : Women who love such are the worst of all

I have been waiting all day, or perhaps longer.
I would have liked to try those wings myself.
It would have been better than this.

MYTH

Long afterward, Oedipus, old and blinded, walked the
roads.   He smelled a familiar smell.   It was
the Sphinx.   Oedipus said, "I want to ask one question.
Why didn't I recognize my mother?"   "You gave the
wrong answer," said the Sphinx.   "But that was what
made everything possible," said Oedipus.   "No," she said.
"When I asked, What walks on four legs in the morning,
two at noon, and three in the evening, you answered,
Man.   You didn't say anything about woman."
"When you say Man," said Oedipus, "you include women
too. Everyone knows that."   She said, "That's what
you think."

RUTH STONE

◫ Until the tardy recognition of the National Books Critics Circle
Award (1999) and National Book Award (2002), the octogenarian
Ruth Stone was known chiefly, and much loved, by her many students
and two generations of woman poets inspired by her talent and tenac-
ity. Stone's collections before and since those awards are equal to or
even stronger than the prizewinning volumes. Her modest profile be-
fore her belated fame was all the more unfortunate since her plain-
spoken work is immediately engaging—direct, insightful, poignant,
funny—and potentially appealing to a wide audience, including peo-
ple who may believe contemporary poetry is not for them.

With her sharp intelligence and wide-ranging curiosity, all things human, as well as quite a few objects beyond human comprehension, form the subjects of Stone's deeply inquisitive art: the facts of daily life, children and the bonds of family and friendship, landscapes and the environment, the intricate wonders of creation revealed by the sciences, human failures and follies, sexuality, aging, poverty and the lives of those on the fringes of society, and, above all, love and loss. An independent spirit, Stone exhibits a strong woman's point of view on the conflicts and often unequal relations between the sexes, but without the solemnity and sour rhetoric typical of certain prominent (and humorless) feminist authors. Skeptical and gifted with a fine eye for the absurd, she abhors dogmatic pronouncements, grand theorizing, vague abstractions, dainty circumlocutions, pomposity, and pretensions social or literary, especially the posturings of fellow practitioners. Instead, the genial but ungentle and undeceived poet prefers to render her critiques with satiric sketches, sardonic asides, witty observations, and (no prude, she) robust, unabashedly earthy humor. As she enters her nineties, Stone has lost none of her gusto for life and none of her artistic gifts, as her exceptionally vigorous latest work amply demonstrates.

Ruth Perkins Stone was born June 8, 1915, in Roanoke, Virginia, but grew up mainly in Indianapolis, where her father's family was prominent. Her father himself was a drummer and sometime typesetter, as well as a steady gambler, who entertained his daughter with music and amusing stories. He personally set and printed up copies of her poems when she was five. Her mother, the poet recalls, recited Tennyson to her while she was still at her breast. Other members of the family were artistic and encouraged the girl, and she learned to read in her grandparents' library when she was three. At the University of Illinois she proved to be precocious in other ways as well, marrying her first husband, a chemist, when she was nineteen. Her second husband, and the love of her life, was the critic and novelist Walter Stone, with whom she had three daughters. In 1952 they moved from Illinois to New York when he took a position in the English Department at Vassar College, in Poughkeepsie.

Stone had already begun publishing poems in a number of little magazines and was awarded the Bess Hokin Prize by *Poetry* in 1953. She also won the Fellowship in Poetry from the *Kenyon Review*, and with the prize money was able to buy a small house in Goshen, Vermont; intended originally as a summer place, it eventually became the poet's permanent residence. In 1959, Walter Stone received a sabbatical, and the family moved to England. While they were abroad he committed suicide, a devastating blow that plunged the poet into years of depression. She was thirty-four at the time of his death, and had a hard struggle raising their three children by herself. Stone never recovered from the loss of her husband, as evidenced by the many love poems and elegies she has written in his memory over almost fifty years.

Stone's first book, *In an Iridescent Time*, appeared in 1959, and soon after she began a precarious, peripatetic life as a visiting writer at several schools. In 1963 she received a two-year fellowship at the Radcliffe Institute, which allowed her to work on her second collection, *Topography and Other Poems*, eventually published in 1971. While at Radcliffe she formed friendships with Maxine Kumin and the novelist and short story writer Tillie Olsen. Stone's third volume, *Cheap*, came out the following year; the title, like that of her next collection, *Second-Hand Coat* (1987), alluded to the difficult economic times the poet often faced over the decades.

From the sixties through the eighties Stone held temporary positions at several institutions, including the University of Wisconsin, Indiana University, the University of California at Davis, Old Dominion, the University of Illinois, Wellesley College, Brandeis, Cooper Union, Harvard, and New York University. Between teaching stints she returned to her house in Vermont and continued writing. The originality and strength of this work garnered high praise as well as several honors: the Shelley Memorial Award (1964), Guggenheim fellowships (1971 and 1975), the Delmore Schwartz Award (1983), a Whiting Writer's Award (1986), and the Paterson Poetry Prize (1988). Finally, in 1989, at age seventy-three, she accepted a regular position as a professor of English offered by the State University of New York–Binghamton, where she taught creative writing until December 2000, when macular degeneration forced her official retirement, though she continued to offer some courses.

After producing a number of limited-edition chapbooks, including *The Solution* (1989), Stone published her fifth full-length collection, *Who Is the Widow's Muse?*, in 1991, followed by *Simplicity* in 1995. In 1996 several of her poet friends and admirers contributed to an essay collection in her honor edited by Wendy Barker and Sandra M. Gilbert, *The House Is Made of Poetry: The Art of Ruth Stone*. With *Ordinary Words* in 1999, she received the major accolade of a National Book Critics Circle Award, then, in 2002, the National Book Award for *In the Next Galaxy*. In 2002 she was also presented the $100,000 Wallace Stevens Award by the Academy of American Poets, for outstanding achievement.

Despite failing eyesight, with transcription help from her daughters Stone completed another extraordinarily deft collection, *In the Dark*, published in 2004, the poet's eighty-ninth year. Reflecting on her art late in her long career, she wrote in "What Is a Poem?":

> Having come this far
> with a handful of alphabet,
> I am forced,
> with these few blocks,
> to invent the universe.

•

GETTING TO KNOW YOU

We slept into one another.
The mattress sloped us to your side.
We shared three daughters.
Miraculous dull day to day
breakfast and dinner.

But compared to all the optic scanning,
the nerve ends of retrospection
in my thirty years of knowing you
cell by cell in my widow's shawl,
we have lived together longer
in the discontinuous films of my sleep
than we did in our warm parasitical bodies.

Thus, by comparison, when the palms
of our hands lay together exchanging oils
and minuscule animals of the skin,
we were relative strangers.

TRAIN RIDE

All things come to an end;
small calves in Arkansas,
the bend of the muddy river.
Do all things come to an end?
No, they go on forever.
They go on forever, the swamp,
the vine-choked cypress, the oaks
rattling last year's leaves,
the thump of the rails, the kite,
the still white stilted heron.
All things come to an end.
The red clay bank, the spread hawk,
the bodies riding this train,
the stalled truck, pale sunlight, the talk;
the talk goes on forever,
the wide dry field of geese,
a man stopped near his porch
to watch. Release, release;
between cold death and a fever,
send what you will, I will listen.
All things come to an end.
No, they go on forever.

JUDITH WRIGHT

◨ For many citizens of Australia, Judith Wright was and is still
considered a prophet and the conscience of the nation, esteemed
equally for her social and environmental activism as for her literary
endeavors. Few writers, particularly poets, have had the immense
degree of real influence and direct impact on national policies and
practices that Wright exerted. Through her poetry and other writ-
ings she helped create a new consciousness of and attitude toward
Australia—its territory and wildlife, its indigenous people, and its
often destructive history—while her pioneering campaigns ulti-
mately produced such unprecedented ecological triumphs as perma-

nent protection of the Great Barrier Reef (from oil drilling) and Fraser Island (from sand mining).

Wright was also instrumental in effecting major cultural shifts that furthered recognition of the rights of the Aborigines and acknowledgment of the abuses inflicted upon them and their land by the colonial settlers, Wright's ancestors among them. No less remarkable, the poet helped foster a new enlightened awareness of woman-man relations and women's sexuality. In the process she altered a long Australian literary tradition that until she arrived (her biographer and several eulogists noted) was centered on "men, horses, and conquest of the land."

Judith Arundell Wright was born May 31, 1915, at Thalgarrah station near Armidale, New South Wales, to a long-established pastoral family. She developed her love of the land as a child, riding her father's large property on her pony. She was educated at home and after the early death of her mother was cared for by an aunt. When her father remarried in 1929, she boarded at the Anglican New England Girls' School in Armidale, which was modeled after strict English "public" schools for boys. (Recalling herself at fourteen, she later wrote: "I was tongue-tied and spotty and beginning to bulge, but I knew I would be a poet.") She then studied English and philosophy at the University of Sydney. She was twenty-five when her first poem was printed.

During World War II she returned home to help out at her father's station, Wallamumbi, after which she worked from 1944 to 1948 as a secretary in Sydney, then for a year as a research officer at the University of Queensland. At the same time she helped edit the literary magazine *Meanjin* and published a poetry collection, *The Moving Image*, in 1946. It was the first of more than fifty books, which would include fifteen volumes of verse as well as literary criticism, biography, history, essays, and writings on environmental and social issues. From the start she refused to conform to conventional expectations for Australian women. In 1950 she met the novelist and independent philosopher Jack McKinney, twenty-four years her senior, and they moved several miles inland from Brisbane to the ecologically rich subtropical region of Mount Tamborine, where their daughter Meredith was born. Unusual for the time, the partners remained unmarried until 1962; he died in 1966. Meredith McKinney, with Patricia Clarke, eventually edited her parents' correspondence in *The Equal Heart and Mind* (2004); she and Clarke also prepared *With Love and Fury: Selected Letters of Judith Wright* (2006).

From the late fifties onward, Wright's literary life and activist interests became intertwined, indeed inseparable, as she made her role as poet gradually into that of a public figure. Beginning with *The Moving Image*, she created a new awareness of the Australian landscape, especially bush country, with its unique diversity of topography and flora and fauna—so wildly different from the tame beauty in Mother England—and its abiding mystery. She also portrayed in sharp vignettes the equally distinctive people inhabiting the land, and its influence on them. "South of My Days," "Metho Drinker," "Country Town," and other poems in the collection have been often anthologized.

In *Woman to Man* (1949), her second, much-discussed volume, Wright took on what in the prudish Australian society of the time were taboo topics: sensual desire and particularly women's sexuality. Explicit and passionate poems like "Woman to Man" and "Woman to Child" created a formidable impression and a heightened recognition of the spiritual dimensions possible in sexual union. Poems from this and the earlier volume have now become part of the curriculum of the Australian school system, and thus a part of the culture.

Wright's next poetry books concentrated on landscape, with *The Two Fires* (1955) emphasizing the destructive effects of English settlement upon the harsh yet fragile terrain and its dispossessed native inhabitants—as well as upon the psyches of the colonists themselves. The poet expressed the multiple desolations of the Aborigines and their culture succinctly in "Bora Ring":

> The song is gone; the dance
> is secret with the dancers in the earth,
> the ritual useless, and the tribal story
> lost in an alien tale.
>
> Only the grass stands up
> to mark the dancing-ring: the apple-gums
> posture and mime a past corroboree,
> murmur a broken chant.
>
> The hunter is gone: the spear
> is splintered underground; the painted bodies

a dream the world breathed sleeping and forgot.
The nomad feet are still.

Only the rider's heart
halts at a sightless shadow, an unsaid word
that fastens in the blood the ancient curse,
the fear as old as Cain.

Wright's intense interest in wildlife is reflected in *Australian Bird Poems* (1961) and *Birds: Poems* (1962), depicted in the poet's typically spare but piquant style. These and her many other nature poems informed the younger generation especially and swayed many Australians to the cause of land conservation and preservation of native species. Over the decades the poet in person proved a very effective, high-profile campaigner against nuclear power plants and rampant commercial development. In protest against what she felt was government collusion with business on environmentally questionable projects, she moved from Mount Tamborine in the mid-seventies.

In 1963 she published *Five Senses*, the first of her several Selected Poems, and a new collection, *City Sunrise*, in 1964. That year, in reaction to the increasing destruction of the Australian rainforest, she co-founded the Wildlife Preservation Society of Queensland, serving as its president until 1976. Amid her increasing involvement in public affairs, committee work, and organizing for several causes, Wright continued to write poetry, publishing collections steadily, if at irregular intervals: *The Other Half* (1966), *Alive: Poems 1971–72* (1973), *Fourth Quarter and Other Poems* (1976), *The Double Tree: Selected Poems 1942–76* (1978), *Phantom Dwelling* (1985), *A Human Pattern: Selected Poems* (1990), and finally *The Flame Tree* (1993). Between these books she also published seven volumes of literary biography and criticism, most notably *Preoccupations in Australian Poetry* (1965) and *Because I Was Invited* (1975).

Besides her work in the Wildlife Preservation Society, Wright was active as a member of the National Parks Association of New South Wales and the South Coast Conservation Council, and as a patron of Amnesty International, the Australian Society of Authors, the National Forests Action Council, and other organizations. In 1975 she became the first woman appointed to the Council of Australian National University. During the last decades of her life, Wright was particularly devoted to redressing the injustices toward the Aborigines, becoming a member of the Aboriginal Treaty Council in 1980.

In 1981 she wrote *The Cry of the Dead*, concerning the maltreatment of native people by settlers in Queensland from the mid-nineteenth century to the 1920s. *We Call for a Treaty* followed in 1985. One of her last public appearances was at a march for reconciliation in Canberra a month before her death.

Over the years Wright's hearing became increasingly impaired, yet she managed to continue to lecture and give very impressive poetry readings. Besides receiving many prizes and several honorary doctorates, in 1992 she became the first Australian to be presented the Queen's Gold Medal for Poetry. Veronica Brady's *South of My Days: A Biography of Judith Wright* appeared in 1998, and various essays and other prose pieces were assembled into an autobiography covering her early years in *Half a Lifetime*, published in 1999. Wright was working on a concluding volume when she died, of a heart attack, on June 25, 2000.

Among numerous memorial tributes, the Australian poet Robert Gray noted that she filled the highest function of a poet, as a moral leader: "She wrote about values, mourning the way land was being destroyed, the way people were being destroyed." The poet and critic Kevin Hart observed shortly after Wright's death, "Whether we know it or not, we all live inside her poems."

FIVE SENSES

Now my five senses
gather into a meaning
all acts, all presences;
and as a lily gathers
the elements together,
in me this dark and shining,
that stillness and that moving,
these shapes that spring from nothing,
become a rhythm that dances,
a pure design.

While I'm in my five senses
they send me spinning
all sounds and silences,
all shape and colour

as thread for that weaver,
whose web within me growing
follows beyond my knowing
some pattern sprung from nothing—
a rhythm that dances
and is not mine.

WOMAN TO CHILD

You who were darkness warmed my flesh
where out of darkness rose the seed.
Then all a world I made in me;
all the world you hear and see
hung upon my dreaming blood.

There moved the multitudinous stars,
and coloured birds and fishes moved.
There swam the sliding continents.
All time lay rolled in me, and sense,
and love that knew not its beloved.

O node and focus of the world;
I hold you deep within that well
you shall escape and not escape—
that mirrors still your sleeping shape;
that nurtures still your crescent cell.

I wither and you break from me;
yet though you dance in living light
I am the earth, I am the root,
I am the stem that fed the fruit,
the link that joins you to the night.

ISHTAR

When I first saw a woman after childbirth
the room was full of your glance who had just gone away.
And when the mare was bearing her foal
you were with her but I did not see your face.

When in fear I became a woman
I first felt your hand.
When the shadow of the future first fell across me
it was your shadow, my grave and hooded attendant.

It is all one whether I deny or affirm you;
it is not my mind you are concerned with.
It is no matter whether I submit or rebel;
the event will still happen.

You neither know nor care for the truth of my heart;
but the truth of my body has all to do with you.
You have no need of my thoughts or my hopes,
living in the realm of the absolute event.

Then why is it that when I at last see your face
under that hood of slate-blue, so calm and dark,
so worn with the burden of an inexpressible knowledge—
why is it that I begin to worship you with tears?

GWENDOLYN BROOKS

Gwendolyn Brooks was born June 7, 1917, in Topeka, Kansas, but her family moved to Chicago when she was a child, and she became a lifelong resident of the South Side. Her mother was a schoolteacher, her father a janitor who had hoped to become a doctor. As a girl she was shy and bookish and had few friends, so her mother encouraged her writing, which began at age seven. To her proud family she became known as "the *female* Paul Laurence Dunbar." She applied herself very seriously to verse—sonnets and ballads were her favorite modes—and in high school she wrote to prominent black writers such as Langston Hughes for advice. When she was fifteen, her mother took her to a reading by Hughes, after which they were introduced. Hughes read the verses she handed him and predicted that one day she would write a book.

Brooks attended Wright Junior College in Chicago, graduating in 1936, and began to contribute poems to the *Chicago Defender* newspaper. She also took poetry workshops at the South Chicago Community Arts Center, where she was encouraged by her instructor, Inez Cunningham Stark, who happened to be on the board of *Poetry*. Brooks made her debut in the magazine in 1944.

Brooks's first book, *A Street in Bronzeville*, appeared in 1945 and was drawn from the lives of diverse people she knew or observed in the neighborhood of the title. Here Brooks demonstrated her mastery of forms, understated humor, and acute social perceptions. In 1949 she published *Annie Allen*, a series of poems depicting the life of a black girl growing to womanhood in inner-city Chicago. The book won the Pulitzer Prize for poetry in 1950, making Brooks the first African American to receive the award. A novel, *Maud Martha*, followed in 1953, and in 1960 another poetry collection, *The Bean Eaters*, which included her most famous piece, "We Real Cool." Of the boys playing truant in the pool hall, the poet later said she thought they felt unwanted, and explained that she placed the word *We* at the ends of the lines for emphasis, "so the reader could give them that little split-second's attention."

WE REAL COOL

THE POOL PLAYERS.
SEVEN AT THE GOLDEN SHOVEL.

We real cool. We
Left school. We

Lurk late. We
Strike straight. We

Sing sin. We
Thin gin. We

Jazz June. We
Die soon.

The missing *We* makes the final line all the more dramatic.

In 1967, at the second Black Writers' Conference at Fisk University, Brooks met many young, militant authors and was impressed by the new generation's call for a separate African-American aesthetic and tradition of literature. Thereafter her own work became more open in form and overtly political in its subjects and rhetoric. In 1968 she published *In the Mecca*, which drew stark portraits of dysfunctional members of a community in growing disarray. Brooks also switched from her major commercial New York publisher to small black-owned houses for her later books, where focus remained on social topics, personalities, and political issues of importance to her large audience in the black community.

In *Riot* (1969) and *Family Pictures* (1970), Brooks focused her attention on the massive urban upheavals and destruction of the late sixties. In 1971 she edited *Jump Bad: A New Chicago Anthology*, and the following year she published *Report from Part One: An Autobiography*. By the end of the seventies her guarded optimism about change had turned to disillusionment, as she witnessed the growing internecine hostilities between the old civil rights movement and the new and more radical Black Power groups. In *Beckonings* (1975) and *To Disembark* (1981), her tone turned acerbic as she agreed with the younger generation's separatist stance and extreme policies advocating drastic measures and even violence to answer the repressions they viewed in the dominant white society. Many critics found Brooks's switch in style from the carefully considered, well-crafted verse of her early career to free-form polemics scant improvement artistically, however pointedly it expressed the poet's solidarity with the angry black community.

Throughout her last decades Brooks read widely around the country, particularly in colleges and schools. She devoted a great deal of time to bringing poetry to children, generously sponsoring poetry programs and prize contests in public grammar and high schools. In 1968 she was named the poet laureate of Illinois, a position she held until her death, and was appointed Consultant in Poetry to the Library of Congress (precursor to the post of Poet Laureate) for 1985–1986. In 1994 the National Endowment for the Humanities named her its annual Jefferson Lecturer, the federal government's highest accolade for achievement in the humanities. Brooks died of cancer on December 3, 2000. Elizabeth Alexander, one of the many younger black poets inspired by her example, edited and introduced *The Essential Gwendolyn Brooks* for the Library of America's American Poets Project in 2005.

KITCHENETTE BUILDING

We are things of dry hours and the involuntary plan,
Grayed in, and gray. "Dream" makes a giddy sound, not strong
Like "rent," "feeding a wife," "satisfying a man."

But could a dream send up through onion fumes
Its white and violet, fight with fried potatoes
And yesterday's garbage ripening in the hall,
Flutter, or sing an aria down these rooms

Even if we were willing to let it in,
Had time to warm it, keep it very clean,
Anticipate a message, let it begin?

We wonder. But not well! not for a minute!
Since Number Five is out of the bathroom now,
We think of lukewarm water, hope to get in it.

AMY CLAMPITT

◨ In 1983 a generous first book of poems appeared that created a sensation. Featuring dense, rich language and an intricate style quite unlike the plainspoken mode in vogue for decades in the United States, the large volume was called *The Kingfisher*, and several critics hailed it as "remarkable," "brilliant," "a major achievement." Helen Vendler, the most influential of all, went so far as to predict that a hundred years hence the collection would "take on the documentary value of what, in the twentieth century, made up the stuff of culture." The author making her "debut" was a virtual unknown named Amy Clampitt, and (all commentators hastened to exclaim) sixty-three years old.

Clampitt had lived all her adult life in New York City, the major hub of the U.S. literary world, and in fact had long been in publishing, but she had labored on the unglamorous side of the industry, mainly as an editor. She had begun sending out poems only in the late 1970s and was quickly printed in *The New Yorker*, the *Atlantic*, *Poetry*, and other leading journals. Then, with the "overnight" success of *The Kingfisher*, the reticent author became an inspiration to countless other aspiring poets, and her unfashionably opulent writing a liberating, even defiant, answer to the long-reigning minimalism of Modernism and its cool, dry, ironic, and generally restrained orthodoxy.

Clampitt's poems are filled with lush descriptions of landscapes of wide variety, packed to bursting with sensuous depictions of plants and animals, brimming over line to line in an onrush of vivid images and sounds. Above all, the poet delights in language—in words themselves—as evidenced in her unusual, sometimes arcane diction. As her later work further demonstrated, Clampitt had one of the largest vocabularies of any poet ever. For full enjoyment of many a poem, the reader would be well advised to keep a dictionary close at hand.

Like Marianne Moore, Clampitt is a precise observer and meticulous recorder of details; thus scientific and other nonliterary lexicons, as well as several foreign tongues, come into play. Particularly in her later books, the sheer verbal profusion can become fatiguing, the syntax confusing—even to the author, one suspects at times, as phrases and clauses pile up and become knotted, like curlicues into snarls. "Precise" can become "precious," and the delicate linguistic balance in her more elaborate pieces can tip from baroque splendor to rococo excess. But at their considerable best, Clampitt's poems are invigorating—virtuoso performances that recreate the wondrous complexity of the world and celebrate its earthly delights.

Eldest of five children, Amy Clampitt was born June 15, 1920, in New Providence, Iowa, a rural community of two hundred. Her family were Quakers of a puritan strain and lived on her grandfather's three-hundred-acre farm, an Eden for a child drawn to the natural world, birds especially. This paradise was lost when she was ten and her father bought Pioneer Farm, a hardscrabble piece of land three miles away. The uprooting marked the sensitive child, and dislocation would become a theme in her work, as in Elizabeth Bishop's. She attended the same consolidated school through twelfth grade, and being tall, shy, bookish, and a bit eccentric, Amy was made fun of by her classmates.

She received a thorough knowledge of the Bible in Sunday school but determined early on that she would not conform to standard expectations, such as settling down and raising a family. She later remarked she did not dream of bringing children into a world of nuclear bombs. Although she was skeptical of organized religion, she did become an Episcopalian in the fifties, but left the church when she felt it did not take a strong enough stand against the Vietnam War.

Clampitt attended Grinnell College in Iowa, and immediately after graduation, in 1941, she moved to New York City. She entered graduate school at Columbia on a fellowship, but dropped out after the first year and took a job as a secretary at Oxford University Press, rising to textbook promotions director. In 1951, in an essay contest sponsored by the press, she won first prize, a trip to England. During the visit she began a romance that ended unhappily in New York (alluded to in the title poem of *The Kingfisher*), but she absorbed and filed in memory the sights of London and the landscapes of the Romantic poets she loved, especially Wordsworth and Keats. (Another favorite was Gerard Manley Hopkins.) On her return she began work on a novel. When no publisher wanted it, she wrote two more, with no better luck. She then became a reference librarian for the National Audubon Society, an ideal job considering her love of wildlife.

In the late sixties Clampitt became actively involved in the antiwar movement, even demonstrating in front of the White House in 1971. She had already worked for the Independent Democrats in Greenwich Village, and while canvassing in 1968 for Senator Eugene McCarthy, the doomed presidential candidate, she met her future longtime partner, Harold Korn, a law professor. She moved in with him in 1973 (a fact unmentioned to her stricter relatives) but kept her small walk-up in a Village brownstone: her own space, until gentrification finally forced her out in her last year.

In the early seventies, after years as a freelance editor, she went to work at the publisher E. P. Dutton. She also began writing poetry for the first time since high school. In 1977 she took a poetry writing course that also offered practice in reading in public, but had an instructor (she wrote at the time) "who I think disapproves of the kind of thing I do." Always independent minded, never part of the New York poetry "scene" or any literary group, Clampitt had worked alone and developed her own style, without concern for current trends. She recalled this response to some early pieces: "'You're in love with words,' I was told (by a poet, yet) in a tone of accusation. When he meant, I guess, was that I tend to use too many of them."

With hesitation she began submitting poems in 1977. Howard Moss, poetry editor of *The New Yorker*, accepted them immediately and gave Clampitt her first publication in 1978, and several more. She soon was contributing to *Poetry* as well. The poet Mary Jo Salter, then a young first reader at the *Atlantic*, was so impressed that she sent the author a fan letter, assuming they were the same age;

they became friends and regular correspondents. The early appearances caught the attention of several critics, as well as the editors of Knopf's new poetry series, who accepted her book manuscript in 1982. Several noted poets were happy to provide blurbs. Vendler, who also sponsored her for a Guggenheim fellowship, wrote: "The poems range from Iowa to Europe, from visual idyll to moral pain, from war to the experiences of women. An assured and distinguished voice resembling no other has been added to the sum of American poetry."

Encouraged by the many enthusiastic reviews of *The Kingfisher* in 1983—and as if to make up for the years in obscurity—Clampitt soon assembled *What the Light Was Like* (1985) from pieces left out of that already big first book and many new poems, again to much praise. But not everyone was pleased: several critics, including some feminists, found her style too cerebral, bookish, and florid, or faulted her devotion to high art. Clampitt continued to go her own way, a braver course than following the crowd, however "correct" their opinions. In 1984 she began studying classical Greek, then toured Greece, preparations for her myth-inspired next collection, *Archaic Figure* (1987). She also published *A Homage to John Keats* in 1984 and edited a collection of *The Essential John Donne* in 1988. Her next full-length poetry book was *Westward* (1990), followed by her last collection, *A Silence Opens* (1994).

After her first success, Clampitt was invited to give readings around the country and taught occasionally, at Amherst, Smith, and the College of William and Mary. She received a fellowship from the Academy of American Poets in 1984, and in 1992 she was awarded a MacArthur "genius" grant. The day she received the news, she went out to buy a small summer place (her first major purchase) in Lenox, Massachusetts. She did not have long to enjoy it.

Early in 1993 she was diagnosed with ovarian cancer, was operated on, and underwent chemotherapy, which greatly weakened her. She was informed that the measures were not successful. Three months before her death she and Hal Korn married, and the poet spent her last days peacefully in Lenox. Mary Jo Salter recalled that she refused intravenous nourishment and was content to look out the window and watch birds at the feeder in the backyard where, the poet observed, "there's so much going on."

Amy Clampitt died September 10, 1994. Her *Collected Poems* appeared in 1997 with a warmly appreciative foreword by Salter,

from which several details here are taken. Willard Spiegelman ed-
ited and provided a valuable introduction to *Love, Amy: The Selected
Letters of Amy Clampitt*, published in 2005.

NOTHING STAYS PUT

In Memory of Father Flye, 1884–1985

The strange and wonderful are too much with us.
The protea of the antipodes—a great,
globed, blazing honeybee of a bloom—
for sale in the supermarket! We are in
our decadence, we are not entitled.
What have we done to deserve
all the produce of the tropics—
this fiery trove, the largesse of it
heaped up like cannonballs, these pineapples, bossed
and crested, standing like troops at attention,
these tiers, these balconies of green, festoons
grown sumptuous with stoop labor?

The exotic is everywhere, it comes to us
before there is a yen or a need for it. The green-
grocers, uptown and down, are from South Korea.
Orchids, opulence by the pailful, just slightly
fatigued by the plane trip from Hawaii, are
disposed on the sidewalks; alstroemerias, freesias
fattened a bit in translation from overseas; gladioli
likewise estranged from their piercing ancestral crimson;
as well as, less altered from the original blue cornflower
of the roadsides and railway embankments of Europe, these
bachelor's buttons. But it isn't the railway embankments
their featherweight wheels of cobalt remind me of, it's

a row of them among prim colonnades of cosmos,
snapdragon, nasturtium, bloodsilk red poppies,
in my grandmother's garden: a prairie childhood,
the grassland shorn, overlaid with a grid,
unsealed, furrowed, harrowed and sown with immigrant grasses,
their massive corduroy, their wavering feltings embroidered

here and there by the scarlet shoulder patch of cannas
on a courthouse lawn, by a love knot, a cross stitch
of living matter, sown and tended by women,
nurturers everywhere of the strange and wonderful,
beneath whose hands what had been alien begins,
as it alters, to grow as though it were indigenous.

But at this remove what I think of as
strange and wonderful, strolling the side streets of Manhattan
on an April afternoon, seeing hybrid pear trees in blossom,
a tossing, vertiginous colonnade of foam, up above—
is the white petalfall, the warm snowdrift
of the indigenous wild plum of my childhood.
Nothing stays put. The world is a wheel.
All that we know, that we're
made of, is motion.

MONA VAN DUYN

◨ Circling a favorite topic in her much-cited poem "Toward a Definition of Marriage," Mona Van Duyn describes the wedded state as "a duel of amateurs" and "the politics of love." On the conflicts of married life, with its many tensions and contests between individual wills, Van Duyn works extensive variations in poems that continually surprise with their odd perspectives and acute insights into the tangled bonds of affection. The course of true love—and of family relations and friendships generally—seldom runs smooth, the poet knows well, but she ultimately discovers lasting rewards amid the traffic of domestic routines.

It is the very ordinariness of daily rounds—the mostly unglamorous underpinnings of civilization—that she celebrates even when those practicalities, especially in the suburban settings of her work, seem unpromising as poetic material. But as the critic William Logan has said, Van Duyn "could make poems from table scraps and newspaper cuttings." He notes that W. H. Auden did likewise, and comparing her poems with Auden's, Logan adds (not necessarily in praise) that they "are often just intelligent talk." In her down-to-earth diction, Van Duyn does share Auden's style. But unlike his easy conversational tone, her voice can seem authentic but awkward, probably deliberately so—to sound more "genuine" or realistic—for in her formal verse she is very artful indeed, especially when employing complex rhyme schemes.

In her high craft and modest understatement, Van Duyn is often compared with Elizabeth Bishop as well. Her precise if slightly eccentric scrutiny also recalls the quirkiness of Marianne Moore, another poet noted for her wry observations on marriage. Unlike Miss Moore, however, Van Duyn had the benefit of practical experience of that institution. And unlike the often troubled Bishop, she enjoyed a very long, steady, and mutually satisfying union with her partner: not so common good fortune that may explain the pervasive optimism in Van Duyn's work. Even her deeply ambivalent feelings toward her parents find resolution, after all, during their old age, especially her mother's grim final years, when the poet finally reaches, at least in the verses of "The Stream," a bittersweet reconciliation. While Van Duyn acknowledges that the human condition is fraught with pain, disappointment, and disillusionment, she also insists that intelligence, grit, and generosity of spirit may ultimately prevail.

In any case, the poet offers the gifts of her wit, clarity of vision (itself a kind of consolation), and empathetic humor about the vagaries of the heart, as when she compares marriage to a picaresque novel, but for the fact that it is

> essentially artless.
> If there were any experts, they are dead, it takes too long.
> How could its structure be more than improvising,
> when it never ends, but line after line plods on,
> and none of the ho-hum passages can be skipped?

Mona Van Duyn was born May 9, 1921, in Waterloo, Iowa, but grew up in Eldora, a small town some thirty miles to the west. She began writing verse while in grammar school, when she acquired her knowledge and love of poetry at the public library, not in the classroom. (She recalled many years later that poetry was used as punishment there: "One was made to stay after school and learn a poem.") She attended Iowa State Teachers College (now Northern Iowa University) in Cedar Falls, where she took her B.A. in 1942. The following year she earned her master's at the University of Iowa, where she met and married Jarvis Thurston and both entered the Ph.D. program in English.

When her husband received a position in 1946 as an assistant professor at the University of Louisville, she became an instructor there. Together in 1947 they founded *Perspective: A Quarterly of Literature*, which they co-edited until 1970. In 1950 both received jobs at Washington University in St. Louis, where they spent their entire careers, Van Duyn in the University College adult education program and only much later, when she was already heavily laden with laurels, as an adjunct and finally a visiting professor in the English Department, until she retired in 1990.

Valentines to the Wide World, Van Duyn's first collection, was published in 1959 and demonstrated her already highly accomplished formal style. It was followed in 1964 by *The Time of Bees*. Both books treat what became her perennial subjects: the complex and fluid dynamics of marriage, the pleasures and challenges of ordinary life (including the darkness of mental illness), and the intricate wonders of the natural world and mankind's interaction with it. From the start she won the admiration of her peers, particularly such masters of technique as James Merrill, Anthony Hecht, Richard Howard, and Richard Wilbur, as well as her Washington colleagues Howard Nemerov and Herbert Morris. Wider recognition arrived in 1970 with *To Take, To See*, which collected her earlier work with several new poems and won both the National Book Award and the Bollingen Prize in 1971. *Bedtime Stories* appeared in 1972, quickly followed by *Merciful Disguises* in 1973, which was reissued in 1982 when she published her poignant *Letters from a Father, and Other Poems*. Although perhaps not as original or moving as her earlier work, *Near Changes* won the Pulitzer Prize in 1991. In 1994 she brought out her *Collected Poems, 1959–1982*, together with a volume of new work entitled *Firefall*, which proved to be her final original book.

Through the years Van Duyn preferred to compose formal verse, but on many occasions she also wrote in free verse. Her switches to more open modes of expression did not however signal philosophical shifts or carry serious political import as with the major midlife stylistic transformations of W. S. Merwin, Adrienne Rich, and others of her contemporaries during the turbulent sixties and seventies. Van Duyn kept her vision finely focused, not on world happenings but on affairs of the heart and the domestic realm.

During her long career Van Duyn received almost every other important accolade that can be bestowed on an American poet, including the Hart Crane Memorial Award and the Shelley Memorial

Prize; fellowships from the Academy of American Poets, the Guggenheim Foundation, and the American Academy of Arts and Sciences; and several prizes from *Poetry*, including the Ruth Lilly Poetry Prize. She was also elected a chancellor of the Academy of American Poets.

Despite the acknowledgments from her fellow artists, critics fluctuated in their assessments decade to decade, and Van Duyn's name never became famous among the larger audience, as reflected in an unfortunate historical footnote: she was not called on to read at the first Clinton inauguration, as ceremony planners seemed unaware of or simply ignored the fact that in 1992–1993 she was serving as the first female Poet Laureate of the United States. Plagued by illness and increasing debilitation during her last decade, Van Duyn was able to produce very little new work but edited a *Selected Poems*, issued in 2003. She died, of bone cancer, in St. Louis on December 1, 2004.

IN BED WITH A BOOK

In police procedurals they are dying all over town,
the life ripped out of them, by gun, bumper, knife,
hammer, dope, etcetera, and no clues at all.
All through the book the calls come in: body found
in bed, car, street, lake, park, garage, library,
and someone goes out to look and write it down.
Death begins life's whole routine to-do
in these stories of our fellow citizens.

Nobody saw it happen, or everyone saw,
but can't remember the car. What difference does it make
when the child will never fall in love, the girl will never
have a child, the man will never see a grandchild, the old maid
will never have another cup of hot cocoa at bedtime?
Like life, the dead are dead, their consciousness,
as dear to them as mine to me, snuffed out.
What has mind to do with this, when the earth is bereaved?

I lie, with my dear ones, holding a fictive umbrella,
while around us falls the real and acid rain.
The handle grows heavier and heavier in my hand.

Unlike life, tomorrow night under the bedlamp
by a quick link of thought someone will find out why,
and the policemen and their wives and I will feel better.
But all that's toward the end of the book. Meantime, tonight,
without a clue I enter sleep's little rehearsal.

THE STREAM

FOR MY MOTHER

Four days with you, my father three months dead.
You can't tell months from years, but you feel sad,

and you hate the nursing home. I've arranged a lunch
for the two of us, and somehow you manage to pinch

the pin from Madrid I bought you closed at the neck
of your best red blouse, put on new slacks, and take

off your crocheted slippers to put on shiny shoes,
all by yourself. "I don't see how you could close

that pin. You look so nice!" "Well, I tried and tried,
and worked till I got it. They didn't come," you said.

"Mother, I'm sorry, this is the wrong day,
our lunch is tomorrow. Here's a big kiss anyway

for dressing up for me. The nurse will come in
tomorrow and help you put on your clothes and pin."

"These last few days her mind has certainly cleared.
Of course the memory's gone," your doctor said.

Next day they bathed you, fixed your hair and dressed
you up again, got a wheelchair and wheeled you past

the fat happy babbler of nonsense who rolled her chair
all day in the hall, the silent stroller who wore

a farmer's cap and bib overalls with rows
of safety pins on the bib, rooms of old babies

in cribs, past the dining hall, on down to a sunny
lounge in the other wing. "Where can I pee,

if I have to pee? I don't like it here, I'm afraid.
Where's my room? I'm going to faint," you said.

But they came with the lunch and card table and chairs
and bustled and soothed you and you forgot the fears

and began to eat. The white tablecloth, the separate
plate for salad, the silvery little coffee pot,

the covers for dishes must have made you feel
you were in a restaurant again after all

those shut-in years. (Dad would never spend the money,
but long ago you loved to eat out with me.)

You cleaned your soup bowl and dishes, one by one,
and kept saying, "This is fun! This is *fun!*"

The cake fell from your trembly fork, so I fed
it to you. "Do you want mine, too?" "Yes," you said,

"and I'll drink your milk if you don't want it." (You'd
lost twelve pounds already by refusing your food.)

I wheeled you back. "Well, I never did *that* before!
Thank you, Jane." "We'll do it again." "Way down *there*,"

you marveled. You thanked me twice more. My eyes were wet.
"You're welcome, Mother. You'll have a good nap now, I'll bet."

I arranged for your old companion, who came twice a day,
to bring you milkshakes, and reached the end of my stay.

On the last night I helped you undress. Flat dugs
like antimacassars lay on your chest, your legs

and arms beetle-thin swung from the swollen belly
(the body no more misshapen, no stranger to see,

after all, at the end than at the beloved beginning).
You chose your flowered nightgown as most becoming.

You stood at the dresser, put your teeth away,
washed your face, smoothed on Oil of Olay,

then Avon night cream, then put Vicks in your nose,
then lay on the bed. I sat beside your knees

to say goodbye for a month. "You know I'll call
every Sunday and write a lot. Try to eat well—"

Tears stopped my voice. With a girl's grace you sat up
and, as if you'd done it lifelong, reached out to cup

my face in both hands, and, as easily
as if you'd said it lifelong, you said, "Don't cry,

don't cry. You'll never know how much I love you."
I kissed you and left, crying. It felt true.

I forgot to tell them that you always sneaked your meat,
you'd bragged, to the man who ate beside you. One night

at home, my heart ringing with what you'd said,
then morning, when the phone rang to say you were dead.

I see your loving look wherever I go.
What is love? Truly I do not know.

Sometimes, perhaps, instead of a great sea,
it is a narrow stream running urgently

far below ground, held down by rocky layers,
the deeds of Mother and Father, helpless soothsayers

of how our life is to be, weighted by clay,
the dense pressure of thwarted needs, the replay

of old misreadings, by hundreds of feet of soil,
the gifts and wounds of the genes, the short or tall

shape of our possibilities, seeking
and seeking a way to the top, while above, running

and stumbling this way and that on the clueless ground,
another seeker clutches a dowsing-wand

which bends, then lifts, dips, then straightens, everywhere
saying to the dowser, it is there, it is not there,

and the untaught dowser believes, does not believe,
and finally simply stands on the ground above,

till a sliver of stream finds a crack and makes its way,
slowly, too slowly, through rock and earth and clay.

Here at my feet I see, after sixty years,
the welling water—to which I add these tears.

DENISE LEVERTOV

⧉ Several cultural streams combined in the life and work of Denise Levertov. From her parents she seemed to inherit a visionary sense of the spiritual dimension of life, though she did not try to transcend the world so much as to penetrate, understand, and appreciate it. Like her parents, too, she was committed to social justice. Her search for harmony in life led her to become a peace activist, and she became prominent among poets who opposed the Vietnam War. She also worked to prevent environmental destruction.

Literary influences in Levertov's work were likewise several and complex. She began writing in a conventional English style, but after moving to the United States she adopted the high Modernist principles of Pound, particularly the use of Imagistic detail. She developed a warm friendship with William Carlos Williams, whose focus on everyday life and common speech came to inform her own approach. Finally she became friends with Robert Creeley and Robert Duncan, adopting their Eastern religious attitudes and various ideas of organic form derived from the poet and theorist Charles Olson, when they were all members of the experimental Black Mountain College in North Carolina. She rejected the self-absorption of the confessional mode (the "me, me, me kind of poem," as she put it), and sought to observe the external world intently and to enact that experience in her poems. In Levertov's secular faith, poetry became a way of discovering meaning, order, and wholeness behind the flux and chaos of surface perceptions.

Levertov was born in Ilford, Essex, England, October 24, 1923. Her mother descended from the Welsh mystic Angel Jones. Her father was related to the founder of the Hasidic branch of Judaism but converted to Christianity and eventually became an Anglican priest. Both worked to promote several human rights causes. Levertov was educated entirely at home in a book-filled environment reminiscent of the Victorian Era. During World War II she served as a nurse in London.

Her first book, *Double Image*, was published in 1946. In 1947 she married an American writer, Mitchell Goodman, and the next year they immigrated to the United States, living first in New York then Massachusetts, where she eventually taught at Brandeis, MIT, and Tufts. Levertov became a citizen in 1955, and by then had acquired a thoroughly American voice, evident in her next collection, *Here and Now* (1956). The book was praised by such older avant-garde figures as Williams and Kenneth Rexroth and new ones like Creeley and Duncan. *With Eyes at the Back of Our Heads* (1959) secured her reputation.

During the tumultuous sixties she joined the anti-war movement. Her husband was arrested with Dr. Benjamin Spock for advising draft resisters. With Daniel Berrigan and her good friend Muriel Rukeyser, she traveled to Hanoi in 1972. Levertov also joined anti-nuclear groups and spoke out against U.S. involvement with repressive regimes in Central America. The Vietnam War and other political issues now figured prominently in her work, notably *The Sorrow Dance* (1967), and some felt her poems of protest departed too radically from the quiet poise of her previous work and were weaker artistically. Among the more effective poems from this period of darkness and near despair is "Tenebrae," which Levertov wrote at the time of the famous March on the Pentagon on October 22, 1967, the first in a chain of events that led to Lyndon Johnson's decision not to run again for president.

Levertov continued her involvement with social causes and went on to publish more than twenty poetry collections, among them: *Relearning the Alphabet* (1970), *To Stay Alive* (1971), *The Freeing of the Dust* (1975), *Collected Earlier Poems 1940–1960* (1979), *Candles in Babylon* (1982), *Poems 1960–1967* (1983), *Oblique Prayers: New Poems* (1984), *Breathing the Water* (1987), *The Sands of the Well* (1996), and *The Life Around Us: Selected Poems on Nature* and *The Stream & the Sapphire: Selected Poems on Religious Themes* (both 1997). Her prose was collected in *The Poet in the World* (1973), *Light Up the Cave* (1981), *New & Selected Essays* (1992), and *Tesserae: Memories & Suppositions* (1995). Levertov taught each spring at Stanford from 1982 to 1993, then lived the rest of her life in Seattle, where she died of lymphoma on December 20, 1997.

THE ACHE OF MARRIAGE

The ache of marriage:

thigh and tongue, beloved,
are heavy with it,
it throbs in the teeth

We look for communion
and are turned away, beloved,
each and each

It is leviathan and we
in its belly
looking for joy, some joy
not to be known outside it

two by two in the ark of
the ache of it.

DIVORCING

One garland
of flowers, leaves, thorns

was twined round our two necks.
Drawn tight, it could choke us,
yet we loved its scratchy grace,
our fragrant yoke.

We were Siamese twins.
Our blood's not sure
if it can circulate,
now we are cut apart.
Something in each of us is waiting
to see if we can survive,
severed.

LISEL MUELLER

☐ Clarity, precision, and direct engagement are the hallmarks of Lisel Mueller's understated art. Her poems convince immediately by the exactness of her observations, then continue to resonate with emotional and philosophical implications. Whether examining nature, meditating on "ordinary" life, or drawing upon memories of separation and loss—Mueller's grandparents perished in the Nazi death camps—the poet speaks as one person to another, with quiet authority. Because English was her second language, acquired in adolescence, she has perhaps an even greater understanding of its nuances and ambiguities than a native speaker. Her diction is impeccable, her phrasing musical, her figures fine and never forced. With her heightened awareness of the power of well-chosen words, she has no need of overblown rhetoric or "poetical" theatrics. In her nine collections spanning five decades, one will find nary a frivolous or ill-conceived piece.

She was born Lisel Neumann in Hamburg, Germany, February 8, 1924. Both her parents were teachers. In 1939, late in the Nazi persecutions, her immediate family managed to get out of Germany and settled in Indiana, where Fritz Neumann became a professor at Evansville College. Lisel was fifteen, and English was, she has written, "a language / I never wanted to understand." But in time it became a means not only for communication but for transformation and comfort. In "Curriculum Vitae" she reveals how the foreign words led to healing and reconciliation. Then, following her mother's death in 1953, English became the vehicle for releasing her deepest feelings, as that loss "hurt the daughter into poetry."

Family matters are the abiding subjects of many of Mueller's poems: the joys and difficulties of child-rearing, the simple satisfactions and even wonders of married life, the myriad daily events (celebrating birthdays, gardening, listening to music) that the less attentive may take for granted but she perceives afresh and savors with unaffected gratitude. Behind the poet's affirmations lies a somber background, however, an unsentimental understanding of history, and thus an abiding melancholy. Mueller's frequent delights in quotidian experience are tinged but also heightened by her sense of their, *our*, transitory nature.

In a memorable phrase from "In Passing," which opens her selected poems, *Alive Together*, and which sounds a leitmotif in much of her work, Mueller states: "what exists, exists / so that it can be lost / and become precious." Thus the importance too of memory, which retrieves and preserves (however imperfectly) the past. Painful though they often are, her recollections become links that sustain and reinforce the bonds of affection. In "Voyager," her haunting tribute to her father, the poet finds in a photographic negative a striking image for this power of recall:

> How can you see, your glasses
> are whitewashed and there are holes
> where your teeth used to be
>
> Nevertheless you smile at me
> across an enormous distance
> as you have so many times
> to let me know you have arrived

While she commemorates the past and finds solace in memory, the poet's most urgent "message" (if that is the word for so undidactic an author) is not so much to dwell on what was or might have been as to become more aware of and exist fully in the here and now— before the gifts life offers are lost.

Lisel attended Evansville College, where she met Paul Mueller, a fellow student. They married in 1943, in the midst of the war while he was on leave from basic training, and she took her B.A. in 1944. In 1950 both enrolled in graduate programs at Indiana University, Lisel in folklore and mythology, Paul in musicology. They eventually built a house in a still-rural area near Libertyville, several miles northwest of Chicago, where Mueller recalled awakening one morning to the unexpected sound of Holsteins, the same breed of cows she had encountered in childhood. The couple lived there for more than forty years, until advancing age and Paul's ailments led them to move into a retirement home in Chicago, where Paul died in 2001.

Mueller's reputation grew slowly but steadily, without benefit of the usual methods today's poetry professionals employ to advance their careers. Lacking an M.F.A., living in relative isolation, and enjoying few literary contacts, she perfected her craft while raising two children. In 1957, the year her first daughter was born, Mueller's first poems appeared in *The New Yorker*. Soon (and frequently) after, she contributed both poetry and prose to *Poetry*, and then to other leading journals. Her second daughter was born in 1962, and in 1965 Mueller published her first collection, *Dependencies* (reissued in paper 1998). She was an instructor for a few years at Elmhurst College and served in the Poets in the Schools program in the mid-seventies. She later taught in the writing program at Goddard College and at the University of Chicago.

Her second full-length collection, *The Private Life*, was selected in manuscript for the Lamont Poetry Award in 1975 and published in 1976. Her translation of *Selected Later Poems of Marie Luise Kaschnitz* and her own third volume, *The Need to Hold Still*, both appeared in 1980. The former won the Jacob Glatstein Prize from *Poetry*, the latter the National Book Award in 1981. *Second Language* was published in 1986, *Waving from Shore* in 1989, and *Learning to Play by Ear* in 1990. *Alive Together: New and Selected Poems* was awarded the Pulitzer Prize in 1997. In 2002 Mueller received the Ruth Lilly Prize from *Poetry* for her lifetime achievement. Although she has now lost most of her sight, the poet remains active and still makes the occasional public appearance, reciting her poems from memory.

NECESSITIES

1.

A map of the world. Not the one in the atlas,
but the one in our heads, the one we keep coloring in.
With the blue thread of the river by which we grew up.
The green smear of the woods we first made love in.
The yellow city we thought was our future.

The red highways not traveled, the green ones
with their missed exits, the black side roads
which took us where we had not meant to go.
The high peaks, recorded by relatives,
though we prefer certain unmarked elevations,
the private alps no one knows we have climbed.
The careful boundaries we draw and erase.
And always, around the edges,
the opaque wash of blue, concealing
the dropoff they have stepped into before us,
singly, mapless, not looking back.

2.

The illusion of progress. Imagine our lives without it:
tape measures rolled back, yardsticks chopped off.
Wheels turning but going nowhere.
Paintings flat, with no vanishing point.
The plots of all novels circular;
page numbers reversing themselves past the middle.
The mountain top no longer a goal,
merely the point between ascent and descent.
All streets looping back on themselves;
life as a beckoning road an absurd idea.
Our children refusing to grow out of their childhoods;
the years refusing to drag themselves
toward the new century.
And hope, the puppy that bounds ahead,
no longer a household animal.

3.

Answers to questions, an endless supply.
New ones that startle, old ones that reassure us.
All of them wrong perhaps, but for the moment
solutions, like kisses or surgery.
Rising inflections countered by level voices,
words beginning with *w* hushed
by declarative sentences. The small, bold sphere
of the period chasing after the hook,
the doubter that walks on water
and treads air and refuses to go away.

4.

Evidence that we matter. The crash of the plane
which, at the last moment, we did not take.
The involuntary turn of the head,
which caused the bullet to miss us.
The obscene caller who wakes us at midnight
to the smell of gas. The moon's
full blessing when we fell in love,
its black mood when it was all over.
Confirm us, we say to the world,
with your weather, your gifts, your warnings,
your ringing telephones, your long, bleak silences.

5.

Even now, *the old things first things,*
which taught us language. Things of day and of night.
Irrational lightning, fickle clouds, the incorruptible moon.
Fire as revolution, grass as the heir
to all revolutions. Snow
as the alphabet of the dead, subtle, undeciphered.
The river as what we wish it to be.
Trees in their humanness, animals in their otherness.
Summits. Chasms. Clearings.
And stars, which gave us the word distance,
so we could name our deepest sadness.

CAROLYN KIZER

▣ Carolyn Kizer's poetry has been called tough-minded and acerbic but could as justly be described as clearheaded and emphatic; empathetic too. Love and loss, hope and disillusionment, and the other opposing forces or facets of the human condition are measured equally in the balance of her lines. Kizer titled her 1984 collection *Yin*, after the Chinese term for the feminine (cold/passive/dark) principle operating in the universe. But just as the *yin* supposes its *yang* (masculine/hot/active/light) counterpart to have meaning and completion, so too in her poems Kizer accepts and even embraces the contrasting and complementary states of experience. Intelligent, witty, feisty, and unafraid to confront unpleasant realities—particularly about male-female and parent-child conflicts—but not hardened by or cynical about them either, Kizer pairs wisdom with compassion in her spirited, adult-strength interpretations of the paradoxes that make the world.

Carolyn Ashley Kizer was born in Spokane, Washington, December 10, 1925. Her father was a prominent attorney, her mother (his second wife) a biology professor with a Ph.D. from Stanford. He was fifty, she in her late forties when their child was born. Kizer was very close to her mother, who imparted a deep love of nature to her adored only child. In "A Muse," her touching memoir in *Yin*, the poet recalls that the very first word she wrote, by chance, in crayon was A-R-T, which to her mother-muse "proved" her precocious child was "*fated* to become an artist." Kizer remembered her father as "authoritarian and severe," polite but remote. After high school in Spokane she attended Sarah Lawrence College, where she studied with Joseph Campbell, the legendary scholar of comparative mythology, and took her B.A. in 1945. She did a year of graduate work at Columbia and then another at the University of Washington.

Kizer did not take a graduate degree but married the wealthy Stimson Bullitt of Seattle; they divorced after the birth of their third child. In 1954 she enrolled in the University of Washington's pioneering creative writing program, founded by Theodore Roethke. Kizer had published a poem in *The New Yorker* at age seventeen, and now, under Roethke's tutelage, she was determined to pursue a writing career. With fellow student David Wagoner, she founded *Poetry Northwest* in 1956, and co-edited the little magazine until 1965 when she accepted an invitation from the State Department to serve as a cultural ambassador (formally a Specialist in Literature) in Pakistan. In 1966 she was named the first director of Literary Programs in the newly established National Endowment for the Arts, where she helped establish policy and assisted several deserving poets. She resigned in 1970 after the chairman, Roger L. Stevens, was dismissed by President Nixon. During the next decades she gave readings around the country, and lectured and served as a poet-in-residence at Stanford, Princeton, Columbia, and other universities.

Kizer published her first book, *The Ungrateful Garden*, in 1961. It was followed by seven other poetry volumes: *Knock upon Silence* (1965), *Midnight Was My Cry: New and Selected Poems* (1971), *Yin* (1984, winner of the Pulitzer Prize), *The Nearness of You: Poems for Men* (1986), *Harping On: Poems 1985–1995* (1996), and *Cool, Calm &*

Collected (2000). Kizer's topics range widely. She has reinterpreted classical myths and retold oriental tales, finding in their perennial truths numerous applications to the present. Many of her poems address the social and political disarray of our time, but they also find abundant satisfactions and deep happiness in daily life, particularly in family relationships. As a feminist author, Kizer has been notably fair in her treatment of *both* sexes; while acknowledging the failings of men and their injustices toward women, she has not hesitated to examine women's own failings or to admit their follies. Some of her most memorable if bittersweet pieces center on children.

For decades Kizer has been a student of Far Eastern cultures (she lived in Nationalist China for a year) and has made several translations from classical and modern Chinese poetry. In 1986 she published *Carrying Over: Translation from Chinese, Urdu, Macedonian, Hebrew and French-African*. She edited *The Essential Clare* in 1992 and compiled *100 Great Poems by Women* in 1995. Her essays on prose, particularly Japanese fiction, are collected in *Picking and Choosing* (1995). Kizer's many awards include the Frost Medal, an American Academy of Arts and Letters Award, and the Theodore Roethke Memorial Poetry Award. She was appointed a life chancellor of the Academy of American Poets in 1995 but resigned in November 1998, along with Maxine Kumin, to protest the absence of blacks and representatives of other minority groups on its board. The ensuing debate led to reorganization of the Academy and broadening of its membership. Kizer is married to John Marshall Woodbridge, an architect and historian. They divide their time between a house in Sonoma and an apartment in Paris.

CHILDREN

What good are children anyhow?
  They only break your heart.
The one that bore your fondest hopes
  will never amount to anything.
The one you slaved to give the chances you never had
  rejects them with contempt.
They won't take care of you in your old age.
  They don't even write home.
They don't follow in your footsteps.
They don't avoid your mistakes.

It's impossible to save them from pain.
    And of course they never listen.

Remember how you hung on the lips
    of your father or grandfather,
Begging for the old stories:
    "Again! Tell it again!
    What was it like 'in olden times'?"
We have good stories too:
    funny, instructive, pathetic.
Forget it. Write them down for your friends.
Your friends, with whom you have that unspoken pact:
Don't ask me about my children, and I won't inquire of yours.

Remember how we used to exchange infant pictures?
How we boasted of cute sayings? How we . . .
    Forget it.
Put away those scrapbooks, with the rusted flute in the closet,
    with the soiled ballet-slippers.
Tear up the clumsy Valentines.
Tear up every crayoned scrap that says, "I love you, Mama."
They don't want us to keep these mementos:
    they find them embarrassing.
These relics of dependent love,
The orange crayon that didn't dare write, "I hate you."
Forget their birthdays, as they forget yours.

Perhaps because they never finish anything,
    not a book, not a school,
Their politics are cruel and sentimental:
Some monster of depravity
    who destroyed millions with his smile,
Who shadowed our youth with terror,
    is a hero to them.
Now he smiles benignly from their walls.

Because they are historyless, they don't believe in history:
    Stalin wasn't so bad.
    The Holocaust didn't really happen.
    Roosevelt was a phony.

But the worst of it is:
  they don't believe we ever believed;
They don't believe we ever had ideals.
They don't believe that we were ever poor.
They don't believe that we were passionate
   —or that we are passionate today!
Forget it. Don't torture yourself.
   You still have some life to salvage.
Get divorced. Go on a diet.
Take up the career you dropped for them twenty years ago.
Go back to the schools they deserted, and sign up for courses:
Study Tranquility 101; take Meditation; enroll for Renewal.

Remember those older friends we used to envy,
  brilliant and glittering with beauty,
Who refused to have children,
  not about to sacrifice their careers;
Who refused the mess, the entrapment,
   as we toiled over chores and homework,
   worried about measles and money—
Have you seen them lately?
They no longer converse in sparkling cadenzas.
They are obsessed with their little dog
  who piddles on the Oriental rug,
  who throws up on the bedspread.

They don't notice his bad breath;
His incessant yapping doesn't seem to disturb them.
To be honest about it,
  the whole apartment smells!
And the way they babble to him in pet names
  instead of talk of Milton, Chaucer, Dante.
The way they caress him makes you fairly ill;
  the way they call him, "Baby."

From PRO FEMINA

I

From Sappho to myself, consider the fate of women.
How unwomanly to discuss it! Like a noose or an albatross necktie

The clinical sobriquet hangs us: codpiece coveters.
Never mind these epithets; I myself have collected some honeys.
Juvenal set us apart in denouncing our vices
Which had grown, in part, from having been set apart:
Women abused their spouses, cuckolded them, even plotted
To poison them. Sensing, behind the violence of his manner—
"Think I'm crazy or drunk?"—his emotional stake in us,
As we forgive Strindberg and Nietzsche, we forgive all those
Who cannot forget us. We *are* hyenas. Yes, we admit it.

While men have politely debated free will, we have howled for it,
Howl still, pacing the centuries, tragedy heroines.
Some who sat quietly in the corner with their embroidery
Were Defarges, stabbing the wool with the names of their ancient
Oppressors, who ruled by the divine right of the male—
I'm impatient of interruptions! I'm aware there were millions
Of mutes for every Saint Joan or sainted Jane Austen,
Who, vague-eyed and acquiescent, worshiped God as a man.
I'm not concerned with those cabbageheads, not truly feminine
But neutered by labor. I mean real women, like *you* and like *me*.

Freed in fact, not in custom, lifted from furrow and scullery,
Not obliged, now, to be the pot for the annual chicken,
Have we begun to arrive in time? With our well-known
Respect for life because it hurts so much to come out with it;
Disdainful of "sovereignty," "national honor," and other
    abstractions;
We can say, like the ancient Chinese to successive waves of
    invaders,
"Relax, and let us absorb *you*. You can learn temperance
In a more temperate climate." Give us just a few decades
Of grace, to encourage the fine art of acquiescence
And we might save the race. Meanwhile, observe our creative
    chaos,
Flux, efflorescence—whatever you care to call it!

II

I take as my theme "The Independent Woman,"
Independent but maimed: observe the exigent neckties
Choking violet writers; the sad slacks of stipple-faced matrons;

Indigo intellectuals, crop-haired and callus-toed,
Cute spectacles, chewed cuticles, aced out by full-time beauties
In the race for a male. Retreating to drabness, bad manners,
And sleeping with manuscripts. Forgive our transgressions
Of old gallantries as we hitch in chairs, light our own cigarettes,
Not expecting your care, having forfeited it by trying to get
       even.

But we need dependency, cosseting, and well-treatment.
So do men sometimes. Why don't they admit it?
We will be cows for a while, because babies howl for us,
Be kittens or bitches, who want to eat grass now and then
For the sake of our health. But the role of pastoral heroine
Is not permanent, Jack. We want to get back to the meeting.

Knitting booties and brows, tartars or termagants, ancient
Fertility symbols, chained to our cycle, released
Only in part by devices of hygiene and personal daintiness,
Strapped into our girdles, held down, yet uplifted by man's
Ingenious constructions, holding coiffures in a breeze,
Hobbled and swathed in whimsy, tripping on feminine
Shoes with fool heels, losing our lipsticks, you, me,
In ephemeral stockings, clutching our handbags and packages.

Our masks, always in peril of smearing or cracking,
In need of continuous check in the mirror or silverware,
Keep us in thrall to ourselves, concerned with our surfaces.
Look at man's uniform drabness, his impersonal envelope!
Over chicken wrists or meek shoulders, a formal, hard-fibered
       assurance.
The drape of the male is designed to achieve self-forgetfulness.

So, Sister, forget yourself a few times and see where it gets you:
Up the creek, alone with your talent, sans everything else.
You can wait for the menopause, and catch up on your reading.
So primp, preen, prink, pluck and prize your flesh,
All posturings! All ravishment! All sensibility!
Meanwhile, have you used your mind today?
What pomegranate raised you from the dead,
Springing, full-grown, from your own head, Athena?

MAXINE KUMIN

☐ "Darlings, it's all a circle," writes Maxine Kumin in "Family Reunion," and it is this sense of connectedness that inspires all her work. Kumin is a poet of attachments: to the family, the community, the natural world, the details of everyday life. In a career spanning five decades, she has been an acute observer of the complex bonds between parents and children, as well as a compassionate witness to the lives, and deaths, of animals. In her reflections on the body, intimate relations, and women's place in the modern world, she recalls her close friend and literary confidante Anne Sexton, though her methods are different. She has also been compared to Robert Frost, in her clear-eyed pictures of New England farm life and variations on the pastoral lyric, and to Elizabeth Bishop, as well, in her precise descriptions and mastery of form.

She was born Maxine Winokur in Germantown, Philadelphia, June 6, 1925. Her mother was a conservatory-trained pianist, "a Bach specialist," the poet recalls in "Life's Work," but her hopes for a career as a professional musician were crushed by her authoritarian father, just as the eighteen-year-old Maxine, an outstanding swimmer, found her own aspirations, to join the Aquacade, blocked by *her* father, who prophesied that she "would come to nothing." Kumin's Jewish family lived next door to a Catholic convent of the teaching Sisters of St. Joseph, and so she attended their grammar school for her first grades. She began writing verse as a child and was encouraged by her high school Latin and English teachers. But when she entered Radcliffe at age seventeen, she found an atmosphere hostile to creative writing. One professor told the aspiring poet she had no talent and "would be better advised to say it with flowers." She did not write for almost a decade. She took her B.A. in 1946 and a master's in 1948.

She married Victor Kumin, an engineer, in 1946, and they soon had a son and two daughters. Her experience was typical of many women in that era, and in a 1977 interview reprinted in *To Make a Prairie* (1980), Kumin remarked:

> It was just after the war, and this is what everyone was desperately doing: the tribe was seen as the saving centrality in a world that had gone totally awry. And I came to poetry as a way of saving myself because I was so wretchedly discontented. It just

wasn't enough to be a housewife and a mother. It didn't gratify great chunks of me.

She began writing again, "in the closet," and sent out light verse to publishers during her third pregnancy. Kumin recalls she made a pact with herself: sell something before this baby is born or give up poetry entirely. She soon began appearing in many popular magazines, including the *Saturday Evening Post*. Her extensive practice in producing short, humorous pieces, with their tight structures, strict metrics, and ingenious rhymes, provided a solid foundation for the work to come.

Kumin's transformation to serious poet began in the late fifties through workshops at the Boston Center for Adult Education with John Holmes. There she met and began her eighteen-year friendship with Anne Sexton, during which they read and critiqued each other's drafts, often daily over a dedicated phone line. Sexton was daring in breaking taboos, writing about incest, abortion, and other topics once considered improper in poetry. Although Kumin did not follow her friend's explicitness in her own work, she credits Sexton for helping her "to put aside academic concerns and be more open, to confront my own being, confront the world around me."

While this openness has grown over the years, Kumin has remained a very conscious artist in control of her material (as Sexton often was not), as concerned with form as with feeling. Like Marianne Moore, Kumin is a poet of reticence, understatement, tact. In her first book, *Halfway* (1961), she treated subjects central throughout her career: family and cultural heritage, humankind's relation to nature, and the tenuousness of life. In *The Privilege* (1965) she further explored memories of her childhood and relationship with her parents, through key moments in her early awareness of her Jewish identity. The book included some of her strongest love lyrics, as well as a journal in verse depicting in ingenious metaphors the natural life surrounding her country home in New Hampshire, where for many years she has raised horses and other animals.

Here as in all her books to follow, Kumin employed a variety of challenging poetic forms and technique, especially when she wished to express intimate feelings and relationships. Far from constricting, she has found such traditional methods liberating, since "form gives you permission to say the hard things." She explained: "It's exactly like building a building . . . you put up these wooden forms, and then you pour the concrete, and then after it's hardened, you knock the wooden forms away. And that's what the formal pattern does for the poem." Using another analogy, she once noted, "When I'm writing free verse, I feel as though I am in Indiana, where it's absolutely flat and you can see the horizon 360 degrees around. . . . I lose, I have no sense of, the line."

Kumin's four collections in the seventies extended her range and established her among the most perceptive writers on the family, nature, and the environment: *The Nightmare Factory* (1970), *Up Country* (1972, winner of the Pulitzer Prize), *House, Bridge, Fountain, Gate* (1975), and *The Retrieval System* (1978). Her new and selected volume *Our Ground Time Here Will Be Brief* followed in 1982, and contains some of Kumin's most touching and well-known poems: "How It Is," an elegy to Sexton; "How It Goes On," on farming; "Changing the Children," on the disappointments of parenting; and "The Envelope," on the continuum of the family. Besides these favorite topics, *The Long Approach* (1985) addressed pressing questions in the larger world: terrorism in the Middle East, famine in Africa, and the renewed threats of nuclear holocaust. In 1987, Kumin published another prose collection, *In Deep: Country Essays*, and in *Nurture* (1989) and *Looking for Luck* (1992) she collected some of her most urgent poems on the fate of animals. For her great concern for their welfare, one critic claimed (as she records in "Nurture") she suffered "from an overabundance of maternal genes." Ignoring such ignorant criticism, she continues:

> Bring me your fallen fledgling, your bummer lamb,
> lead the abused, the starvelings, into my barn.
> Advise the hunted deer to leap into my corn.

But Kumin's long experience with the gritty realities of life on a working farm prevent her from harboring any easy, sentimental views of nature. In one of her best-known poems, "Woodchucks," for example, she describes her frustration as a gardener in unsuccessful warfare against the destructive rodents. Finally, after cyanide fails, she resorts to a .22 shotgun—"I, a lapsed pacifist fallen from grace / puffed with Darwinian pieties for killing"—and manages to eliminate all but one old "wily fellow," and her sense of shame.

In the late nineties she published *Connecting the Dots* (1996) and her *Selected Poems 1960–1990* (1997). Then, in 1998, Kumin suffered near-fatal injuries when her horse panicked and overturned the carriage she was driving. She was seventy-three at the time. Ninety-five percent of people in such accidents die before reaching an emergency room, and almost all survivors are paralyzed, she later was told. The long and arduous process through which she relearned such basic functions as how to walk and to write is recorded in her 2000 memoir, *Inside the Halo and Beyond: The Anatomy of a Recovery.* Still highly productive after a half century of distinguished publications, Kumin presented *The Long Marriage* in 2001, *Jack and Other New Poems* in 2005, and *Still to Mow* in 2007, as well as *Bringing Together: Uncollected Early Poems 1958–1988* in 2003.

Kumin is also the author of six novels; a collection of short stories; more than twenty children's books, four written with Anne Sexton; and two other books of essays, *Women, Animals, and Vegetables* (1994) and *Always Beginning: Essays on a Life in Poetry* (2000). Among her many honors are an American Academy of Arts and Letters award, a National Endowment for the Arts grant, and fellowships from the Academy of American Poets, the National Council on the Arts, and the Bunting Institute. She served as Consultant in Poetry to the Library of Congress (1981–1982) and Poet Laureate of New Hampshire (1989–1994), and is a former chancellor of the Academy of American Poets. She has taught at Tufts, Washington University, Brandeis, Princeton, and MIT, among other institutions.

Early and late, when addressing personal, social, and political issues, whether in poetry or prose, Kumin has done so through the individual instance. Avoiding easy rhetoric, she persuades by illuminating the worth of all she cherishes with strict attention to detail and great care for language itself. "Well," she has said, "words are the only 'holy' for me."

THE ENVELOPE

It is true, Martin Heidegger, as you have written,
I fear to cease, even knowing that at the hour
of my death my daughters will absorb me, even
knowing they will carry me about forever
inside them, an arrested fetus, even as I carry
the ghost of my mother under my navel, a nervy
little androgynous person, a miracle
folded in lotus position.

Like those old pear-shaped Russian dolls that open
at the middle to reveal another and another, down
to the pea-sized irreducible minim,
may we carry our mothers forth in our bellies.
May we, borne onward by our daughters, ride
in the Envelope of Almost-Infinity,
that chain letter good for the next twenty-five
thousand days of their lives.

A CALLING

Over my desk Georgia O'Keeffe says
I have no theories to offer and then
takes refuge in the disembodied
third person singular: *One works
I suppose because it is the most
interesting thing one knows to do.*
O Georgia! Sashaying between
first base and shortstop as it were
drawing up a list of all the things
*one imagines one has to do . . .
You get the garden planted. You
take the dog to the vet. You
certainly have to do the shopping.*

Syntax, like sex, is intimate.
One doesn't lightly leap from person
to person. *The painting*, you said,
*is like a thread that runs
through all the reasons for all the other
things that make one's life.*
O awkward invisible third person,
come out, stand up, be heard!
Poetry is like farming. It's
a calling, it needs constancy,
the deep woods drumming of the grouse,
and long life, like Georgia's, who
is talking to one, talking to me,
talking to you.

ANNE SEXTON

☐ Anne Sexton came to poetry relatively late, and in dire circumstances, while recovering from a nervous breakdown and a suicide attempt. Her psychiatrist suggested she try writing poetry, and what she began as therapy she then pursued in earnest as a professional. Her aim in both endeavors was to uncover repressed emotions. Like Sylvia Plath, Sexton has been classified as a "confessional" poet, though the interests of both were wider than mere self-revelation. Also like Plath, she studied with Robert Lowell, but both women came to their distinctive styles largely on their own. Sexton herself rejected the "confessional" label, saying she was an "imagist" dealing with "reality and its hard facts." As catharsis, her poetry provided temporary relief; as psychic remedy it ultimately failed. But in the practice of the art, Sexton created a career and a body of work that moved far beyond what might have been expected, given her background and psychological burdens.

Sexton was born Anne Gray Harvey in Newton, Massachusetts, November 9, 1928. Her father was a successful businessman (woolens), her mother a frustrated writer. She grew up in apparently well-to-do surroundings, but life at home was not pleasant. Her father was an alcoholic, and both parents may have abused her. As a child she was closest to her great-aunt; when "Nana" had a breakdown, Sexton was devastated. She had trouble in school, which she disliked, and eventually she was sent to a boarding school, where she began to write poems. She attended Garland Junior College for a year, then, at nineteen, she eloped with Alfred Muller "Kayo" Sexton II. While he was serving in the Korean War, she became a fashion model. She also had a number of affairs, which first led her to seek counseling. In 1953 her first daughter was born, and her husband took a job as a salesman in her father's business. Her aunt died in 1954, and in 1955, after the birth of her second daughter, Sexton went into therapy again. Her depressions grew worse, she was abusive to her children, attempted suicide several times, and occasionally was institutionalized.

In 1956, following her doctor's advice she joined writing groups in Boston and met Lowell, Plath, George Starbuck, and Maxine Kumin, who became her closest writer-friend and confidante. She became proficient in formal verse, and her early poems were praised for their technical skill. Sexton was deeply affected by W. D. Snodgrass's *Heart's Needle* but said she had not read Lowell's *Life Studies* when she started writing. (Among the earliest books of so-called confessional poetry, both volumes appeared in 1959.) In 1960 she published *To Bedlam and Part Way Back*, and followed up with *All My Pretty Ones* in 1962. Here the poet dealt with her breakdowns and recovery, and tried to come to terms with her unresolved feelings about her parents, both of whom died in 1959. The books were pioneering—presenting deep personal problems directly as well as from a distinctively female point of view—and resonated with many readers. Awards followed: a Robert Frost fellowship to the Bread Loaf Writers' Conference, a Radcliffe Institute fellowship, a Guggenheim fellowship, and prizes from literary magazines. Eventually she received the Shelley Memorial Prize, a Ford Foundation grant, a traveling fellowship from the American Academy of Arts and Letters, and the Pulitzer Prize, for *Live or Die* (1966).

Sexton was a glamorous figure and became highly popular as a reader. She received honorary degrees and taught at Colgate and then, from 1969 until her death, at Boston University. In 1969 her play *Mercy Street* was produced off-Broadway, and in 1972 she published a collection of prose poems, *Transformations*. But it was with *Love Poems* (1969) that she achieved her greatest critical and popular success: perhaps an ironic achievement, for as her celebrity grew her marriage suffered and her husband became abusive. (Nonetheless she helped him in business when he broke from her father's company.) Behind the polished image, old problems persisted. Sexton suffered longer bouts of depression and grew ever more dependent on therapists, medications, and her friends. Her alcoholism and repeated suicide attempts kept friends on edge and alienated many, which increased her isolation.

In 1973, Sexton decided to end her marriage. Her physical and mental heath declined noticeably while relations with her daughters, already difficult, became further strained. As her later work met with less favor, the poet began to lose confidence. Ordinarily a brilliant performer on stage, she now began to give readings backed by a rock group. Despite the several pressures, she continued to write. She published *The Book of Folly* in 1972 and *The Death Notebooks* in 1974, and completed work on *The Awful Rowing Toward God* (1975). Now divorced and living alone, she had affairs and continued therapy, without relief. On October 4, 1974, she met Maxine Kumin for lunch, then drove home and asphyxiated herself in the garage.

Linda Gray Sexton edited her *Words for Dr. Y: Uncollected Poems with Three Stories* (1978) and, with Lois Ames, *Anne Sexton: A Self-Portrait in Letters* (1977); *The Complete Poems* came out in 1981. Linda Wagner-Martin, Diana Hume George, J. D. McClatchy, and several others have produced critical studies. Diane Wood Middlebrook's *Anne Sexton: A Biography* (1991) created controversy by including material from Sexton's first therapist.

HOUSEWIFE

Some women marry houses.
It's another kind of skin; it has a heart,
a mouth, a liver and bowel movements.
The walls are permanent and pink.
See how she sits on her knees all day,
faithfully washing herself down.
Men enter by force, drawn back like Jonah
into their fleshy mothers.
A woman *is* her mother.
That's the main thing.

THE TRUTH THE DEAD KNOW

FOR MY MOTHER, BORN MARCH 1902, DIED MARCH 1959
AND MY FATHER, BORN FEBRUARY 1900, DIED JUNE 1959

Gone, I say and walk from church,
refusing the stiff procession to the grave,
letting the dead ride alone in the hearse.
It is June. I am tired of being brave.

We drive to the Cape. I cultivate
myself where the sun gutters from the sky,
where the sea swings in like an iron gate
and we touch. In another country people die.

My darling, the wind falls in like stones
from the whitehearted water and when we touch
we enter touch entirely. No one's alone.
Men kill for this, or for as much.

And what of the dead? They lie without shoes
in their stone boats. They are more like stone
than the sea would be if it stopped. They refuse
to be blessed, throat, eye and knucklebone.

ADRIENNE RICH

◨ As a poet, feminist critic and theorist, and teacher, Adrienne Rich has long been a provocative and inspirational figure in American letters and in the women's movement. Major changes in the author's personal life, reflected in the evolution of her style, have also mirrored transformations in American society as a whole since the sixties. Rich's incisive critiques of women's traditional domestic and sexual roles, the use and misuse of language for social and political power, and issues of justice and injustice have been influential in reshaping basic notions about identity and responsibility, not only in academic circles but also among a large general audience. For Rich, the personal truly is political. As a poet and witness she has tried to recover the forgotten and to speak for those who cannot; and, contrary to W. H. Auden's dictum, she has become that rarity, a poet who has made something happen.

Rich was born in Baltimore, Maryland, May 16, 1929, and enjoyed a privileged upbringing in a prosperous household. Her mother and physician father had a wide circle of highly cultured friends, and amid many books she grew up in a stimulating intellectual and artistic atmosphere. In 1951, the year she graduated from Radcliffe, Auden selected her highly formal first book, *A Change of World*, for the Yale Younger Poets prize, commending it for its technical mastery and "detachment from the self and its emotions"—academic restraints Rich and many others would reject in the artistic revolution soon to come. In 1953 she married Alfred Conrad, a Harvard economist, and had three sons within five years. Amid the burdens of child-rearing, she managed to meet and make friends with other emerging poets of her generation, including W. S. Merwin, Sylvia Plath, and Ted Hughes, then living in Cambridge. She also formed a close friendship with Robert Lowell. Gradually she grew conflicted about her roles as a woman and a writer.

In her bitter *Snapshots of a Daughter-in-Law* (1963), written over eight years, Rich spoke more freely, in both subjects and style, about language itself, barriers, and decisions in a "life I didn't choose," signaling her move from safe conformity toward risky liberation. The book was not well received. *Necessities of Life* appeared next, in the midst of great personal and social turmoil in 1966, when Rich and her husband moved to New York City. The poet taught in a remedial program for poor, mainly nonwhite, entering college students. She and her husband also became active in anti-war protests. Finding parallels between Vietnam and sexual politics, Rich became more seriously involved in the women's movement as well. In 1970 she and her husband went their separate ways, and he later committed suicide.

Leaflets (1969) was followed by *The Will to Change* (1971), then *Diving into the Wreck* (1973), which won the National Book Award. Rich declined to accept the prize as an individual but rather on behalf of all silenced women. Written with cinematic immediacy, the volume marked a further change of style. Her descriptions of psychic scarring resonated with an ever-growing audience; the collection remains in print and has become a modern classic. By the mid-seventies the poet's political stance had become still more militant, and in 1976 she came out publicly as a lesbian. The same year she published her ground-breaking analysis *Of Woman Born: Motherhood as Experience and Institution*. The study initially provoked controversy, particularly for its scathing dissection of the medical establishment's co-opting and often benighted control of the birth process, but this book too has become a classic. *Twenty-One Love Poems* (1977) was included in her much-discussed collection *Dream of a Common Language* (1978), where Rich explicitly treats the subject of lesbian love and sensuality in her poetry for the first time.

Rich's prolific works thereafter have traced her personal and political explorations in poems increasingly candid in their revelations about her life and outspoken in their message about the damage done not only to women but to society as a whole by male-dominated power structures. While she has continued to return to these fundamental themes, Rich has also written on large historic topics, depicted the lives of pioneering women (Emily Dickinson, the neglected astronomer Caroline Herschel, the artists Paula Becker and Clara Rilke), and reflected on the several meanings of love in modern society, particularly for herself as a lesbian, and on her artistic identity and Jewish heritage. Her voluminous output also includes anti-war poetry and, in her recent work, an exploration of the American ideal and its betrayals, including racism.

Rich's many later collections include: *A Wild Patience Has Taken Me This Far* (1981), *The Fact of a Doorframe: Poems Selected and New* (1984), *Your Native Land, Your Life* (1986), *Time's Power* (1989), *An Atlas of the Difficult World* (1991), *Dark Fields of the Republic: Poems 1991–1995* (1995), *Midnight Salvage: Poems 1995–1998* (1999), *Fox: Poems 1998–2000* (2001), and *The School Among the Ruins: Poems 2000–2004* (2004), winner of the National Book Critics Circle Award. Nearing eighty, Rich continues to be highly productive, publishing in 2007 yet another generous collection, *Telephone Ringing in the Labyrinth, Poems: 2004–2006*. Besides *Of Woman Born*, Rich's influential prose works were collected in *On Lies, Secrets and Silence: Selected Prose, 1966–1978* (1979), which includes her provocative essay "Compulsory Heterosexuality and Lesbian Existence"; *Blood, Bread and Poetry: Selected Prose, 1979–1986* (1986); *What Is Found There: Notebooks on Poetry and Politics* (1993); and *Arts of the Possible: Essays and Conversations* (2001).

Among her many other awards are the Bollingen Prize, fellowships from the Academy of American Poets and the MacArthur Foundation, the first Ruth Lilly Poetry Prize, and a Lannan Foundation Lifetime Achievement Award. In 2006 the National Book Foundation presented her its Medal for Distinguished Contribution to American Letters. Her acceptance speech on that occasion has been printed in *Poetry and Commitment* (2007). Rich has taught at Columbia, Brandeis, Rutgers, Cornell, and Stanford, among other universities, and lives in northern California.

"I AM IN DANGER—SIR—"

"Half-cracked" to Higginson, living,
afterward famous in garbled versions,
your hoard of dazzling scraps a battlefield,
now your old snood

mothballed at Harvard
and you in your variorum monument
equivocal to the end—
who are you?

Gardening the day-lily,
wiping the wine-glass stems,
your thought pulsed on behind
a forehead battered paper-thin,

you, woman, masculine
in single-mindedness,
for whom the word was more
than a symptom—

a condition of being.
Till the air buzzing with spoiled language
sang in your ears
of Perjury

and in your half-cracked way you chose
silence for entertainment,
chose to have it out at last
on your own premises.

—1964

From TWENTY-ONE LOVE POEMS

III

Since we're not young, weeks have to do time
for years of missing each other. Yet only this odd warp
in time tells me we're not young.
Did I ever walk the morning streets at twenty,
my limbs streaming with a purer joy?
did I lean from any window over the city
listening for the future
as I listen here with nerves tuned for your ring?
And you, you move toward me with the same tempo.
Your eyes are everlasting, the green spark
of the blue-eyed grass of early summer,
the green-blue wild cress washed by the spring.
At twenty, yes: we thought we'd live forever.
At forty-five, I want to know even our limits.

I touch you knowing we weren't born tomorrow,
and somehow, each of us will help the other live,
and somewhere, each of us must help the other die.

XI

Every peak is a crater. This is the law of volcanoes,
making them eternally and visibly female.
No height without depth, without a burning core,
though our straw soles shred on the hardened lava.
I want to travel with you to every sacred mountain
smoking within like the sibyl stooped over her tripod,
I want to reach for your hand as we scale the path,
to feel your arteries glowing in my clasp,
never failing to note the small, jewel-like flower
unfamiliar to us, nameless till we rename her,
that clings to the slowly altering rock—
that detail outside ourselves that brings us to ourselves,
was here before us, knew we would come, and sees beyond us.

—1974–1976

FOR THE RECORD

The clouds and the stars didn't wage this war
the brooks gave no information
if the mountain spewed stones of fire into the river
it was not taking sides
the raindrop faintly swaying under the leaf
had no political opinions

and if here or there a house
filled with backed-up raw sewage
or poisoned those who lived there
with slow fumes, over years
the houses were not at war
nor did the tinned-up buildings

intend to refuse shelter
to homeless old women and roaming children

they had no policy to keep them roaming
or dying, no, the cities were not the problem
the bridges were non-partisan
the freeways burned, but not with hatred

Even the miles of barbed-wire
stretched around crouching temporary huts
designed to keep the unwanted
at a safe distance, out of sight
even the boards that had to absorb
year upon year, so many human sounds

so many depths of vomit, tears
slow-soaking blood
had not offered themselves for this
The trees didn't volunteer to be cut into boards
nor the thorns for tearing flesh
Look around at all of it

and ask whose signature
is stamped on the orders, traced
in the corner of the building plans
Ask where the illiterate, big-bellied
women were, the drunks and crazies,
the ones you fear most of all: ask where you were

—1983

SYLVIA PLATH

Sylvia Plath's roles as woman and as persona in her poems are difficult to separate. This confusion was compounded when she was made a totemic figure and appropriated by feminist causes, even though she died before the rise of the modern women's movement. As many women identified with her real-life drama and the frustration, anger, and pain expressed in her writing, the poet became a powerful icon of that debilitating modern phenomenon, the divided self.

Plath was born in Winthrop, Massachusetts, October 27, 1932. Her autocratic immigrant father, Otto, was an entomologist (he wrote the standard text on *Bumblebees and Their Ways*, 1934) and taught German at Boston University; her mother, Aurelia, had been his student. When he died, following a foot amputation caused by long-undiagnosed (and perhaps willfully concealed) diabetes, Aurelia recalled that eight-year-old Sylvia told her: "I'll never speak to God again." She never recovered from the loss, and her rage and grief were later expressed in her most provocative poems. A diligent student, Plath read widely in high school, and in her senior year her first published story appeared in *Seventeen*. She attended Smith College (1951–1955) on a full scholarship. Plath's upbringing was conventional, and she harbored conventional expectations as well as artistic aspirations. While she was an academic overachiever, she also wanted to be popular. The preliberation fifties dictated that young women seek marriage and thus renounce careers, but Plath wanted both.

Always extremely competitive, she won prizes for her poetry, then a guest editorship at *Mademoiselle* in her junior year. (She interviewed Marianne Moore and Richard Wilbur.) Denied entrance to a Harvard writing course that summer, she had a nervous breakdown and attempted suicide. She was institutionalized at McLean's, a psychiatric hospital in nearby Belmont. (Robert Lowell and the mathematician Robert Nash are numbered among its many famous ex-patients.) After treatment, which was paid for by the woman who sponsored her scholarship at Smith, Plath returned to school the next term, on schedule. These events would be related in her autobiographical novel *The Bell Jar*, published under the name "Victoria Lucas" shortly before her death. Plath graduated with highest honors and won a Fulbright fellowship to study for her master's in England. She chose Newnham College, Cambridge.

Having read some of Ted Hughes's work in a little magazine, Plath was impressed by his poems and was anxious to meet him. At a college party in February 1956 she sought out the dashing and brilliant figure, who had graduated from Cambridge two years earlier. It was love (and lust) at first sight. Following a passionate four-month courtship, the handsome couple married on Bloomsday, June 16, 1956, in London's Bloomsbury district. That summer Plath typed up her husband's poems and sent them to a first-book contest in New York. The book, *The Hawk in the Rain*, won the prize—the judges were W. H. Auden, Stephen Spender, and Marianne Moore—as well as publication. The volume gathered uniformly rave reviews on both sides of the Atlantic, launching Hughes's career. When her own first-book manuscript was rejected (she had submitted it for prize publication in the Yale Younger Poets series), Plath wrote her mother: "I am so happy *his* book is accepted *first*. It will make it so much easier when mine is accepted."

In 1957 the couple went to the United States, Plath with a teaching job at Smith, Hughes at the University of Massachusetts. After these experiences both decided against academic careers. In Boston and at Yaddo, the noted artists' colony, they worked on their books, Plath on *The Colossus*, Hughes on a new collection, *Lupercal*. Plath also audited a writing seminar conducted by Robert Lowell, then on the brink of his "confessional" style. In the class she became friends with Anne Sexton, who had also had brushes with suicide. Sexton later recalled: "We talked death and this was life for us." Despite their intimacy, Plath considered Sexton a rival, as she did Adrienne Rich, soon to be a leader in the women's movement. Unlike Rich, Plath was not keen on sisterhood and expressed distaste for celibacy, barrenness, and aging. Her ambivalence toward female identity and feelings of alienation from the body are evident in such poems as "The Moon and the Yew Tree," "Edge," and "Tulips."

In December 1959, Plath and Hughes returned to England. Ted's reputation continued to grow, particularly as he gave poetry readings and talks on the BBC. Their first child, Frieda, was born in 1960. Soon after, a London publisher brought out *The Colossus*. While the reviews were not glowing, critics praised the collection for its intelligence, expert use of language, and technical skill. Plath had learned her lessons from Yeats, Eliot, and especially Auden, but perhaps too well. Thoroughly trained in the New Criticism that then dominated English studies and teaching, her studied lines displayed high discipline within dense rhetorical structures. In the summer of 1961 the family moved to the village of North Tawton in Devon, where, amid many domestic chores, Plath wrote a great deal—not in her laborious old way but in looser modes, and "at top speed," Hughes recalled, "as one might write an urgent letter." He had suggested a change of method and had set her various exercises in description. The transition from formal to freer styles is apparent in "The Moon and the Yew Tree," written at this time, which begins, "I simply cannot see where there is to get to," and ends: "And the message of the yew tree is blackness—blackness and silence."

Darkness soon descended in earnest. Plath had a miscarriage, followed by an appendectomy, the occasion for "Tulips." She soon became pregnant with another child, and Nicholas was born in January 1962. Shortly after, the BBC produced her radio play "Three Women." It was then that Plath discovered that Hughes was having an affair with another woman, the beautiful Assia Wevill, a translator who worked in advertising. (The two met, and apparently were immediately enamored, when Assia and her husband rented the Hugheses' flat upon their move to Devon.) Following a confrontation, the poets separated, Ted moving back to London.

Their marriage had in fact been faltering for some time. Hughes seemed happy to leave. But for Plath too, despite the hardship of caring for two small children alone, the separation may have proved a liberation, artistically. From the beginning of their relationship, Plath may have felt insecure, then ever more in the shadow of her formidable, increasingly famous husband. Some have suggested that, besides acting as her mentor, Hughes became a father-substitute, and in both roles she sought his approval. All her life she had tried to fulfill others' expectations, and when the marriage broke up, the perfectionist felt she had failed, and was devastated.

In any case, at the end of September, Plath also returned to the city with the two children and took a small flat. Isolated, ill, and under great emotional strain, she now composed the most important works of her life. Through the exceptionally cold winter she continued to write at a prodigious rate—a poem, sometimes two or three, a day (or night, when the children were sleeping)—producing in her final months enough work to fill three posthumous volumes. Among them were the searing "Lady Lazarus," in which Plath speaks directly about suicide in a fantasy of resurrection, and "Daddy," a return (like "The Colossus" earlier) to unresolved conflicts over her father, now a figure of patriarchy and much larger societal oppression, described with hyperbolic allusions to the Nazis and the Holocaust. Arresting as the poem and its metaphors are, not all critics have found these analogues successful or even appropriate, and some readers have taken offense that Plath should equate her private emotions and misfortunes with an historic tragedy of such monstrous proportions. The poet's apologists argue that when the persona says: "Daddy, I have to kill you" and "I have always been scared of *you*" and "Every woman adores a fascist," Plath is addressing not only her personal demons but the dilemmas of many other women or the situation for women in male-dominated societies generally.

Extreme psychological conditions that the poet transformed in her art were not amenable to control in her life, unfortunately. On February 11, 1963, after putting the children to bed, sealing their room, and laying out bread and milk, Sylvia Plath put her head in the oven and asphyxiated herself. *The Bell Jar* had just been published, to fair reviews. Omitting a few poems he found too painful, Ted Hughes rearranged the manuscript she left and had planned to call *Ariel*, and the book was published in 1965. Two other collections followed, *Crossing the Water* (1971) and *Winter Trees* (1972).

Hughes had custody of Frieda and Nicholas, who were respectively three and not yet one at the time of their mother's death. Eventually Hughes moved back to Devon, with Assia, who helped care for the children. The couple had a child, Alexandra Tatiana (called Shura), born in 1965; several months after her birth, Assia left her husband to be with Hughes. He did not marry her, however, and in fact Assia felt that he never would. In March 1969, Wevill killed their daughter and herself, like Plath with gas.

Both Ted and Sylvia had projected striking profiles that fit perfectly the romantic image of passionate poets. Following Plath's death, and more after Wevill's, Hughes was cast in the role of villain. Ironically, Plath's suicide brought her fame, even immortality, far beyond the limited renown in literary circles that a poet might usually expect. But her demise clouded Hughes's reputation during a thirty years' war led by academic critics who, taking cues from his estranged wife's late poems, cast him as a destructive force and turned Plath into a victim and feminist emblem. Through the years Hughes remained silent and declined to defend himself, even when he was assaulted and his readings were disrupted by shouts of "murderer." (The more rabid devotees repeatedly tried to chisel off the name Hughes from Plath's tombstone.) He said he preferred not "to be dragged out into the bullring and . . . goaded into vomiting up every detail of my life with Sylvia."

Hughes's edition of *The Collected Poems* was published in 1981. It received the 1982 Pulitzer Prize, making Plath the only poet to be so honored posthumously. In 1982 Hughes co-edited, with Frances McCullough, *The Journals of Sylvia Plath*, which provoked more attacks for its missing pages of the last journal. In his Foreword to the book, Hughes explained that he destroyed the last part "because I did not want her children to have to read it (in those days I regarded forgetfulness as an essential part of survival)." Nonetheless scholars felt it a betrayal of both the poet and her work, some of the most significant portions of which were produced during the period covered in the entries from that fateful winter of 1962 until her death.

Finally in 1998, only months before his own death, Hughes broke his long silence with *The Birthday Letters*, in which he gives a detailed portrait of his marriage to Plath through poetic letters addressed as if to her. Contrary to the partisan image, Hughes portrays Plath as brilliant but violent, mad, and thus doomed. He professes his love for her, but says that despite his efforts to make her happy, it became impossible since she continued her obsession with her dead father, and ultimately it killed her. (Named poet laureate in 1984, Hughes died, having produced dozens of poetry volumes, translations, children's books, and anthologies, October 28, 1998.)

Plath wrote to her mother almost daily, and in 1975 Aurelia Plath edited a collection of correspondence from 1950 to 1963 in *Letters Home*. *The Unabridged Journals of Sylvia Plath*, edited by Karen V. Kukil, was published in 2000. It was followed in 2004 by *Ariel: The Restored Edition: A Facsimile of Plath's Manuscript, Reinstating Her Original Selection and Arrangement*.

DADDY

You do not do, you do not do
Any more, black shoe
In which I have lived like a foot
For thirty years, poor and white,
Barely daring to breathe or Achoo.

Daddy, I have had to kill you.
You died before I had time—
Marble-heavy, a bag full of God,
Ghastly statue with one gray toe
Big as a Frisco seal

And a head in the freakish Atlantic
Where it pours bean green over blue

In the waters off beautiful Nauset.
I used to pray to recover you.
Ach, du.

In the German tongue, in the Polish town
Scraped flat by the roller
Of wars, wars, wars.
But the name of the town is common.
My Polack friend

Says there are a dozen or two.
So I never could tell where you
Put your foot, your root,
I never could talk to you.
The tongue stuck in my jaw.

It stuck in a barb wire snare.
Ich, ich, ich, ich,
I could hardly speak.
I thought every German was you.
And the language obscene

An engine, an engine
Chuffing me off like a Jew.
A Jew to Dachau, Auschwitz, Belsen.
I began to talk like a Jew.
I think I may well be a Jew.

The snows of the Tyrol, the clear beer of Vienna
Are not very pure or true.
With my gipsy ancestress and my weird luck
And my Taroc pack and my Taroc pack
I may be a bit of a Jew.

I have always been scared of *you*,
With your Luftwaffe, your gobbledygoo.
And your neat mustache
And your Aryan eye, bright blue.
Panzer-man, panzer-pan, O You—

Not God but a swastika
So black no sky could squeak through.
Every woman adores a Fascist,
The boot in the face, the brute
Brute heart of a brute like you.

You stand at the blackboard, daddy,
In the picture I have of you,
A cleft in your chin instead of your foot
But no less a devil for that, no not
Any less the black man who

Bit my pretty red heart in two.
I was ten when they buried you.
At twenty I tried to die
And get back, back, back to you.
I thought even the bones would do.

But they pulled me out of the sack,
And they stuck me together with glue.
And then I knew what to do.
I made a model of you,
A man in black with a Meinkampf look

And a love of the rack and the screw.
And I said I do, I do.
So daddy, I'm finally through.
The black telephone's off at the root,
The voices just can't worm through.

I've killed one man, I've killed two—
The vampire who said he was you
And drank my blood for a year,
Seven years, if you want to know.
Daddy, you can lie back now.

There's a stake in your fat black heart
And the villagers never liked you.
They are dancing and stamping on you.
They always *knew* it was you.
Daddy, daddy, you bastard, I'm through.

MORNING SONG

Love set you going like a fat gold watch.
The midwife slapped your footsoles, and your bald cry
Took its place among the elements.

Our voices echo, magnifying your arrival. New statue.
In a drafty museum, your nakedness
Shadows our safety. We stand round blankly as walls.

I'm no more your mother
Than the cloud that distills a mirror to reflect its own slow
Effacement at the wind's hand.

All night your moth-breath
Flickers among the flat pink roses. I wake to listen:
A far sea moves in my ear.

One cry, and I stumble from bed, cow-heavy and floral
In my Victorian nightgown.
Your mouth opens clean as a cat's. The window square

Whitens and swallows its dull stars. And now you try
Your handful of notes;
The clear vowels rise like balloons.

EDGE

The woman is perfected.
Her dead

Body wears the smile of accomplishment,
The illusion of a Greek necessity

Flows in the scrolls of her toga,
Her bare

Feet seem to be saying:
We have come so far, it is over.

Each dead child coiled, a white serpent,
One at each little

Pitcher of milk, now empty.
She has folded

Them back into her body as petals
Of a rose close when the garden

Stiffens and odors bleed
From the sweet, deep throats of the night flower.

The moon has nothing to be sad about,
Staring from her hood of bone.

She is used to this sort of thing.
Her blacks crackle and drag.

LINDA PASTAN

◨ Steadily over three decades, writing with great care but little fanfare, Linda Pastan has created a body of work that has established her as the premiere contemporary American poet of family life. Within the domestic circle Pastan has found more than enough subjects and insights to fill a dozen volumes: the complex relations between husband and wife, the abiding ties between the generations, the challenges of motherhood and child-rearing, the myriad demands and rewards of daily life when it is lived with full engagement of mind and heart. She is a keen observer who conveys her discoveries directly, in lucid but subtly rhythmic lines. Steering clear of self-consciously literary devices, she finds the unexpected but inevitably right image or metaphor, usually drawn from nature, to convey her insights.

When her first collection, *A Perfect Circle of Sun*, appeared in 1971, Pastan was praised for showing what Emerson said was the "invariable mark of wisdom": her ability "to see the miraculous in the common." But it might be fairer to say the poet is less concerned with miracles than with the mysteries within the mundane. Like

Emily Dickinson, whose concision, unusual angles of sight, and deep skepticism she shares, Pastan avoids easy, sentimental reflections, preferring to let her clear-eyed, ironic approach to human desires and behavior bring her closer to the realities of the human condition, including those that may be most difficult and disappointing.

While Pastan's poems are often witty, and invariably reveal the unusual in the quotidian, there is also an undercurrent of melancholy in her verse. The persona speaking her poems is always a real, physical person in the real and evanescent world. Much of what she considers is bittersweet and painful—separation and longing, the diminishments of age, the loss of those she loves, and in recent years the recognition of her own inevitable demise. But in the face of much sorrow the poet offers an affirmation: "All I can try to do / is set it to music."

Linda Olenik Pastan was born in New York City, in the Bronx, May 27, 1932. Her father was a doctor, her mother a homemaker and "the perfect surgeon's wife." An only child, she was often lonely but read widely. (She alludes to the fact in a piece collected in *An Early Afterlife*: "In the English Novel, where I spent my childhood.") She began writing poems, mostly about her close-knit family, when she was ten or eleven. She graduated from Radcliffe College, then received her M.A. from Brandeis, where she studied with J. V. Cunningham, likewise a poet of wit and succinctness. Like many other women of her generation, she married early, as was expected, and started a family. She did not take up writing again seriously until fairly late, for a poet. Recalling this moment of decision in a 2006 interview with Linda Sue Grimes, she explained:

> I was a product of the '50s—what I called the perfectly polished floor syndrome. I had to have a homemade dessert on the table for my husband every night, and this was when I was in college. . . . And I felt that I couldn't be the perfect wife and mother that I was expected to be, and commit myself to something as serious as my poetry, and I wasn't going to do that half-heartedly. It was all or nothing. And I stopped writing for almost ten years, and I was very unhappy about it during those years. And my husband finally said he was tired of hearing what a good poet I would have been if I hadn't gotten married. Let's do something about it.

Pastan's poems soon began appearing in the leading literary magazines. Following her well-received debut in *A Perfect Circle of the Sun*, she produced *Aspects of Eve* (1975) and the remarkable collection *The Five Stages of Grief* (1978). Of the book, May Sarton wrote: "Nothing is [in Pastan's work] for effect. There is no self-pity, but in this new book she has reached down to a deeper layer and is letting the darkness in. These poems are full of foreboding and acceptance, a wry unsentimental acceptance of hard truth." One of the lighter but ruefully wise pieces in the collection may be the definitive statement on the subject of the "25th High School Reunion":

> We come to hear the endings
> of all the stories
> in our anthology
> of false starts:
> how the girl who seemed
> as hard as nails
> was hammered
> into shape;
> how the athletes ran
> out of races;
> how under the skin
> our skulls rise
> to the surface
> like rocks in the bed
> of a drying stream.
> Look! We have all
> turned into
> ourselves.

In an interview on the Lehrer Newshour in 2003, Pastan discussed her habit of conciseness: "I have a natural impulse to condense. I'd like to write long narrative poems. I'd like to write a novel. And any time I start anything long, I keep trying to take out anything extraneous, anything that doesn't belong, and I end up with a small lyric poem that just happens." The process of arriving at a small poem "that just happens" is a long one, Pastan noted: "But each poem of mine goes through something like one hundred revisions."

Following these demanding methods, in the eighties Pastan was still able to produce four major volumes: *Waiting for My Life* (1981); *PM/AM: New and Selected Poems* (1982), nominated for the

National Book Award; *A Fraction of Darkness* (1985); and *The Imperfect Paradise* (1988), nominated for the *Los Angeles Times* Book Award. The nineties brought *Heroes in Disguise* (1991), *An Early Afterlife* (1995), and *Carnival Evening: New and Selected Poems 1968–1998* (1998), which occasioned Pastan's second National Book Award nomination. Most recently she has published *The Last Uncle* (2002) and *Queen of a Rainy Country* (2006).

Unlike the majority of contemporary women poets, Pastan has not held a regular academic position, though she gives readings of her work regularly throughout the country, and for twenty years was on the staff of the Bread Loaf Writers' Conference in Middlebury, Vermont. She has received the Dylan Thomas Award, a Pushcart Prize, and the Bess Hokin Prize and Ruth Lilly Poetry Prize from *Poetry*, among other accolades. She also received the Radcliffe College Distinguished Alumnae Award, and from 1991 to 1994 she served as the poet laureate of Maryland. The mother of three and grandmother of seven, Linda Pastan lives in Potomac, Maryland, near Washington, with her husband, Dr. Ira Pastan, the founder and head of the Laboratory of Molecular Biology at the National Cancer Institute.

WHAT WE WANT

What we want
is never simple.
We move among the things
we thought we wanted:
a face, a room, an open book
and these things bear our names—
now they want us.
But what we want appears
in dreams, wearing disguises.
We fall past,
holding out our arms
and in the morning
our arms ache.
We don't remember the dream,
but the dream remembers us.
It is there all day
as an animal is there

under the table,
as the stars are there
even in full sun.

PROSODY 101

When they taught me that what mattered most
was not the strict iambic line goose-stepping
over the page but the variations
in that line and the tension produced
on the ear by the surprise of difference,
I understood yet didn't understand
exactly, until just now, years later
in spring, with the trees already lacy
and camellias blowsy with middle age
I looked out and saw what a cold front had done
to the garden, sweeping in like common language,
unexpected in the sensuous
extravagance of a Maryland spring.
There was a dark edge around each flower
as if it had been outlined in ink
instead of frost, and the tension I felt
between the expected and actual
was like that time I came to you, ready
to say goodbye for good, for you had been
a cold front yourself lately, and as I walked in
you laughed and lifted me up in your arms
as if I too were lacy with spring
instead of middle-aged like the camellias,
and I thought: So this is Poetry.

THE OBLIGATION TO BE HAPPY

It is more onerous
than the rites of beauty
or housework, harder than love.
But you expect it of me casually,
the way you expect the sun

to come up, not in spite of rain
or clouds but because of them.

And so I smile, as if my own fidelity
to sadness were a hidden vice—
that downward tug on my mouth,
my old suspicion that health
and love are brief irrelevancies,
no more than laughter in the warm dark
strangled at dawn.

Happiness. I try to hoist it
on my narrow shoulders again—
a knapsack heavy with gold coins.
I stumble around the house,
bump into things.
Only Midas himself
would understand.

FLEUR ADCOCK

▣ Claimed by her native New Zealand and by England, her long-
time home, and acclaimed in both halves of the hemisphere, Fleur
Adcock has become recognized as one of the finest poets in the
Commonwealth, male or female, of the last forty years. She is now
one of the most popular as well. In her down-to-earth subjects and
plainspoken style, Adcock is an immediately engaging if frequently
unpredictable author. Although her poems typically start with pro-
saic situations presented in a matter-of-fact manner, their fluid lines
can shift by degrees and rise to more rarefied levels or swerve quite
suddenly into surprising, even startling, new regions. Adcock views
the human condition with open eyes and an astringent mind—and
is not afraid to speak it. What she says can press the limits some con-
sider proper in poetry. The discrepancies between the decorous de-
meanor of her personas and their indecorously candid comments
create the sharp frissons in Adcock's edgier verses.
   Amor and *Eros* closely intertwine throughout her work, the
contrasts and conflicts between love and lust provoking some of her

most pungent observations—and wickedly amusing punch lines. For her wry, deadpan, and decidedly unsentimental approach to sex, Adcock's poems in this vein have been termed "anti-erotica." Indeed, in her most famous (or notorious) piece, "Against Coupling," Adcock dares to talk freely and quite offhandedly about a once-taboo topic, "the solitary act," and its practical advantages. But her gentle, more vulnerable side is equally compelling. On the subjects of displacement and loss, Adcock is particularly acute. On the complications of ordinary social relationships, she is likewise adroit and enlightening. But on vagaries of intimate attachments in their many varieties and phases, psychological and physical, she is unsurpassed.

Adcock's range of topics is in fact quite wide, drawn from immediate experience and the everyday realities of domestic life as well as from the facts of history and their continuing fallout. She has repeatedly exemplified the latter through the lives of her immigrant ancestors and their travails, as in her striking depiction of "The Voyage Out," in which during the hundred days in steerage a young mother tries to protect "the daughter / she rocked unborn in the swaying hammock / beneath her ribs." The poet has been particularly concerned throughout her career to record the lives of women who have been marginalized and ignored by official histories, as in her sketches of anonymous unlucky patients in "The Soho Hospital for Women."

(Kareen) Fleur Adcock was born February 10, 1934, in Papakura, Auckland, New Zealand. She started school there but from 1939 spent most of her childhood in England, where her parents were engaged in the war effort. In 1947 she returned with them to New Zealand, but not happily. (In a 2000 interview in *Thumbscrew* with Julian Stannard she remembered her desire to get out of the country and "to come back to England from which I had been reluctantly dragged away at the age of 13.") She studied classics at Victoria University in Wellington, where she met and married the part-Polynesian poet and novelist Alistair Te Ariki Campbell in 1952, when she was eighteen. Their first son, Gregory, was born shortly after she took her degree in 1954. She earned her master's in 1956 and gave birth to another son, Andrew, in 1957. The following year she divorced Campbell and took a job as a lecturer in classics at the University of Otago, in Dunedin, and worked in the university library. She returned to Wellington in 1962 and resumed her library work. That year she married the writer Barry Crump, briefly. In

1963 they divorced, and Adcock at last returned to England with her son Andrew. (The older boy remained with his father.)

In London Adcock worked as a librarian in the Foreign and Commonwealth Office. It was thirteen years before she returned to New Zealand: a visit, she has said, "which I found very traumatic, engaging with parts of my past I had tried to forget about." Back in Great Britain in 1976 she received two creative writing fellowships, which she used first at Charlotte Mason College in Ambleside then at the Universities of Newcastle upon Tyne and Durham in the north of England. By the early eighties she was writing fulltime, composing her own poetry while translating, editing, and presenting programs on the BBC.

Adcock had already appeared in little magazines in New Zealand (such few as there were) before she emigrated. Her first book, *The Eye of the Hurricane*, was published there in 1964, after she had settled in England. Her second book, *Tigers*, combining poems from the debut volume with new work, came out in 1967 (from Oxford University Press, as have many of her subsequent volumes). In these books as in much of her early (and later) poetry, Adcock's classical background is evident in her skillful deployment of demanding forms, strict meter, rhyme, and other traditional resources. In her first years in London she became involved with The Group, an informal gathering of poets who discussed each other's work. (Members included Edward Lucie-Smith, Anthony Thwaite, George MacBeth, Peter Porter, occasionally Ted Hughes, and other notables.) Adcock found the criticism, which was "quite severe and analytical," particularly useful to her for getting rid of "woolly" passages. "I just wrote another poem which was tauter, less sloppy," she recalled in the *Thumbscrew* interview. "And, yes, in any case I like poems that make sense and use normal grammar and all the things which are unfashionable in certain societies."

Adcock has acknowledged the early influence of Robert Graves, evident in her historical pieces, and W. H. Auden, whose conversational tone and topicality she emulates (as in recent poems about British prime minister Tony Blair and other pols). She also credits Ezra Pound's early work (but not the *Cantos*), as can be seen in her arresting images and concrete language. She has noted the paucity of prominent women poets—and thus female mentors or exemplars—in the sixties, apart from Marianne Moore, Stevie Smith, and perhaps a couple of others. She did read the early, more conven-

tional work of Sylvia Plath (who, coincidentally, died the week be-
fore Adcock arrived in London), but has said that Plath was "no
model" for her. She says she did not care "at all" either for the work
of Anne Sexton, "the archetypal confessional poet for me."

In its consummate but unobtrusive technique, Adcock's work in
fact resembles that of Elizabeth Bishop. And though she does not al-
lude to him, in her critical and satiric pieces she displays more than
a touch of Philip Larkin, whose biting wit and "less deceived" atti-
tude toward contemporary mores and manners she obviously shares.
Like Larkin, she is particularly skeptical of modern romance and
other species of self-delusion, and it is this no-nonsense attitude,
coupled with abundant sardonic humor, that has won her, like that
acerbic master, a wide audience beyond the restricted realm of po-
etry circles and academia.

Adcock published four collections in the seventies that bought
her increasing admiration, from critics and general readers alike.
High Tide in the Garden (1971) depicts her daily life in England, cen-
tered on her house in East Finchley, with frequent backward glances
to her earlier experiences in New Zealand. In *The Scenic Route* (1974)
the poet considers her Irish immigrant ancestors, whose experiences
(carefully researched and vividly recreated) she returns to frequently
in later work, along with several brief, imagistic travel pieces. Com-
posed following her unhappy return visit to New Zealand, *The Inner
Harbour* (1979) is a darker collection, as the poet reflects on her
repatriated son, contemplates fundamental questions of love and
death, and attempts a reconciliation with the past, particularly her
ambivalent relation to her homeland. In *Below Loughrigg* (also 1979)
Adcock examines the continuing influence of the Lake Poets and the
English Romantic tradition in poems that were the immediate prod-
uct of her sojourn on the writing fellowships. In 1981, with her pro-
file now foremost among her compatriots writing verse, she was
asked to edit *The Oxford Book of Contemporary New Zealand Poetry.*

With the strong reception of her first *Selected Poems* in 1983,
Adcock was firmly established in the first rank of poets writing in
English. For many critics this early work remains her most affecting
and enduring. Several poems in her later collections have shown
looser form, their more relaxed, fluid structures aptly reflecting the
surreal world of the unconscious. Her many other poems on histor-
ical themes, by contrast, are fact-based, and flatter or more prosaic,
but nonetheless fascinating particularly for their reconstructions of

the immigrant experience. Meanwhile, in the eighties Adcock continued to produce other impressive work as well. In 1983 she published a collection of translations, *The Virgin and the Nightingale: Medieval Latin Poems*. In 1986 she collaborated with the composer Gillian Whitehead on a song cycle, *Hotspur: A Ballad for Music*, and brought out a volume of new poems, *The Incident Book*.

Although she harbored reservations about certain poets she considered extreme in their feminist positions, such as Adrienne Rich (as she noted in her preface), and with a personal antipathy toward confessionalism, she compiled *The Faber Book of 20th Century Women's Poetry*, published in 1987. In 1988 she collected her newest work in *Meeting the Comet*, followed in 1991 by *Time-Zones*, containing poems that track the lives and translocations of several of her ancestors, ministers to miscreants, to New Zealand. Also in 1991 a new edition of her *Selected Poems* was issued as well as her translation from the Romanian of *Letters from Darkness*, poems by the anti-Ceauşescu activist Daniela Crasnaru. In 1994 she edited another volume of translations, from medieval Latin, *Hugh Primas and the Archpoet*. *Looking Back*, her ninth collection of original work, appeared in 1997, followed by her splendid *Collected Poems 1960–2000* in 2000.

Among her several accolades, Adcock received the Cholmondeley Award for Poetry in 1976 and a New Zealand National Book Award in 1984. In 1996 she was awarded an OBE (Officer of the Order of the British Empire) for her contributions to New Zealand literature. Elizabeth II presented her the Queen's Medal for Poetry in 2006, making Adcock one of only seven women to be given this highest recognition for the art in the Commonwealth.

ADVICE TO A DISCARDED LOVER

Think, now: if you have found a dead bird,
not only dead, not only fallen,
but full of maggots: what do you feel—
more pity or more revulsion?

Pity is for the moment of death,
and the moments after. It changes
when decay comes, with the creeping stench
and the wriggling, munching scavengers.

Returning later, though, you will see
a shape of clean bone, a few feathers,
an inoffensive symbol of what
once lived. Nothing to make you shudder.

It is clear then. But perhaps you find
the analogy I have chosen
for our dead affair rather gruesome—
too unpleasant a comparison.

It is not accidental. In you
I see maggots close to the surface.
You are eaten up by self-pity,
crawling with unlovable pathos.

If I were to touch you I should feel
against my fingers fat, moist worm-skin.
Do not ask me for charity now:
go away until your bones are clean.

POEM ENDED BY A DEATH

They will wash all my kisses and fingerprints off you
and my tearstains—I was more inclined to weep
in those wild-garlicky days—and our happier stains,
thin scales of papery silk . . . Fuck that for a cheap
opener; and false too—any such traces
you pumiced away yourself, those years ago
when you sent my letters back, in the week I married
that anecdotal ape. So start again. So:

They will remove the tubes and drips and dressings
which I censor from my dreams. They will, it is true,
wash you; and they will put you into a box.
After which whatever else they may do
won't matter. This is my laconic style.
You praised it, as I praised your intricate purled
embroideries; these links laced us together,
plain and purl across the ribs of the world . . .

AUDRE LORDE

◨ "Art for art's sake doesn't really exist for me. What I saw was wrong, and I had to speak up," Audre Lorde remarked in the early eighties, recalling her start as an activist author. "I loved poetry, and I loved words. But what was beautiful had to serve the purpose of changing my life, or I would have died." A decade later she re-iterated her artistic goals: "I want my poems—I want all of my work—to engage, and to empower people to speak, to strengthen themselves into who they most want and need to be and then to act, to do what needs being done." Concerning her own struggles to be heard, she added, "And I will not allow my work to be trivi-alized because what I am writing is not only about me, it is about the lives of many voiceless people, and the life of the planet that we share."

Lorde identified herself as "a black feminist lesbian mother poet," and all the facets and facts of her life were inextricably related in her long effort to expose racial and sexual stereotypes and raise awareness of the deep damage they cause. She was both an author and an exemplar, particularly for the minorities whose frustrations she shared and whose anger and aspirations she expressed in her intensely visceral poetry and urgent prose. Drawing from her own painful experiences, Lorde applied her vision to ever larger communities, describing the growing consciousness among marginalized people of the need for change. In successive books from the sixties to the early nineties, she not only recorded but helped promote major phases of the several civil rights movements—for blacks, women, and gays—that transformed American society.

Youngest of three daughters, Audre Geraldine Lorde was born February 18, 1934, in New York City, in segregated Harlem, to immigrants from the West Indies whose hopes of a better life disappeared in the Great Depression. As a child Lorde suffered severe myopia and learned to speak belatedly, at age four, while learning to read at the same time. From her mother she heard tales of the Caribbean isles and acquired her love for words—and respect for their power. As a young girl she often responded to questions by repeating a poem, and by the seventh grade she began writing her own. In Catholic grammar schools she experienced condescension and other forms of racial prejudice, but at Hunter College High School the outsider met other aspiring poets and found support among her fellow rebels. She became an editor on the school magazine and had a love poem published in *Seventeen*.

In 1954, Lorde attended the National University of Mexico, where she came to terms with her identity as a lesbian and her vocation as a poet. She received her B.A. from Hunter College in 1959, then studied for her master's in library science at Columbia while supporting herself as a medical clerk, ghostwriter, and factory worker, and in other jobs. She also became active in the lively gay culture in Greenwich Village, long a haven for artists and bohemians, and for American homosexuals a rare enclave of free expression in the preliberation era.

After taking her M.L.S. degree in 1961 Lorde worked as a librarian at the Mount Vernon Public Library. She married Edward Rollins, an attorney, in 1962, with whom she had a son and a daughter; they divorced in 1970. Lorde began publishing in the early sixties, including in Langston Hughes's *New Negro Poets, USA* (1962) and a number of black literary journals. She also became active in the civil rights and nascent anti-war and feminist movements. In 1968 she published her first poetry collection, *The First Cities*, with help from the poet Diane di Prima, a classmate at Hunter High.

With a grant from the National Endowment for the Arts, that year she became a poet in residence at Tougaloo College, a black institution in Mississippi. It proved a transformative experience which, in the aftermath of the King and Kennedy assassinations, fired her writing with a new sense of the need for action. While at Tougaloo she met Frances Clayton, who became her lover of many years, and wrote the poems that became her second book, *Cables to Rage*, published in 1970. The collection centered on love, loneliness, childbirth, and child-rearing, and occasioned her coming out in print as a lesbian. Other poems treated themes that would become leitmotifs throughout Lorde's later work: violence, the destructive force of lies and silence, the difficulties in finding love and dealing with loss, and her hope for social reform and spiritual renewal through personal relationships and stronger communal bonds, especially among women.

From a Land Where Other People Live (1973) was an angrier book, as the author viewed oppression and prejudice from a global perspective and with increasing impatience for justice. The collection was nominated for the National Book Award. Centering on her native city, Lorde published *New York Head Shop and Museum* in 1974. The poems depicted the extreme poverty, urban blight, and not-so-benign neglect that continued to demoralize inhabitants of the inner city: reminders of the lingering dysfunction following the riots and social upheavals of the sixties. In 1976, with support from Adrienne Rich, W. W. Norton brought out *Coal*, Lorde's first book to be issued by a mainstream publisher. It included her first two books and introduced a wider audience to the poet's examinations of the oppression of women and affirmations of the power of love, reconciliation, and sisterhood. Norton also brought out *The Black Unicorn* (1978), Lorde's ambitious survey of black history and African mythology, in which the poet found examples of pride, persistence, moral strength, and perennial wisdom.

In 1977, Lorde was diagnosed with breast cancer and underwent a mastectomy. She kept a journal of her experiences, with reflections on the disease, Western attitudes toward it, and her decision to fight to survive rather than behave as a victim. *The Cancer Journals* appeared in 1980, including her notes, an essay on her experience as a black lesbian feminist, and an address she delivered in 1977, "The Transformation of Silence into Language and Action." The book received an award from the American Library Association in 1981. In 1982 Lorde published *Zami: A New Spelling of My Name*, a self-described "biomythography" tracing her life after cancer treatment. Six years after her operation she was again diagnosed with cancer; she recorded her experience and reflections in *A Burst of Light* (1988), which won a National Book Award.

Lorde published new work with selections from her first five books in *Chosen Poems—Old and New* in 1982 (revised, enlarged, and retitled *Undersong* in 1992), *Sister Outsider: Essays and Speeches* in 1984, and an entirely new poetry volume, *Our Dead Behind Us*, in 1986. Lorde taught English at John Jay College of Criminal Justice in New York City from 1979 to 1981, and from 1981 to 1987 she was a professor of English at Hunter College, where she was named Thomas Hunter Professor in 1987. She was a founder of Kitchen Table: Women of Color Press, publisher and distributor exclusively of works by women of color, as well as a founder of Sisters in Support of Sisters in South Africa. She was named poet laureate of New York for 1991–1992.

Audre Lorde died of cancer on November 17, 1992. Her last poetry collection, *The Marvelous Arithmetics of Distance—Poems 1987–1992*, appeared posthumously in 1993 and *The Collected Poems of Audre Lorde* in 1997.

NOW THAT I AM FOREVER WITH CHILD

How the days went
While you were blooming within me
I remember each upon each—
The swelling changed planes of my body—
And how you first fluttered, then jumped
And I thought it was my heart.

How the days wound down
And the turning of winter
I recall, with you growing heavy
Against the wind. I thought
Now her hands
Are formed, and her hair
Has started to curl
Now her teeth are done
Now she sneezes.
Then the seed opened.
I bore you one morning just before spring—
My head rang like a fiery piston
My legs were towers between which
A new world was passing.

From then
I can only distinguish
One thread within running hours
You . . . flowing through selves
Toward you.

MARY OLIVER

◨ Mary Oliver is probably the most popular American poet now writing on nature. But while animals and plants figure in all her work (and virtually no human beings, except her speakers), Oliver is not a "nature poet" in the old Romantic mold. At the start of the Industrial Revolution in the early nineteenth century, William Wordsworth and poets who followed him turned to Nature in part to escape the increasing ugliness of urban civilization. Through communion with the natural world, they also aspired to escape or transcend earthly bounds and somehow reach a realm where death held no sway—as Wordsworth indicated in his famous ode, "Intimations of Immortality." Oliver's expectations have been otherwise. Nature in its earthly complexity and transient beauty, here and now, is more than sufficient to evoke awe, give joy, and sustain the spirit. This is the nature of *her* transcendence. But along with exuberance at its wonders, the poet also expresses and accepts the hard truth about nature, including the dark side. She puts the matter plainly in "Poppies": "of course / loss is the great lesson."

Oliver was born September 10, 1935, in Maple Heights, Ohio, a pastoral area that to the child "was an extended family," and thus she felt an immediate affinity with the natural world. After a year at Ohio State University, she transferred to Vassar College but left after one year. Although she would later conduct many poetry seminars and workshops, she never studied in one herself; in fact she never took a degree. She did take a number of dull jobs—deliberately, she explained to an interviewer, because "if you have an interesting job you get interested in it." Oliver preferred to direct her attention to her real work, writing, and persevered at it in relative obscurity for some twenty years. Her first book, *No Voyage, and Other Poems*, appeared in 1963 (enlarged edition 1965), followed by *The River Styx, Ohio* (1972), then *The Night Traveler* and *Twelve Moons* (both 1978), as well as a chapbook, *Sleeping in the Forest* (1979). Although they were solid accomplishments, the volumes did not attract great attention beyond Oliver's small but steadily growing group of fans.

When *American Primitive*, her remarkable fifth collection, appeared in 1983, the literary world seemed taken by surprise, and the book went on to win the Pulitzer Prize. Each succeeding book has been eagerly awaited by her now considerable audience; the collections have generally received strong notices from the critics as well. *Dream Work* appeared in 1986, *House of Light* in 1990, and then her first *New and Selected Poems* in 1992, which won the National Book Award.

In these and subsequent books Oliver examines the world with an eye any naturalist would envy. So intense are her life studies that, in following her supple lines, readers may be flattered to think the keen perceptions she expresses are their own. Her descriptions of flora and fauna are as exact as her figures for their ways of being are brilliant. In her poem "Entering the Kingdom," she voices the wish, "To learn something by being nothing / A little while but the rich / Lens of attention." What she has seen is both wondrous and harsh: in the wild world, all is not sweetness and light. Or as she puts it in "Skunk Cabbage": "What blazes the trail is not necessarily pretty."

In her encompassing vision, the world is a continuum, where violence is part of the natural cycle of birth, growth, death, and decay, of departure and renewal. She finds consolation in the thought that "nothing in this world moves / but as a positive power," and in "A Certain Sharpness in the Morning Air," she asks:

> for it's true, isn't it,
> in our world,
> that the petals pooled with nectar, and the polished thorns
> are a single thing . . .
> that love itself, without its pain, would be
> no more than a shruggable comfort.

In her close reading of nature and its intricate organization, she also forces a reconsideration of humankind's cherished assumptions. In "Some Questions You Might Ask," she wonders if our definition of the soul isn't too limited:

> Is the soul solid, like iron?
> Or is it tender and breakable, like
> the wings of a moth in the beak of the owl?
>
> . . .
>
> Why should I have it, and not the anteater
> who loves her children?
> Why should I have it, and not the camel?
> Come to think of it, what about the maple trees?

In its diversity the natural world is filled with marvels, the poet finds, and they are all the more to be valued because they are mutable and mortal. She asks in "The Summer Day": "Doesn't everything die at last, and too soon? / Tell me, what is it you plan to do / with your one wild and precious life?" Oliver's own response has been:

> . . . I want to love this world
> as though it's the last chance I'm ever going to get

to be alive
and know it.

("October")

Oliver's other books of the nineties include *White Pine: Poems and Prose Poems* (1994), *Blue Pastures* (1995), *West Wind: Poems and Prose Poems* (1997), *Winter Hours: Prose, Prose Poems, and Poems* (1999). She also wrote two guides to poetry writing, *A Poetry Handbook* (1994) and *Rules for the Dance: A Handbook for Writing and Reading Metrical Verse* (1998), drawn from her decades of experience in the classroom. Oliver began teaching in 1972 as an instructor at the Fine Arts Workshop in Provincetown, Massachusetts, her home on Cape Cod, which has remained a place of inspiration and renewal for the poet. At various intervals she has been a visiting professor or writer-in-residence at several institutions, including Case Western Reserve, Bucknell, Sweet Briar, and Bennington.

Even during extended periods of teaching, Oliver continued to make Provincetown her permanent residence, living there for more than forty years with her companion Mary Malone Cook, a photographer who also acted as her agent. When Cook died in 2005, after a long decline with increasing debility, it was a devastating loss. Oliver turned to the church and found a measure of solace in the local Episcopalian community, at least for a time. Her grief and the direct involvement with a religious group had a profound effect upon the poet's outlook, and subsequently upon her work.

Throughout her career, while the poetry showed an undefined but deeply felt spiritual foundation, it stemmed primarily from the long American tradition of transcendentalism propounded in the mid-nineteenth century by the philosophical Ralph Waldo Emerson and Henry David Thoreau, and found affinities in the all-embracing vision of a kindred soul, Walt Whitman—not conventional faith or the doctrines of any specific denomination. This work inspired confidence and continues to move even nonbelievers or skeptics because of what might be called Oliver's earth-centered spirituality, a kind of secular faith. But her most recent poems, particularly several pieces collected in *Thirst* (2006), represent a major shift, reflecting the alteration in her personal life, and with it perhaps a new sense of insight and urgency. For the first time Oliver's poems are explicit in their declaration of faith, some in fact very direct in professing Christian belief.

And yet, and yet . . . several lines still leave a sense of uncertainty or at least ambivalence as well, especially on the question of the existence of an afterlife or a personal heaven. In "On Thy Wondrous Works I Will Meditate," the poet seems to question her worthiness and perhaps that of religious doctrine itself. As for the question of trying to be good: "*To what purpose? / Hope of Heaven?* Not that. But to enter / the other kingdom: grace, and imagination, // and the multiple sympathies: to be as a leaf, a rose, / a dolphin, a wave rising. . . ." In another poem from the collection, "In the Storm," she seems resigned to the fact

> Belief isn't always easy.
> But this much I have learned—
> if not enough else—
> to live with my eyes open.
>
> I know what everyone wants
> is a miracle.

Oliver's other recent books include *The Leaf and the Cloud* (2000), *What Do We Know* (2002), *Owls and Other Fantasies: Poems and Essays* (2003), and the large *New and Selected Poems*, Volume Two (2004), comprising her later books beginning with *White Pine* (1994) with several previously uncollected pieces. *Why I Wake Early: New Poems* and *Blue Iris: Poems and Essays* also appeared in 2004, as did another prose collection, *Long Life: Essays and Other Writings*. *Our World*, combining Oliver's prose with photographs by Molly Malone Cook, appeared in 2007, and a new poetry volume, *Red Bird*, in 2008.

Oliver finds that inspiration often strikes during her regular walks when, she told an interviewer, "I enter some arena that is neither conscious nor unconscious. . . . I see something and look at it and look at it. I see myself going closer and closer just to see it better, as though to see its meaning out of its physical form. And then, I take something emblematic from it and then it transcends the actual." The result is a kind of epiphany. As she says in "Poppies," "that light / is an invitation / to happiness, / and that happiness . . . is a kind of holiness, / palpable and redemptive."

"I think that appreciation is a very valuable thing to give to the world," she has said. "And that's the kind of happiness I mean." Through the imagination it is possible to merge momentarily with the nonhuman and thus, she notes, "you can live more lives than

your own. You can escape your own time, your own sensibility, your
own narrowness of vision."

ROSES, LATE SUMMER

What happens
to the leaves after
they turn red and golden and fall
away? What happens

to the singing birds
when they can't sing
any longer? What happens
to their quick wings?

Do you think there is any
personal heaven
for any of us?
Do you think anyone,

the other side of that darkness,
will call to us, meaning us?
Beyond the trees
the foxes keep teaching their children

to live in the valley.
So they never seem to vanish, they are always there
in the blossom of light
that stands up every morning

in the dark sky.
And over one more set of hills,
along the sea,
the last roses have opened their factories of sweetness

and are giving it back to the world.
If I had another life
I would want to spend it all on some
unstinting happiness.

I would be a fox, or a tree
full of waving branches.
I wouldn't mind being a rose
in a field full of roses.

Fear has not yet occurred to them, nor ambition.
Reason they have not yet thought of.
Neither do they ask how long they must be roses, and then what.
Or any other foolish question.

THE PLACE I WANT TO GET BACK TO

is where
    in the pinewoods
        in the moments between
            the darkness

and first light
    two deer
        came walking down the hill
            and when they saw me

they said to each other, okay,
    this one is okay,
        let's see who she is
            and why she is sitting

on the ground, like that,
    so quiet, as if
        asleep, or in a dream,
            but, anyway, harmless;

and so they came
    on their slender legs
        and gazed upon me
            not unlike the way

I go out to the dunes and look
    and look and look
        into the faces of the flowers;
            and then one of them leaned forward

and nuzzled my hand, and what can my life
bring to me that could exceed
that brief moment?
For twenty years

I have gone every day to the same woods,
Not waiting, exactly, just lingering.
Such gifts, bestowed,
can't be repeated.

If you want to talk about this
come to visit. I live in the house
near the corner, which I have named
Gratitude.

MARGE PIERCY

◧ Unlike certain well-fixed writers who profess solidarity with the proletariat, from the podium, or proclaim sympathy for the under-privileged and downtrodden, from the safety of their studies, Marge Piercy actually comes from the ranks of the working poor and knows firsthand the grinding routines, insecurities, and indignities of life as lived on the margins. And unlike "engaged" authors who boldly pen essays or manifestos and sign petitions in support of the current high-profile cause, but after a season are heard no more, Piercy has remained true to her basic principles—and actually labored in the field to promote the ideals she holds dear—for four decades. Although she is called a political poet, not always in praise, she is not a self-righteous preacher or polemicist. She has not sacrificed aesthetics to ideology. In her vibrant work the poetry, not mere rhetoric, has prevailed, in lines informed with sharp intelligence, elevated by memorable language, and, despite all, brightened by a persistent sense of humor. Whatever the topic she takes on, Piercy makes persuasive conversation, and good company.

Questions of social justice create the major motifs of her work: economic betterment for the impoverished, equal treatment for women and advancement of civil rights generally, freedom of expression and individual liberation, including (and especially) in sexual and interpersonal relations. In Piercy's poems ethical, economic, and psychological issues are never treated in the abstract but through the individual instance, particularly as drawn from her own life. Piercy's Jewish heritage, a cultural and spiritual awareness instilled by her maternal grandmother, the daughter of a rabbi, has also inspired many of her most joyful and reflective pieces of fiction and verse. Philosophical and feisty, Piercy possesses remarkable energy: she has produced, thus far, seventeen poetry collections and seventeen novels as well as other prose pieces, a play, a textbook, and several recordings.

Marge Piercy was born March 31, 1936, in Detroit, Michigan, where her father repaired machinery at Westinghouse Electric. Robert Piercy was of Welsh-English ancestry and grew up in coal-mining country in Pennsylvania. Like many other factory workers during the depression, he became unemployed, and thus times were hard for the family, which included Piercy's half-brother Grant, fourteen years her senior, with whom she had a sometimes difficult relationship. The poet's later efforts at understanding and connecting with him (ultimately unsuccessful, given his problems) were recorded in her poignant collection *What Are Big Girls Made Of?* (1997). Piercy's mother Bert Bernice Bunnin (her father had wanted a boy, hence the male first name) grew up poor and had to leave school in tenth grade to go to work and help support the family.

Piercy's relationship with the strong, long-suffering Bert was loving but complicated, as revealed in several poems. In her autobiographical *Parti-Colored Blocks for a Quilt* (1982), the poet credits her mother for teaching her to observe, be curious, and love reading: "She had contempt for people who did not notice. . . . We would give each other three random words to make stories around. We would try to guess the stories of people we saw on the bus," she remembers. Less fondly, the poet has recalled hard times in the rough neighborhoods of her childhood, where breadwinners often beat their wives and children, as she relates in "Family values":

> . . . No one ever spoke
> of it. No one called the police and besides
> didn't he have a right? He was the father.
> He brought home what was left of his paycheck.
> . . .
> Families were strong
> then, yes, strong as gulags

Drunkenness, drug abuse, anti-Semitism, rape, and other violence were also common in those unlamented "good old days." As the daughter grew more independent, she and her mother quarreled, and finally Piercy left home, at age seventeen. The two were not truly reconciled until late in her mother's life.

First in her family to attend college, Piercy enrolled in the University of Michigan where she won Hopwood prizes for both fiction and poetry and graduated Phi Beta Kappa in 1957. With the prize money she traveled briefly in France, then took an M.A. at Northwestern University, where she held a fellowship, and in 1958 married a French Jewish particle physicist. He expected traditional sex roles in the marriage and did not take her writing seriously; they divorced in 1959. She was twenty-three and moved to Chicago, where she lived in poverty and worked at several part-time jobs (secretary, model, switchboard operator, clerk), then as a poorly paid instructor at the Indiana University extension in Gary, where she also became involved in the civil rights movement.

During this time Piercy wrote novels featuring working-class women but could not get them published. In 1962 she remarried, this time to a computer scientist; they had an open relationship, with other men and women often living with them, first in Cambridge then in San Francisco. They eventually returned east to Boston and, upset with the U.S. course in Vietnam, they joined the anti-war movement. Piercy became a political organizer but continued to write fiction in what spare time she could find. In 1965 she and her husband moved to Brooklyn, where she became active in the radical Students for a Democratic Society, working with the SDS office in New York. She also became involved in the women's movement just as its second wave was beginning, around 1966, writing articles and organizing consciousness-raising groups. She was driven to feminism, in part, by the crude, old-fashioned misogyny she encountered among male anti-war activists, as recorded in her essay "The Grand Coulee Dam" (1969).

Piercy's health deteriorated in the late sixties—as did the anti-war movement, when the once closely knit activist community broke down into warring factions and became infiltrated by government provocateurs. (The huge extent of the CIA's wiretapping and other illegal spying on organizers, demonstrators, and journalists—an operation code-named Chaos—was confirmed in hundreds of long-secret documents declassified, though still heavily censored, and released by the agency in June 2007. It also worked in secret with police departments across the country.) After eight years of protests and other opposition nationwide, the war not only continued but escalated, and a sense of futility set in. Amid the gloom, Piercy managed to write both fiction and verse—she would continue to write in both forms simultaneously in the years to come—and her first poetry collection, *Breaking Camp*, was published in 1968. It was followed by the poems of *Hard Loving* in 1969, which also saw the appearance of her first novel, *Going Down Fast* (reprinted 1981). *Dance the Eagle to Sleep*, her second, was printed in 1970.

In 1971, Piercy and her husband moved to Cape Cod, which became her permanent home. At the small house they had built in Wellfleet, Piercy began work on new poems and the novel *Small Changes* (1973) and, as she has related, felt liberated artistically and regained her health. She took up gardening avidly (in the bleakness of depression Detroit her mother had cultivated a small garden that cheered her daughter) and became active in the women's movement on the Cape. She began traveling to Boston to do research as well as to visit friends; she has continued to work for feminist and various other political and environmental causes, alternating between both places as her bases. Ever productive, Piercy completed *Small Changes* and two more poetry volumes, *To Be of Use* (1973) and *Living in the Open* (1976). In the meantime her partner had become disaffected and the relationship effectively ended by 1976, though the final break occurred only years later.

By the mid-seventies Piercy was well established and widely hailed as both a poet and fiction writer, her reputation further enhanced with two novels, the utopian fantasy *Woman on the Edge of Time* (1976) and the realistic *The High Cost of Living* (1978), as well as another poetry collection, *The Twelve-Spoked Wheel Flashing* (also 1978). In addition she began presenting lectures and poetry readings across the country and was invited to teach as a visiting writer at many universities and conferences. Over the years she has been a writer-in-residence at Kansas University, Purdue, Holy Cross, Buffalo, and Cincinnati, among other schools. She has also given workshops at the Indiana, Aspen, Port Townsend, and other prestigious writers' conferences.

In 1982, Piercy married her current husband, the novelist and playwright Ira Wood, whom she had met several years earlier and with whom she wrote the drama *The Last White Class* (1979). Piercy has described the union as a very close, mutually supportive relationship. Together they have also published a novel, *Storm Tide* (1998), and composed a manual and source book, *So You Want to Write* (2001), based on workshops they have given around the country. In 1997 they founded the Leapfrog Press, a small literary publishing house.

In 1980, Piercy published *The Moon Is Always Female*, a strong and varied collection containing many of her finest poems on her favorite subjects that has been called a feminist classic; the poems below are taken from that volume. In the "Lunar Cycle" section of the book, Piercy presents spirited statements on central feminist issues, as in the ironically titled "Right to life":

> A woman is not a basket you place
> your buns in to keep them warm. Not a brood
> hen you can slip duck eggs under.
> Not the purse holding the coins of your
> descendants till you spend them in wars.
> Not a bank where your genes gather interest
> and interesting mutations in the tainted
> rain, any more than you are.
>
> . . .
>
> I will choose what enters me, what becomes
> flesh of my flesh. Without choice, no politics,
> no ethics lives. I am not your cornfield,
> not your uranium mine, not your calf
> for fattening, not your cow for milking.
> You may not use me as your factory.
> Priests and legislators do not hold
> shares in my womb or my mind.
> This is my body. If I give it to you
> I want it back. My life
> is a non-negotiable demand.

In a lighter vein, in "Cats like angels," she drolly compares notes on her tastes in men, using aptly homely images. Dispensing with the stringent standards of youth, she adopts the looser, more comfortable expectations of middle age, now preferring, she says,

> men with rumpled furrows and the slightly
> messed look at ease of beds recently

well used.
    We are not all supposed
to look like undernourished fourteen year
old boys, no matter what the fashions
ordain. You are built to pull a cart,
to lift a heavy load and bear it,
to haul up the long slope, and so
am I, peasant bodies, earthy, solid
shapely dark glazed clay pots that can
stand on the fire. When we put our
bellies together we do not clatter
but bounce on the good upholstery.

In 1982 *Circles on the Water: Selected Poems* appeared, as well as the essay collection *Parti-Colored Blocks for a Quilt*. The novel *Braided Lives* and a new poetry collection, *Stone, Paper, Knife*, came out in 1983. Piercy's other, very well-received poetry volumes include *My Mother's Body* (1985), *Available Light* (1988), *Mars and Her Children* (1992), *Early Grrrl* (1999), *The Art of Blessing the Day: Poems with a Jewish Theme* (also 1999), *Colors Passing Through Us* (2003), and *The Crooked Inheritance* (2006). Besides several other novels, she has also written a memoir, *Sleeping with Cats* (2002). Helpful criticism of her work has been gathered by Sue Walker and Eugenie Hamner in *Ways of Knowing: Essays on Marge Piercy* (1992).

Perhaps the best summary of Piercy's philosophy and the goal of her poetic endeavor can be found in the closing lines of her long poem, "The art of blessing the day":

What we want to change we curse and then
pick up a tool. Bless whatever you can
with eyes and hands and tongue. If you
can't bless it, get ready to make it new.

•

MY MOTHER'S NOVEL

Married academic woman ten
years younger holding that microphone
like a bazooka, forgive

me that I do some number of things
that you fantasize but frame
impossible. Understand:
I am my mother's daughter,
a small woman of large longings.

Energy hurled through her
confined and fierce as in a wind
tunnel. Born to a mean
harried poverty crosshatched
by spidery fears and fitfully
lit by the explosions
of politics, she married her way
at length into the solid workingclass:
a box of house, a car she could
not drive, a TV set kept turned
to the blare of football,
terrifying power tools, used wall
to wall carpeting protected
by scatter rugs.

Out of backyard posies
permitted to fringe
the proud hanky lawn
her imagination hummed
and made honey,
occasionally exploding
in mad queen swarms.

I am her only novel.
The plot is melodramatic,
hot lovers leap out of
thickets, it makes you cry
a lot, in between the revolutionary
heroics and making good
home-cooked soup.
Understand: I am my mother's
novel daughter: I
have my duty to perform.

FOR STRONG WOMEN

A strong woman is a woman who is straining.
A strong woman is a woman standing
on tiptoe and lifting a barbell
while trying to sing Boris Godunov.
A strong woman is a woman at work
cleaning out the cesspool of the ages,
and while she shovels, she talks about
how she doesn't mind crying, it opens
the ducts of the eyes, and throwing up
develops the stomach muscles, and
she goes on shoveling with tears
in her nose.

A strong woman is a woman in whose head
a voice is repeating, I told you so,
ugly, bad girl, bitch, nag, shrill, witch,
ballbuster, nobody will ever love you back,
why aren't you feminine, why aren't
you soft, why aren't you quiet, why
aren't you dead?

A strong woman is a woman determined
to do something others are determined
not be done. She is pushing up on the bottom
of a lead coffin lid. She is trying to raise
a manhole cover with her head, she is trying
to butt her way through a steel wall.
Her head hurts. People waiting for the hole
to be made say, hurry, you're so strong.

A strong woman is a woman bleeding
inside. A strong woman is a woman making
herself strong every morning while her teeth
loosen and her back throbs. Every baby,
a tooth, midwives used to say, and now
every battle a scar. A strong woman
is a mass of scar tissue that aches

when it rains and wounds that bleed
when you bump them and memories that get up
in the night and pace in boots to and fro.

A strong woman is a woman who craves love
like oxygen or she turns blue choking.
A strong woman is a woman who loves
strongly and weeps strongly and is strongly
terrified and has strong needs. A strong woman is strong
in words, in action, in connection, in feeling;
she is not strong as a stone but as a wolf
suckling her young. Strength is not in her, but she
enacts it as the wind fills a sail.

What comforts her is others loving
her equally for the strength and for the weakness
from which it issues, lightning from a cloud.
Lightning stuns. In rain, the clouds disperse.
Only water of connection remains,
flowing through us. Strong is what we make
each other. Until we are all strong together,
a strong woman is a woman strongly afraid.

FOR THE YOUNG WHO WANT TO

Talent is what they say
you have after the novel
is published and favorably
reviewed. Beforehand what
you have is a tedious
delusion, a hobby like knitting.

Work is what you have done
after the play is produced
and the audience claps.
Before that friends keep asking
when you are planning to go
out and get a job.

Genius is what they know you
had after the third volume
of remarkable poems. Earlier
they accuse you of withdrawing,
ask why you don't have a baby,
call you a bum.

The reason people want M.F.A.'s,
take workshops with fancy names
when all you can really
learn is a few techniques,
typing instructions and some-
body else's mannerisms

is that every artist lacks
a license to hang on the wall
like your optician, your vet
proving you may be a clumsy sadist
whose fillings fall into the stew
but you're certified a dentist.

The real writer is one
who really writes. Talent
is an invention like phlogiston
after the fact of fire.
Work is its own cure. You have to
like it better than being loved.

LUCILLE CLIFTON

Lucille Clifton writes in a minimalist style to maximal effect. Most of her poems are quite brief, less than a dozen usually short lines, composed with artful simplicity in a deliberately limited vocabulary, avoiding the usual poetic devices and even titles as well as conventional capitalization and punctuation. But within these chosen confines, Clifton boldly sketches vignettes in which personalities, voices, backgrounds, and the very atmosphere of her scenes come palpably to life. The poet is particularly acute in dramatizing black history and oppression from the days of slavery to the turbulence of the recent past—often as represented by her own family— and in depicting the daily experiences of "ordinary people": their challenges, sufferings, aspirations, and resilience amid often extremely unpromising circumstances. Countering negative stereotypes and demeaning simplifications, the characters and scenarios in many poems project images of the strength and ingenuity of African-American working-class people thriving (as she puts it with biting terseness) "in the inner city / or / like we call it / home."

Besides revealing contemporary realities and reaffirming the complex humanity too often slighted or ignored by the media and mere statistics, Clifton recalls the diverse cultural legacies that have enriched and helped sustain black life for centuries. In her narratives and meditations she skillfully retells traditional tales to retrieve ancient wisdom. She recasts African and Native American mythology and folklore and reimagines biblical characters from both Testaments to draw updated messages, and in general tries to preserve the past and reinterpret it in ways meaningful to the present. In the several facets of her art, Clifton has, in short, returned to the ancient roles of the poet—as historian, teacher, spiritual guide, moral authority— but without the old pretensions or the posturing typical of some current producers of modishly "sophisticated" but less substantial work. She herself puts the matter more simply: "I write to celebrate life."

Lucille Sayles Clifton was born June 27, 1936, in Depew, New York. Her father worked in local steel mills, her mother was a laundress; neither had a formal education, but they made sure their children had plenty of books. Her father, Samuel, prepared a genealogy that became the basis for Clifton's first-person accounts in *Generations: A Memoir* (1976), which traces family origins from a great-great-grandmother, Caroline Sale, who was kidnapped from Dahomey (Benin) as a child and sold in New Orleans in 1830.

In 1953, at age sixteen, Lucille gained early admission to Howard University, where she majored in drama and met the writers Sterling A. Brown and Toni Morrison, and Fred J. Clifton, whom she married in 1958. They eventually had six children. In 1955 she transferred to Fredonia State Teachers College, acted, and began writing the concise poems characteristic of her mature style. In 1969, Robert Hayden, a noted poet of the older generation, submitted her work for the YM-YWHA Poetry Center Discovery

Award; she won the prize, which included publication of her first collection, *Good Times*. Centered on the topics that would inspire most of her subsequent volumes—her family and African heritage, the struggle against racism and economic hardship, and the American dream deferred—*Good Times* was named one of the best books of 1969 by the *New York Times*, instantly placing Clifton among the most prominent black writers.

Her career as a children's writer began soon after, with publication of two illustrated books of verse in 1970, *The Black ABC's* and *Some of the Days of Everett Anderson*, the initial volume in a long and very popular series about a young black boy growing up in the inner city. She has now written some twenty children's books, most specifically addressed to young black readers. Meanwhile, after working as a claims clerk for the State of New York, she was an assistant in the Office of Education in Washington until she became poet-in-residence at Coppin State College in Baltimore in 1971. From 1979 to 1982 she was poet laureate of Maryland.

During the seventies Clifton completed three new poetry volumes: *Good News About the Earth* (1972), *An Ordinary Woman* (1974), and *Two-Headed Woman* (1980), which won the Juniper Prize and was nominated for the Pulitzer. *Two-Headed Woman* is particularly notable for Clifton's strong feminist stand, which counters common Western prejudices or myths that portray black women at extremes as either sly seductresses or hapless victims. In *Generations* (1976) Clifton represents the larger black diaspora through the individual stories spoken by various members of her family using the black vernacular. In 1987 she collected all her poetry volumes to this point in *Good Woman: Poems and a Memoir, 1969–1980*, which was also nominated for the Pulitzer Prize. The same year she published *Next: New Poems*, a book mostly of elegies, including remembrances of her mother, who died at only forty-four in 1959, and of her husband of almost fifty years in 1984. Other pieces commemorate the great Chief Crazy Horse, the fallen at Gettysburg, the victims of Nagasaki, and the massacred at Jonestown.

Clifton's most recent collections include *Quilting: Poems 1987–1990* (1991), *The Book of Light* (1993), *The Terrible Stories* (1995, nominated for the National Book Award), *Blessing the Boats: New and Selected Poems, 1988–2000* (winner of the National Book Award), and *Mercy* (2004). Her several other honors include an Emmy Award, a Lannan Foundation Literary Award, a grant from the National Endowment for the Arts, the Ruth Lilly Prize, and the Shelley Memorial Award. In 1999, Clifton was elected a chancellor of the Academy of American Poets. She has appeared numerous times on television programs, including the *Today Show*, *Nightline*, and Bill Moyers's series, "The Power of the Word." She has been a visiting writer at a number of universities and is now Distinguished Professor of Humanities at St. Mary's College of Maryland.

THE LOST BABY POEM

the time i dropped your almost body down
down to meet the waters under the city
and run one with the sewage to the sea
what did i know about waters rushing back
what did i know about drowning
of being drowned

you would have been born into winter
in the year of the disconnected gas
and no car   we would have made the thin
walk over genesee hill into a canada wind
to watch you slip like ice into strangers' hands
you would have fallen naked as snow into winter
if you were here i could tell you these
and some other things

if i am ever less than a mountain
for your definite brothers and sisters
let the rivers pour over my head
let the sea take me for a spiller
of seas   let black men call me stranger
always   for your never named sake

MARGARET ATWOOD

Poet, fiction writer, literary essayist, cultural historian, journalist, children's writer, anthologist, teacher—in her several endeavors Margaret Atwood has been exceptionally original and influential for more than four decades, attaining the stature, now very rare, of all-around person of letters. Equally unusual for a contemporary author, she has been not only prolific in multiple genres but highly proficient in each of them, gaining a huge popular audience while garnering the respect of serious critics and scholars. Underlying and reinforcing her literary work are Atwood's forceful ideas as a leading feminist and committed environmental and human rights activist. It is not surprising, then, that power has been a, if not *the*, central subject in Atwood's diverse, far-ranging writings. Questions of dominance—with several related, recurring subtopics on the struggle for survival—are illustrated in her poetry and fiction through a broad range of piquant particulars, small scale and large, from the complex, perennial dynamics between the sexes to the ongoing (and imagined future) political, environmental, and economic contests waged worldwide for control.

Although she is now more famous for her fiction, Atwood began as a poet and so she has remained. Well into the eighties she brought out superb poetry collections at two- or three-year intervals between her probing novels (and sometimes both verse and prose in the same year), along with important anthologies and collections of her own short stories, nonfiction, or literary criticism. If her prose presents her public persona, Atwood's poetry offers more private, concentrated, and intense expressions of her views on humankind's dysfunctional relations with nature and on the psychosexual dimensions of intimate attachments—revealed as too often off-balance and destructive, and as self-defeating on the world stage as in domestic scenarios. In her poems Atwood's voice is bracingly direct, her language spare, elemental. But her lines are highlighted with luminous images drawn from ordinary experience while her themes are often elaborated with clever recasting of plots and personages from mythology. Atwood is particularly adept at portraying situations of conflict from the perspective of a female protagonist, and her lines move with propulsive force toward dramatic conclusions.

Atwood's early poetry, well represented in her *Selected Poems 1965–1976* (1976), is probably her strongest and remains fresh: continually surprising both for bold ideas and vigorously inventive use of language. The landscapes she depicts—whether the expanses of primeval nature or the arenas of "civilized" society or the interior realm of untidy thoughts and inchoate emotions—are frequently bleak, sometimes grotesque, and usually fraught with menace: unset-tling reading. The sense of unease is intensified by Atwood's gift for finding the uncanny amid the ordinary, her disarming wit, and espe-cially her deceptively even tenor and ironic understatement. On many occasions, however, when scenes of cruelty and violation demand it, she also speaks with carefully controlled rage. The epigraph to the anti-love songs of *Power Politics* offers a terse example of the tone:

> *you fit into me*
> *like a hook into an eye*
>
> *a fish hook*
> *an open eye*

Margaret Eleanor Atwood was born in Ottawa, Ontario, No-vember 18, 1939. Her father was a zoologist whose researches in forest entomology (tree-eating insects specifically) took him regu-larly to the backwoods of northern Quebec. The family usually ac-companied him, and thus Margaret did not attend school for a full academic year until the eighth grade. But she read constantly and eclectically, everything from the classics to comic books, while de-veloping a keen interest in the rugged Canadian terrain. Her knowl-edge of the subject is reflected in *Wilderness Tips and Other Stories* (1991). The family moved to Toronto in 1946, and following high school Atwood entered Victoria College at the University of Toronto in 1957. Her teachers included the noted poet Jay Macpherson and the distinguished literary critic Northrup Frye, whose interpretive theories based on myth and Jungian psychology left a lasting impression on the young writer.

Atwood graduated in 1961 with honors. The same year she pri-vately printed her first book, *Double Persephone*, poems based on the character in Greek myth—a favorite figure or trope for women po-ets in later decades—and the book won the E. J. Pratt Medal, the first of her myriad awards. On a Woodrow Wilson fellowship she at-tended Radcliffe, at the time Harvard's women's college, and took an A.M. in 1962. She did coursework at Harvard for a Ph.D. in Victo-rian literature in 1962–1963 and 1965–1967, but did not finish her dissertation. (She would eventually be awarded almost a score of honorary doctorates.) Meanwhile she produced her second poetry collection, *The Circle Game*, in 1964 (revised 1966), which won the Governor General's Award for poetry.

In the early seventies Atwood worked as an editor at the small House of Anansi Press in Toronto, which in 1972 issued the pioneering literary study that first brought her national attention, and notoriety, *Survival: A Thematic Guide to Canadian Literature*. For her fellow citizens, as inhabitants of a vast land with large tracts still wild and inhospitable, the idea of survival carried special resonance (and still does). Likewise, lingering questions of Canadian independence and a distinct national identity held strong, if deeply ambivalent, import following centuries of colonial control by Britain as well as cultural dominance by both the Old Country and the hugely powerful neighbor to the south. When she broached these touchy topics in *Survival*, boldly and irreverently, Atwood provoked a huge controversy, then serious reexamination of the issues, which changed perceptions throughout the country about Canada's literary heritage. With equal insouciance she revisited the topic in 1995 in *Strange Things: The Malevolent North in Canadian Literature*, based on lectures she delivered at Oxford.

Following two more small poetry books and her first novel, Atwood published five collections in quick succession that firmly established her as the new leader among Canadian poets and one of the most significant authors of her generation: *The Animals of That Country* (1968), *The Journals of Susanna Moodie* (1970, based on the true story of a nineteenth-century Canadian pioneer), *Procedures for Underground* (also 1970), *Power Politics* (1971), and *You Are Happy* (1974). During this period she also made her name as a novelist, beginning with *The Edible Woman* (1969), *Surfacing* (1972), and *Lady Oracle* (1976).

Atwood's accomplishments as a poet began to be eclipsed by the acclaim that followed the publication of her next novels: *Life Before Man* (1976), *Bodily Harm* (1981), and the extremely successful *The Handmaid's Tale* (1985), a grim vision of the future that was shortlisted for Britain's Booker Prize and won the Arthur C. Clarke Award. It was made into a film, with a screenplay by Harold Pinter, in 1990. As in the poems, Atwood's themes in the novels and "speculative fictions" usually center on matters of survival, with her heroines caught in personal or professional power struggles. Atwood takes a strong feminist position in the novels, most often using satire and shrewdly sardonic observations of social rituals to make her points.

In the late sixties Atwood also began her academic career, with teaching stints in British Columbia, Montreal, Alberta, and then

York University in Toronto. In the seventies and eighties she held a number of writer-in-residence posts, at the University of Toronto, New York University, and institutions in Australia, Alabama, and Texas. In 1968 she married her first husband; they divorced in 1973. She then married the novelist Graeme Gibson, and they moved north of Toronto with his two sons by a previous marriage; their daughter was born in 1976. In 1982 she published *Second Words: Selected Critical Prose*, and was accorded the signal honor and influential position of editing *The New Oxford Anthology of Canadian Verse*.

Nearly all of Atwood's novels from the late eighties onwards were finalists or recipients of major Canadian and British prizes, including *Cat's Eye* (1988), *The Robber Bride* (1993), *Alias Grace* (1996), *The Blind Assassin* (2000), *Oryx and Crake* (2003), and *The Penelopiad* (2005). From the late seventies to 2006 she published nine collections of short fiction as well, in addition to editing three further anthologies of short stories, two of them for Oxford. She also wrote or collaborated on a half dozen children's books, and besides the nonfiction collections mentioned, brought out *Negotiating with the Dead: A Writer on Writing* (2002) and *Writing with Intent: Essays, Reviews, Personal Prose—1983–2005* (2005).

During these highly productive decades, Atwood's output in poetry diminished in quantity, and was sometimes of uneven quality compared with the superlative earlier work. Following the *Selected Poems* of 1976, she published *Two-Headed Poems* (1978), *True Stories* (1981), *Interlunar* (1984), *Selected Poems II: Poems Selected and New 1976–1986* (1987), *Morning in the Burned House* (1996), *Eating Fire: Selected Poems, 1965–1995* (1998), and *The Door* (2007). Although Atwood has returned to favorite topics and retained her trademark techniques in her later work—startling figures, arresting metaphors, satiric humor, mythological allusions, dramatic denouements— poems in more recent books, especially the longer pieces, can sometimes seem studied in their effects, predictable in their rhetoric or unsubtle in their "messages." They are also less economical in their means. Telling it "slant" (as Emily Dickinson advised), and keeping it shorter, might have produced stronger results. Even so, Atwood is a consistently *engaging* poet late and soon. Her work brims with important ideas and unusual perceptions delivered with remarkable turns of phrase and indelible images.

Atwood has used her renown to further causes she supports. In the mid-eighties she was an officer of the Writers' Union of Canada and president of International P.E.N., which has been instrumental in freeing writers held as political prisoners under repressive regimes. After Carolyn Forché could not find a publisher for her poems about the civil war in El Salvador, Atwood helped get the work into print. When her novel *The Blind Assassin* won the 2000 Booker Prize, the most prestigious and at £50,000 the most lucrative literary award in England, Atwood donated the money to environmental groups.

Many major studies of her life and work have appeared over the last twenty years. Some of the more useful include *Margaret Atwood* by Barbara Hill Rigney (1987); *Critical Essays on Margaret Atwood*, edited by Judith McCombs (1988); *Margaret Atwood: Conversations*, twenty-one interviews edited by Earl Ingersoll (1990); *Margaret Atwood: Writing and Subjectivity: New Critical Essays*, edited by Colin Nicholson (1994); *Margaret Atwood* by Coral Ann Howells (1996); *Margaret Atwood: A Biography* (1998) and *Margaret Atwood: A Critical Companion* (2004) by Nathalie Cooke; *Margaret Atwood Revisited* by Karen F. Stein (Twayne World Authors series, 1999); and *The Cambridge Companion to Margaret Atwood*, edited by Coral Ann Howells (2006).

THE ANIMALS IN THAT COUNTRY

In that country the animals
have the faces of people:

the ceremonial
cats possessing the streets

the fox run
politely to earth, the huntsmen
standing around him, fixed
in their tapestry of manners

the bull, embroidered
with blood and given
an elegant death, trumpets, his name
stamped on him, heraldic brand
because

(when he rolled
on the sand, sword in his heart, the teeth
in his blue mouth were human)

he is really a man

even the wolves, holding resonant
conversations in their
forests thickened with legend.

     In this country the animals
     have the faces of
     animals.

     Their eyes
     flash once in car headlights
     and are gone.

     Their deaths are not elegant.

     They have the faces of
     no-one.

HABITATION

Marriage is not
a house or even a tent

it is before that, and colder:

the edge of the forest, the edge
of the desert
     the unpainted stairs
at the back where we squat
outside, eating popcorn

the edge of the receding glacier

where painfully and with wonder
at having survived even
this far

we are learning to make fire

CARRYING FOOD HOME IN WINTER

I walk uphill through the snow
hard going
brown paper bag of groceries
balanced low on my stomach,
heavy, my arms stretching
to hold it turn all tendon.

Do we need this paper bag
my love, do we need this bulk
of peels and cores, do we need
these bottles, these roots
and bits of cardboard
to keep us floating
as on a raft
above the snow I sink through?

The skin creates
islands of warmth
in winter, in summer
islands of coolness.
The mouth performs
a similar deception.

I say I will transform
this egg into a muscle
this bottle into an act of love

This onion will become a motion
this grapefruit
will become a thought.

From SONGS OF THE TRANSFORMED

PIG SONG

This is what you changed me to:
a greypink vegetable with slug
eyes, buttock
incarnate, spreading like a slow turnip,

a skin you stuff so you may feed
in your turn, a stinking wart
of flesh, a large tuber
of blood which munches
and bloats. Very well then. Meanwhile

I have the sky, which is only half
caged, I have my weed corners,
I keep myself busy, singing
my song of roots and noses,

my song of dung. Madame,
this song offends you, these grunts
which you find oppressively sexual,
mistaking simple greed for lust.

I am yours. If you feed me garbage,
I will sing a song of garbage.
This is a hymn.

RAT SONG

When you hear me singing
you get the rifle down
and the flashlight, aiming for my brain,
but you always miss

and when you set out the poison
I piss on it
to warn the others.

You think: *That one's too clever,*
she's dangerous, because

I don't stick around to be slaughtered
and you think I'm ugly too
despite my fur and pretty teeth
and my six nipples and snake tail.
All I want is love, you stupid
humanist. See if you can.

Right, I'm a parasite, I live off your
leavings, gristle and rancid fat,
I take without asking
and make nests in your cupboards
out of your suits and underwear.
You'd do the same if you could,

if you could afford to share
my crystal hatreds.
It's your throat I want, my mate
trapped in your throat.
Though you try to drown him
with your greasy person voice,
he is hiding / between your syllables
I can hear him singing.

CROW SONG

In the arid sun, over the field
where the corn has rotted and then
dried up, you flock and squabble.
Not much here for you, my people,
but there would be
if
if

In my austere black uniform
I raised the banner
which decreed *Hope*
and which did not succeed
and which is not allowed.
Now I must confront the angel
who says Win,
who tells me to wave any banner
that you will follow

for you ignore me, my
baffled people, you have been through
too many theories
too many stray bullets
your eyes are gravel, skeptical,

in this hard field
you pay attention only
to the rhetoric of seed
fruit stomach elbow.

You have too many leaders
you have too many wars,
all of them pompous and small,
you resist only when you feel
like dressing up,
you forget the sane corpses . . .

I know you would like a god
to come down and feed you
and punish you. That overcoat
on sticks is not alive
                        there are no angels
but the angels of hunger,
prehensile and soft as gullets.
                    Watching you
my people, I become cynical,
you have defrauded me of hope
and left me alone with politics . . .

[Ellipses in original.]

MARILYN HACKER

Marilyn Hacker has been as progressive in her political and so-
cial ideals as she has been proficient in using traditional poetic meth-
ods to express her artistic vision and commitment to the cause of
liberation. In a career now spanning four decades, she has recorded
major transformations of the times through the lens of her own ex-

periences as a Jewish lesbian feminist living intensely in the continual flux of multicultural New York and, increasingly, Paris. In a series of well-wrought collections, Hacker has depicted with intellectual clarity and emotional subtlety the complex dynamics of friendship, the invigorating if turbulent force of erotic desire and entanglement, and the profound dread, enduring heartache, and irreparable loss brought by the epidemics of AIDS and cancer. Remarkably, given her outspokenness and the prickliness of poetry cliques, Hacker's work has gained the admiration of her peers across a wide spectrum of styles and philosophies, ultraliberal to conservative, even during periods when sharp polarizations on political-artistic issues have roiled the literary world.

Marilyn Hacker was born on Thanksgiving Day, November 17, 1942, in New York City and grew up in the Bronx. Her parents were trained as chemists, but her father was unable to find work in his field during the depression, while her mother's hope for a career as a doctor was denied because of the quotas against women and Jews in medical schools. (Hacker once dryly observed that her mother's master's degree entitled her "to work as a saleswoman at Macy's.") She became a teacher in the public schools instead, and the principal support of the family. Her father eventually got a teaching position at City College but died young, from pancreatic cancer.

Hacker was admitted to the elite Bronx High School of Science, thrived in its high-powered intellectual atmosphere for three years, then, at age fifteen, enrolled early in New York University where she pursued her interests in both science and the arts, especially French literature. She dropped out a year before graduation to marry a high school classmate, Samuel Delany, a science fiction writer. Maintaining an open marriage (each had liaisons with both sexes), they settled in the East Village on the Lower East Side of Manhattan, and Hacker took commercial editorial jobs. Their daughter was born in 1974, but they soon separated and eventually divorced in 1980, though they remained friends.

Returning to school, Hacker edited the university literary magazine and earned her B.A. in Romance languages. In 1970 she moved to London, where she ran an antiquarian bookstore, and began making trips to Paris to acquire books. At age twenty-six she also started submitting poems to magazines and was soon printed in *Epoch*, the *London Magazine*, and other journals. The poet and translator Richard Howard accepted several pieces for *New American Review*; then he became a mentor. With his help, her first book, *Presentation Piece*, was accepted for publication in 1974. It made a strong impression, winning both the Lamont Prize from the Academy of American Poets and a National Book Award. She was thirty-one.

Separations followed in 1976 and *Taking Notice* in 1980. The first three volumes were reissued as *First Cities: Collected Early Poems 1960–1979*, in 2003. The critics marveled at Hacker's self-assurance in these books, especially the mastery shown in her sonnets, sestinas, villanelles, canzones, couplets, and other forms. With vivid language and deft technique, the poet exposed a sometimes grim urban reality where love both illuminated and disappointed, as she tried to "maul the pain / to shape." But the sense of world-weariness was brightened by flashes of wit, as in the satires of famous poets in these "Occasional Verses":

> "Your breasts are like melons, your mouth like dark plums,"
> said Petrarch. Said Laura, "Why can't we be chums?"
>
> "Your glance is a torrent and I die of thirst,"
> said William. Said Maud, "Revolution comes first."

Loss is a major leitmotif in the early work, and the forces of history only increased the bereavement, catastrophically, as the eighties descended into the AIDS crisis with its seemingly unremitting suffering and premature deaths. For homosexual communities, where the epidemic struck first, the losses evoked a sense of rage and frustration and helplessness—all the more devastating since only a few years earlier there were celebrations for what appeared to be a new age of freedom and social justice following the advances of the gay liberation movement in the seventies.

Against this dark background, Hacker portrayed a more positive, if often fraught, side of gay life in *Love, Death, and the Changing of the Seasons* (1986, reprinted 1995), which chronicled in graphic detail and colloquial speech her passionate affair with a younger woman carried on in New York, Paris, and elsewhere, and the range of emotions—lust, longing, joy, jealousy, betrayal—she experienced in the process. Hacker narrated the story through a sequence of sonnets (and the occasional villanelle), as if to contain by formal measures the powerful feelings her obsession aroused. During this period she also published *Assumptions* (1985) and *Going Back to the River* (1990), which received a Lambda Literary Award. Her first selected volume, titled *The Hang-Glider's Daughter*, was also released in 1990 by Onlywomen Press in London.

Hacker's *Selected Poems, 1965–1990* appeared in 1994 and received the Poets' Prize. The same year she published a new and very somber collection, *Winter Numbers*, which won the Lenore Marshall Poetry Prize from *The Nation*, as well as her second Lambda Literary Award. In these stark poems Hacker meditated on the passing of several loved ones to cancer and to AIDS. (The numbers in the title refer to both poetic meters and the weeks and days counted down from the moment of dread diagnoses.) But the poet was not only a witness to the pain of others; she became a fellow sufferer, as she too was discovered to have cancer, of the breast, and experienced the physical and spiritual toll exacted by the disease and the treatments for it. Adding to the melancholy of this time, shortly after undergoing chemotherapy Hacker learned she had lost the editorship of the prestigious *Kenyon Review*, a position she had held for four years (1990–1994), provoking controversy in some quarters because of the number of emerging minority authors she chose to print.

Beginning in the mid-eighties, Hacker's trips to Paris became more frequent and her stays longer, and in 1989 she bought a small apartment there; she now divides her time between the city and New York. Over the years she has met many French poets and has translated several into English, notably Claire Malroux and Vénus Khoury-Ghata. She also co-edited a special bilingual issue of *Poetry* (October 2000) devoted to contemporary French poetry. In 2002 she published her ninth collection, *Squares and Courtyards*, in which she records further losses from AIDS and cancer, then reflects on her experiences with gratitude for the quotidian in a forty-page sequence, "Paragraphs from a Daybook."

Hacker's most recent volume is *Desesperanto: Poems 1999–2000* (2005). The title is an amalgam of *desespoir*, French for despair, and the Spanish *esperanto*, for one who hopes (and the name of the artificial universal language). With smoldering anger she considers in "Morning News" the current spate of bloody conflicts around the world, violence that has become a commonplace to citizens who, safe in their own houses, read of the savagery in "the newspaper, whose photographs / make sanitized excuses for the war." The volume alternates between the two extremes of the title, sadness especially in several elegiac pieces for dead and ailing friends, but with hope too particularly when, displaying her virtuosity in several sonnets and blank verse, the poet portrays the rich daily life in the City of Light with its present-day multiracial and cultural diversity.

Hacker's other awards include the Conners Prize from the *Paris Review*, the John Masefield Memorial Award from the Poetry Society of America, and fellowships from the Guggenheim and Ingram Merrill foundations. She has taught at a number of schools, including her alma mater, and is now a professor of French in the Graduate Center of the City University of New York.

INVOCATION

This is for Elsa, also known as Liz,
an ample-bosomed gospel singer, five
discrete malignancies in one full breast.
This is for auburn Jacqueline, who is
celebrating fifty years alive,
one since she finished chemotherapy,
with fireworks on the fifteenth of July.
This is for June, whose words are lean and mean
as she is, elucidating our protest.
This is for Lucille, who shines a wide
beam for us with her dark cadences.
This is for long-limbed Maxine, astride
a horse like conscience. This is for Aline
who taught her lover to caress the scar.
This is for Eve, who thought of AZT
as hopeful poisons pumped into a vein.
This is for Nanette in the Midwest.
This is for Alicia, shaking back dark hair,
dancing one-breasted with the Sabbath bride.
This is for Judy on a mountainside,
plunging her gloved hands in a glistening hive.
Hilda, Patricia, Gaylord, Emilienne,
Tania, Eunice: this is for everyone
who marks the distance on a calendar
from what's less likely each year to "recur."
Our saved-for-now lives are life sentences
—which we prefer to the alternative.

MORNING NEWS

Spring wafts up the smell of bus exhaust, of bread
and fried potatoes, tips green on the branches,
repeats old news: arrogance, ignorance, war.
A cinder-block wall shared by two houses
is new rubble. On one side was a kitchen
sink and a cupboard, on the other was
a bed, a bookshelf, three framed photographs.

Glass is shattered across the photographs;
two half-circles of hardened pocket bread
sit on the cupboard. There provisionally was
shelter, a plastic truck under the branches
of a fig tree. A knife flashed in the kitchen,
merely dicing garlic. Engines of war
move inexorably toward certain houses

while citizens sit safe in other houses
reading the newspaper, whose photographs
make sanitized excuses for the war.
There are innumerable kinds of bread
brought up from bakeries, baked in the kitchen:
the date, the latitude, tell which one was
dropped by a child beneath the bloodied branches.

The uncontrolled and multifurcate branches
of possibility infiltrate houses'
walls, windowframes, ceilings. Where there was
a tower, a town: ash and burnt wires, a graph
on a distant computer screen. Elsewhere, a kitchen
table's setting gapes, where children bred
to branch into new lives were culled for war.

Who wore this starched smocked cotton dress? Who wore
this jersey blazoned for the local branch
of the district soccer team? Who left this black bread
and this flat gold bread in their abandoned houses?
Whose father begged for mercy in the kitchen?

Whose memory will frame the photograph
and use the memory for what it was

never meant for by this girl, that old man, who was
caught on a ball field, near a window: war,
exhorted through the grief a photograph
revives. (Or was the team a covert branch
of a banned group; were maps drawn in the kitchen,
a bomb thrust in a hollowed loaf of bread?)
What did the old men pray for in their houses

of prayer, the teachers teach in schoolhouses
between blackouts and blasts, when each word was
flensed by new censure, books exchanged for bread,
both hostage to the happenstance of war?
Sometimes the only schoolroom is a kitchen.
Outside the window, black strokes on a graph
of broken glass, birds line up on bare branches.

"This letter curves, this one spreads its branches
like friends holding hands outside their houses."
Was the lesson stopped by gunfire? Was
there panic, silence? Does a torn photograph
still gather children in the teacher's kitchen?
Are they there meticulously learning war-
time lessons with the signs for house, book, bread?

SHARON OLDS

For its direct treatment of family life, personal relations, and human physicality, Sharon Olds's poetry has been widely praised by those who admire what is for them its brave if often painful candor. Her work has been severely criticized for like reasons by those who find the intimate revelations of the poet's own history and her graphic presentations of the body less sincere than sensational. Olds follows in the footsteps of the first generation of confessional poets, notably Anne Sexton. In her work, as in much other autobiographically derived writing, the line between truth-telling and self-indulgence is sometimes thin and may, like beauty or bane, depend upon the preconceptions of the beholder. In any case, her frequent journeys into the interior can be unsettling explorations of the human psyche, made more unnerving by the odd humor, naive tone, or flat affect Olds projects. But, the poet insists, only by confronting what is concealed, especially the traumas of her and our own personal histories, can sanity or wholeness be found.

Sharon Olds was born in San Francisco on November 19, 1942, and was raised, to use her words, as a "hellfire Calvinist." She attended Stanford, then took her graduate degrees from Columbia, and has since made her home in New York City. Her first collection, *Satan Says* (1980), won the San Francisco Poetry Center Award and attracted immediate attention for its explicit language and startling imagery. Her second volume, *The Dead and the Living* (1983), which won the Lamont Prize and the National Book Critics Circle Award, drew inspiration from historical photographs as well as portraits of her parents, grandparents, and children, drawing parallels between public and private lives.

Following *The Gold Cell* (1987), Olds published *The Father* (1992), a book of memories of life growing up with an alcoholic, abusive father, and her struggles at reconciliation, particularly during his last days as he lay dying of cancer. In recent volumes, *The Wellspring* (1996) and *Blood, Tin, Straw* (1999), Olds has returned to her "family romance" and perennial questions of the relation between mind and body, the tangled bonds of affection, and a variety of social issues. In 2002 she published *Strike Sparks: Selected Poems, 1980–2002*, followed in 2003 by a new collection, *The Unswept Room*, which returns to many topics of her earlier work, particular family relationships and her deceased parents, while coming to terms with her own mortality. Throughout her work Olds applies cinematic techniques, editing and splicing past with present events, offering close-ups from her personal life against wide-angle shots of larger historical contexts.

For many years Olds has taught at New York University, where she chaired the creative writing program. She has also conducted workshops at Goldwater Hospital, a facility for the physically disabled on Roosevelt Island. She appears frequently around the country, reciting her work (often with her colleague Galway Kinnell) and giving writing classes. Olds was named New York State poet laureate for 1998–2000, and was elected for a six-year term as a chancellor of the Academy of American Poets in 2007.

THE LANGUAGE OF THE BRAG

I have wanted excellence in the knife-throw,
I have wanted to use my exceptionally strong and accurate arms
and my straight posture and quick electric muscles
to achieve something at the center of a crowd,
the blade piercing the bark deep,
the haft slowly and heavily vibrating like the cock.

I have wanted some epic use for my excellent body,
some heroism, some American achievement
beyond the ordinary for my extraordinary self,
magnetic and tensile, I have stood by the sandlot
and watched the boys play.

I have wanted courage, I have thought about fire
and the crossing of waterfalls, I have dragged around

my belly big with cowardice and safety,
my stool black with iron pills,
my huge breasts oozing mucus,
my legs swelling, my hands swelling,
my face swelling and darkening, my hair
falling out, my inner sex
stabbed again and again with terrible pain like a knife.
I have lain down.

I have lain down and sweated and shaken
and passed blood and feces and water and
slowly alone in the center of a circle I have
passed the new person out
and they have lifted the new person free of the act
and wiped the new person free of that
language of blood like praise all over the body.

I have done what you wanted to do, Walt Whitman,
Allen Ginsberg, I have done this thing,
I and the other women this exceptional
act with the exceptional heroic body,
this giving birth, this glistening verb,

and I am putting my proud American boast
right here with the others.

TOPOGRAPHY

After we flew across the country we
got in bed, laid our bodies
delicately together, like maps laid
face to face, East to West, my
San Francisco against your New York, your
Fire Island against my Sonoma, my
New Orleans deep in your Texas, your Idaho
bright on my Great Lakes, my Kansas
burning against your Kansas, your Kansas
burning against my Kansas, your Eastern
Standard Time pressing into my
Pacific Time, my Mountain Time
beating against your Central Time, your
sun rising swiftly from the right my
sun rising swiftly from the left your
moon rising slowly from the left my
moon rising slowly from the right until
all four bodies of the sky
burn above us, sealing us together,
all our cities twin cities,
all our states united, one
nation, indivisible, with liberty and justice for all.

LOUISE GLÜCK

🔲 "I am attracted to ellipsis, to the unsaid, to suggestion, to elo-
quent, deliberate silence. The unsaid, for me, exerts great power,"
Louise Glück has remarked. These absences speak volumes in her
spare, even stark, but always highly evocative work. Glück's subjects
are the most fundamental—foremost love and flawed or failed rela-
tionships, in their many permutations and ramifications, especially
loss and loneliness—and her language is lean, even simple, pared of

superfluous details and modifiers that usually situate and individuate persons, places, and actions in poems.

Thus stripped to essentials, Glück's poems seem to exist in an almost timeless realm, like the archetypes of myth and fairy tale that the author has often adapted. And for all the emotional resonance and tension in her lines, the diction and overall tone display a kind of classical poise, an elemental purity. One can imagine people two or three centuries hence having little trouble understanding most of her poems, without footnotes. "I do not think that more information always makes a richer poem," she has noted. Alluding to ruins and other damaged or incomplete works that forcibly call to mind the cultures and larger contexts they bespeak, she added: "It seems to me that what is wanted, in art, is to harness the power of the unfinished." All art requires active audience participation, of course, but more than most Glück's suggestive poems invite the reader to "complete" them.

Louise Elisabeth Glück was born April 22, 1943, in New York City and was raised on Long Island. As a child she grew up with a feeling of guilt over the death of her older sister in infancy, a bereavement that lingers and is evidenced as a recurring theme of irreparable loss in Glück's poetry. She has attributed her psychic survival to poetry and psychoanalysis. At Sarah Lawrence College and Columbia University she studied with Leonie Adams and Stanley Kunitz but did not take a degree. She has taught at several schools, including Columbia, Iowa, Warren Wilson, Goddard, and, for more than twenty years, Williams College. She is now an adjunct professor of English and writer in residence at Yale.

Glück's debut collection was *Firstborn*, published in 1968 and winner of the Poet's Prize from the Academy of American Poets, followed by *The House on Marshland* (1975), *Descending Figure* (1980), and *The Triumph of Achilles* (1985), which won the National Book Critics Circle Award as well as prizes from the *Boston Globe* and the Poetry Society of America. The collections were reissued in 1995 in *The First Four Books of Poems*. While each is a distinctive accomplishment, the generally brief poems and short sequences in the early volumes share a characteristic atmosphere of disillusionment, cold clarity, and latent anger, as an oddly dispassionate speaker reveals fragments of a life marked by family dysfunction, alienation, difficult and unrequited love, marital tension, anorexia, and other disquieting psychological or spiritual states. The suppressed emotions and generally flat affect of the personas add an eerie quality to already bleak but continually fascinating scenarios.

All of Glück's subsequent volumes have won prizes, sometimes multiple awards, and mark different points of departure or approaches, some very original indeed, to her favorite topics of love and loss. *Ararat* (1990), winner of the Bobbitt National Prize for Poetry from the Library of Congress, is probably Glück's most personal collection: an unsparing family portrait of a shallow and silent father, an emotionally repressed mother, a withdrawn and obedient child, all scarred by the devastating death of an infant daughter-sibling. In the course of the searching, deeply felt poems, the speaker confronts several painful truths and comes to a measure of self-understanding, acceptance, and finally forgiveness. The much-discussed *Wild Iris* (1992) won the William Carlos Williams Award and the Pulitzer Prize, and comprises a unified sequence of fifty-four poems that meditate on the relation of God and the natural world, from the perspective (and through the voices) of flowers—and in a striking exception, "Witchgrass," a weed that mocks the pruning gardener: "I was here first, / before you were here . . . And I'll be here when only the sun and moon / are left, and the sea, and the wide field. / I will constitute the field." In the larger philosophical context, Glück (like Wallace Stevens) proposes that in a disillusioned modern world following the loss of faith in a caring God, it becomes the function of the poet to recognize and celebrate the things of the wondrous natural world as our earthly and only paradise.

In 1994, Glück won a P.E.N. nonfiction award for her critical prose collected in *Proofs and Theories: Essays on Poetry*, which offers apologies for her own aesthetics and methods, as well as thought-provoking examinations of the craft in general and the function and often frustrating life of the poet in particular. In *Meadowlands* (1996) Glück ingeniously intertwines her version of the mythical Odysseus and Penelope with a present-day married couple, playing off the contrasts and parallels between the two unlucky pairs, sometimes to comic effect. *Vita Nuova* (1992), another original book-length sequence that reconsiders life and love, received the Book Award in Poetry from *The New Yorker*. *The Seven Ages*, a provocative and at times disturbing contemplation of death, appeared in 2001, and in 2006 *Averno*, a highly original reinterpretation of the myth of Persephone and Demeter interleaved with scenes of contemporary mother-daughter conflicts.

Among several other awards, Glück won the 2001 Bollingen Prize in Poetry from Yale for her lifetime achievement, a Lannan Literary Award, the Sara Teasdale Memorial Prize, the MIT Anniversary Medal in 2000, and fellowships from the National Endowment for the Arts and the Guggenheim and Rockefeller foundations. A member of the American Academy and Institute of Arts and Letters, she was elected a chancellor of the Academy of American Poets in 1999. She was the judge for the prestigious Yale Series of Younger Poets for 2003–2007, and in 2003–2004 she was the Poet Laureate of United States.

A FABLE

Two women with
the same claim
came to the feet of
the wise king. Two women,
but only one baby.
The king knew
someone was lying.
What he said was
Let the child be
cut in half; that way
no one will go
empty-handed. He
drew his sword.
Then, of the two
women, one
renounced her share:
this was
the sign, the lesson.
Suppose
you saw your mother
torn between two daughters:
what could you do
to save her but be
willing to destroy
yourself—she would know
who was the rightful child,

the one who couldn't bear
to divide the mother.

EROS

I had drawn my chair to the hotel window, to watch the rain.

I was in a kind of dream or trance—
in love, and yet
I wanted nothing.

It seemed unnecessary to touch you, to see you again.
I wanted only this:
the room, the chair, the sound of the rain falling,
hour after hour, in the warmth of the spring night.

I needed nothing more; I was utterly sated.
My heart had become small; it took very little to fill it.
I watched the rain falling in heavy sheets over the darkened city—

You were not concerned; I could let you
live as you needed to live.

At dawn the rain abated. I did the things
one does in daylight, I acquitted myself,
but I moved like a sleepwalker.

It was enough and it no longer involved you.
A few days in a strange city.
A conversation, the touch of a hand.
And afterward, I took off my wedding ring.

That was what I wanted: to be naked.

ELLEN BRYANT VOIGT

◻ Ellen Bryant Voigt is a well-grounded poet. Her work is firmly
based on experience, the hard-earned knowledge and heightened
awareness acquired in her several roles as a woman, daughter, wife,

mother, musician, and teacher. Her style is plainspoken, poised, direct in treating the fundamental realities of love, marriage, family relations, work, illness, death, and the multiple challenges of leading a meaningful life in the modern world. Like Elizabeth Bishop, Voigt is a reticent author and avoids rhetorical displays. The elegant structures and subtle techniques of her economical verses reveal themselves gradually upon rereading, while the full meanings and intense emotions that inform her seemingly uncomplicated lines emerge only upon further reflection. Like Bishop's, Voigt's art conceals its artfulness.

Voigt grew up on a farm, and her formative years within a close-knit extended family and small community doubtless contributed to the solidity of her poetry, its substantial content and clarity, and to the sustaining wisdom it imparts. Yet her work is never merely "practical," let alone plodding; all she composes moves with confident grace. Voigt is also an accomplished pianist, and a thorough musicality shapes the sure rhythms, crisp intonation, and supple phrasing of her lines. In its overall timbre, the voice in her poetry speaks with Frost's "sound of sense." Her unsentimental pastoral pieces also recall his, except that where Frost paints his sketches of nature to point up specific truths or to draw out explicit moral lessons, Voigt prefers to let her poetic landscapes, portraits, and narratives speak for themselves.

She was born May 9, 1943, in Danville, Virginia, a rural area whose old-fashioned, family-centered culture, now vanished, the poet retrieves in several vivid lyrics and longer sequences. Her father was a farmer, her mother an elementary school teacher: strong individuals both whose redoubtable character and endearing personalities are portrayed in several of Voigt's most poignant lines. The poet recalls her father singing in a barbershop quartet and her own piano-playing in church. She has credited Bach and Brahms as influences on her poetry, and one can discern their contrapuntal methods in the fugal arrangements of several of her lyrics and especially the sequences. (She is also fond of themes and variations.) Intending a career as a concert artist, she enrolled at Converse College in South Carolina; attracted first by its music conservatory, she became increasingly drawn to poetry.

After taking her B.A. in 1964, she entered the Writers' Workshop at the University of Iowa, as one of only three women in her large class, and earned her M.F.A. in 1966. En route to that degree she married Francis Voigt, a college dean, in 1965; they have two children. In 1966 she began teaching at Iowa Wesleyan. Then, in 1970, she took a position in Vermont at Goddard College, where she founded the first low-residency creative writing program; the format has since been adopted at several schools. She taught creative writing at MIT from 1979 to 1982, and since 1981 has been on the faculty of the M.F.A. program at Warren Wilson College in North Carolina. Voigt has also been a frequent visiting writer at universities and writers' conferences across the country.

Claiming Kin, her first collection, appeared in 1976 to high praise. Here the poet presents decidedly un-Romantic views of rural life (poisonous snakes, headless chickens, separated calves bawling for their mothers), but juxtaposed to the harshness of nature and "the vast, disordered world" is the music of Bach and the great civilizing force enacted "At the Piano." In 1983, Voigt published her second book, *The Forces of Plenty*: a somewhat ironic or ambivalent title, as much of the volume considers the negative aspects of middle age, with its inevitable personal diminishments and the mounting losses in the family. Particularly moving are the poems in the elegiac sequence "To My Father" and the poet's meditations on the power of music in "A Fugue."

Her superb third volume, *The Lotus Flowers* (1987), is also filled with memories of the family romance and demonstrates the wisdom of Yeats's remark, quoted as the epigraph of the book: "Man is in love and loves what vanishes." Among the highlights of the consistently powerful collection are "Visiting the Graves," recollections of school days in "The Field Trip," "The Farmer" and the story of a disappointed wife of a farmer in "Amaryllis," striking accounts of unhappy incidents with animals involving her father ("Night Shade") and her grandfather ("Short Story"), and especially the portrait of the poet's dark-haired mother in her youth in "The Photograph" with its haunting closing lines:

> The horseshoe hung in the neck of the tree sinks
> deeper into heartwood every season.
> Sometimes I hear the past
> hum in my ear, its cruel perfected music,
> as I turn from the stove
> or stop to braid my daughter's thick black hair.

Voigt's achievement in that book is rivaled by work in *Two Trees* (1992), particularly the musical sequences "At the Piano" and

"*Variations*: At the Piano," as well as the five-part title poem and its companion six-part "Variations: Two Trees," in which Voigt reworks the story of Adam and Eve from Genesis into modern moral fables.

Kyrie followed in 1995: a National Book Critics Circle Award finalist and a *tour de force* (an overused term but truly appropriate in this instance) in which Voigt presents a long sequence of loose sonnets based on two enormous, simultaneous catastrophes of the early twentieth century, World War I and the flu epidemic of 1918. She quotes from Alfred W. Crosby's book, *America's Forgotten Pandemic: The Influenza of 1918*, as her epigraph: "Nothing else—no infection, no war, no famine—has ever killed so many in as short a period." Voigt interweaves the two tragic strands, depicting several scenes of the devastating effects of the disease in the United States with vignettes of the disaster Over There through letters from a doughboy who, amid deepening gloom, valiantly tries to keep up the spirits of the folks back home.

Shadow of Heaven (2002), a National Book Award finalist, likewise carries a melancholy tone but expresses (like the music of Brahms) autumnal depths of feeling within beautifully constructed forms. The collection is notable especially for "Long Marriage," "Practice," the fifteen-part sequence "The Garden, Spring, the Hawk," and another brilliant sequence, in seven sections, devoted to scenes from the life of her mother and father, "The Art of Distance." The finest poems from this and her previous volumes are joined, together with a large and truly extraordinary group of more recent pieces, in *Messenger: New and Selected Poems, 1976–2006* (2007), demonstrating yet again (if proof is still necessary) that Voigt ranks among the most accomplished poets of her generation.

She has also published a collection of essays on the craft of poetry, *The Flexible Lyric* (2002). Among her several other awards are fellowships from the National Endowment for the Arts and the Guggenheim Foundation, Pushcart Prizes in 1983 and 1991, prizes from the Poetry Society of America, and Lila Wallace–Reader's Digest awards from 1999 to 2002. In 2003 she was elected a chancellor of the Academy of American Poets, and from 1999 to 2003 she served as poet laureate of Vermont, her home of many years. In awarding Voigt the 2002 James Merrill fellowship from the Academy of American Poets, the judges wrote in the citation: "For over thirty years, Ellen Bryant Voigt has extended our knowledge of what

it means and feels like to be totally human in this America, and she
has done this in a body of work that plumbs the human spirit and
the mysteries of the world in which it lives and dies."

AMARYLLIS

Having been a farmer's daughter
she didn't want to be a farmer's wife, didn't want
the smell of ripe manure in all his clothes,
the corresponding flies in her kitchen,
a pail of slop below the sink,
a crate of baby chicks beside the stove, piping
beneath their bare lightbulb, cows calling at the gate
for him to come, cows standing in the chute
as he crops their horns with his long sharp shears.
So she nagged him toward a job in town;
so she sprang from the table, weeping, when he swore;
so, after supper, she sulks over her mending
as he unfolds his pearl pocketknife
to trim a callus on his palm.
Too much like her mother, he says, not knowing
any other reason why she spoils the children,
or why he comes in from the combine with his wrenches
to find potatoes boiled dry in their pot,
his wife in the parlor on the bench
at her oak piano—not playing
you understand, just sitting like a fern
in that formal room.
                              So much time to think,
these long hours: like her mother,
each night she goes to bed when her husband's tired,
gets up when he gets up, and in between tries
not to move, listening to the sleep of this good man
who lies beside and over her. So much time alone,
since everything he knows is practical.
Just this morning, he plunged an icepick
into the bloated side of the cow unable to rise,
dying where it fell, its several stomachs having failed—
too full, he said, of sweet wet clover.

LESSON

Whenever my mother, who taught
small children forty years,
asked a question, she
already knew the answer.
"Would you like to" meant
you would. "Shall we" was
another, and "Don't you think."
As in, "Don't you think
it's time you cut your hair."

So when, in the bare room,
in the strict bed, she said
"You want to see?" her hands
were busy at her neckline,
untying the robe, not looking
down at it, stitches
bristling where the breast
had been, but straight at me.

I did what I always did:
not weep—she never wept—
and made my face a freshly
white-washed wall: let her
write, again, whatever
she wanted there.

NIKKI GIOVANNI

Of the several young black writers who emerged during the civil rights ferment of the late sixties, Nikki Giovanni has had probably the most visible career. Outspoken and marvelously self-assured, Giovanni presented an impressive image of the assertive new generation of African-American authors who gave voice to the heady feelings of empowerment sparked by the Black Liberation movement. Impatient with the older, slower, more pacifist methods of opposing social injustice, they were anxious to reignite the long effort for racial equality and were more than willing to be impolite and "in your face" to be heard. Energized by firebrands like Amiri Baraka (formerly LeRoi Jones) at the second Black Writers' Conference held at Fisk University in 1967, Giovanni and others who attended were eager to answer the call for black separatism and to do their part by creating a distinct black literature independent of white-dominated American-English-European literary traditions and conventions, or the dictates of mainstream media generally.

Considering themselves integral to the larger political revolution, these aspiring black writers embraced their educational roles in raising consciousness (to use the catchphrase of the era), especially by identifying and celebrating the movement's bold new ideas (under the general heading of Black Power), new images (Black Is Beautiful), and new leadership, which for Giovanni and many of her peers came to be epitomized by the militant Black Panther party. To accomplish their aims, the younger poets (and some of the older ones too, like Gwendolyn Brooks) focused on the current realities of black life—particular people, places, experiences good and bad, and, above all, their own dialect.

Giovanni herself was especially drawn to the concrete details of daily life in the black community and political issues of the hour, and thus her early work was highly topical. For the same reason (as with proletarian writings of earlier eras) many of Giovanni's efforts—viewed now, some forty years on—seem perhaps of more importance as vivid records of social history than as "timeless art." And that, she says, is exactly what she intended. "Poetry is but a reflection of the moment," she has declared (in her prose collection *Sacred Cows*, 1988), immediately adding, "The universal comes from the particular." But besides her political observations, the particulars that have most absorbed the poet's attention have been the details of her own life.

She was born Yolande Cornelia Giovanni, Jr., June 7, 1943, in Knoxville, Tennessee, but spent much of her childhood in Cincinnati. In 1957 she returned to Knoxville to live with her maternal grandparents. In high school she was encouraged by her English and French teachers, and at the end of her junior year she was able to enroll early at Fisk. She was expelled her first semester, for an unauthorized visit to her grandparents, and moved to Cincinnati, where she attended night classes at the University of Cincinnati. In 1964 she returned to Fisk, where she majored in history and took a workshop in which she met several leaders of the Black Arts Movement, including Jones/Baraka. As the civil rights movement heated up, Giovanni helped reestablish a chapter of the Student Nonviolent Coordinated Committee (SNCC) that Fisk had earlier banned.

She graduated in 1967 with honors and, back in Cincinnati, began working on the poems that would make up her self-published first book, *Black Feeling, Black Talk* (1969), and edited a revolutionary journal called *Conversation*. She also organized the city's first Black Arts Festival. At a conference she met H. Rap Brown (before the SNCC national director became a Black Panther extremist), moved to Delaware to work at a settlement house, then received a Ford Foundation fellowship for graduate studies at the University of Pennsylvania School of Social Work. In 1968 she dropped out and wrote most of *Black Judgement*. On hearing of the assassination of Martin Luther King, Jr., on April 4 she drove to Atlanta to attend the funeral.

She then moved to New York and entered the School of Fine Arts at Columbia. She took courses in creative writing but was informed that she could not write, and left without an M.F.A. In 1969 she began teaching at Queens College. Having printed *Black Feeling* at her own expense, she decided to publicize it herself as well. She rented Birdland, the famous jazz club on West Forty-fourth Street, to throw a book party. It was so well promoted that the huge crowd gathering outside attracted the attention of reporters at the nearby *New York Times*, who were surprised so many had shown up for a poetry reading. The story was printed on the first page of the Metro section of the paper. Within eight months, Giovanni had sold some ten thousand copies. With a grant from the Harlem Council for the Arts, she then completed *Black Judgement*. Combined with her first book, it was issued by a commercial publisher in 1970. In August she gave birth to her only child, Thomas Watson Giovanni, and that fall she began teaching at Rutgers.

Giovanni's career was no less eventful during the following decade. In 1970 her NikTom press issued *Night Comes Softly*, one of the first anthologies of poetry by black women. The following year she appeared on the television program *Soul!* (including a show with Lena Horne, the subject of her poem "For a Woman Whose Voice I Like"), and read to large audiences in Harlem. She printed *Spin a Soft Black Song* and recorded her first album, *Truth Is on Its Way*, to great success. An interview she taped with James Baldwin, in London, was broadcast and a transcript was published in late 1971.

In 1972 *Truth* received an award as Best Spoken Word Album and Giovanni was invited to read at Lincoln Center. She also published *My House*, named one of the best books of 1973 by the American Library Association. In 1973, too, Giovanni completed a taped dialogue with the pioneering activist poet Margaret Walker, and *Ladies' Home Journal* gave her one of its Women of the Year Awards in a ceremony broadcast from the Kennedy Center. (Not all black writers were pleased, considering her acceptance a "sellout.") To celebrate her thirtieth birthday she gave a reading at Lincoln Center in New York City. At the request of the U.S. State Department she traveled to Africa, presenting lectures in Ghana, Nigeria, Tanzania, and Zambia. She also published *Ego Tripping and Other Poems for Young Readers* and recorded another album, *Like a Ripple on a Pond.*

Giovanni has always favored conversational speech in poetry, and live performances and recordings have formed an essential part of her career. Indeed, projected orally the force of her personality gives her poems meaning and resonance they may lack standing alone in print and read silently on the page. Curiously for a writer, Giovanni has expressed deep skepticism about the written word and the artifices of formal composition. In her often-cited "My House," the self-conscious speaker asks: "does this really sound / like a silly poem"? She also asserts that "english isn't a good language / to express emotion through / mostly i imagine because people / try to speak english instead / of trying to speak through it."

Such pronouncements, like other of her critical remarks, do not bear close scrutiny: she does not explain why or how any other language is (or could be) fitter for communication, though elsewhere she finds African oral traditions superior in their expressiveness. Giovanni prides herself on "truth-telling" (what author does not?), but the poet-polemicist routinely privileges the people, experiences, and attributes of her race, especially the female portion, as in the very popular "Ego Tripping (there may be a reason why)," her unabashedly extravagant celebration of the Black Woman. This bias, though unfair, illogical, and no more commendable than any other ethnic prejudice, is of course flattering to that part of her audience (already converted) to whom it is addressed.

While she has praised the opposite sex on occasion, notably in "Beautiful Black Men," Giovanni has no delusions about their persistent, unenlightened attitudes—even in the egalitarian era of revolution—and she scores the continued arrogant, unequal, and ill treatment by black males toward black women. She puts the matter succinctly in "Woman Poem": "it's a sex object if you're pretty / and no love / or love and no sex if you're fat / get back fat black woman be a mother / grandmother strong thing but not woman."

During the seventies and eighties she gave as many as two hundred readings and lectures a year while releasing a new book or album (sometimes both) almost every other year. She was invited to join a number of public service panels and commissions, and continued to teach. Among others, she held visiting professorships at Ohio State, St. Joseph's College, the University of Minnesota, and Virginia Polytechnic Institute in Blacksburg. The last position become permanent in 1989, and she is currently professor of English and the Gloria D. Smith Professor of Black Studies.

Giovanni has been a favorite speaker at commencement exercises, by the late nineties accumulating almost a score of honorary doctorates. Over the years many other literary and civic awards have been bestowed, including presentations of the keys to a dozen cities. She was elected to the Ohio Women's Hall of Fame and named an Outstanding Woman of Tennessee, as well as the first recipient of the Rosa Parks Woman of Courage Award. She has also been named Woman of the Year for *Ebony*, *Mademoiselle*, and *Essence*, and won the NAACP Image Award three times.

Most recently Giovanni published her *Selected Poems*, with a foreword and detailed chronology by Virginia C. Fowler, in 1996; *Love Poems* in 1997; *Blues for All the Changes: New Poems* in 1999; and *Quilting the Black-Eyed Pea: Poems and Not-Quite Poems* in 2002. *The Collected Poetry of Nikki Giovanni: 1968–1998* was released in 2003. She has also published several children's books. In 2003 her popular prose works were reissued in *The Prosaic Soul of Nikki Giovanni*, including her personal history of the sixties, *Gemini: An Extended Autobiographical Statement on My First Twenty-Five Years of Being a Black Poet* (nominated for the National Book Award) and the essay collections *Sacred Cows . . . And Other Edibles* (winner of the Ohioana Library Award) and *Racism 101*. In 1995, Giovanni was diagnosed with lung cancer and underwent surgery successfully. She later edited, with Karen L. Stanford, *Breaking the Silence: Inspirational Stories of Black Cancer Survivors*, published in 2005.

LEGACIES

her grandmother called her from the playground
    "yes, ma'am" said the little girl
    "i want chu to learn how to make rolls" said the old
woman proudly
but the little girl didn't want
to learn how because she knew
even if she couldn't say it that
that would mean when the old one died she would be less
dependent on her spirit so
the little girl said
    "i don't want to know how to make no rolls"
with her lips poked out
and the old woman wiped her hands on
her apron saying "lord
    these children"
and neither of them ever
said what they meant
and i guess nobody ever does

EAVAN BOLAND

After Seamus Heaney, Eavan Boland is the best-known contemporary Irish poet. While well versed in the bardic tradition, she has long had a quarrel with older Irish literature, which idealized women, made them emblems, or (more often) simply ignored them. Like Heaney, she has forged a lyrical but insistent voice that speaks of and to the realities of the modern world. Like him too, she is preoccupied with history, but concerned most about what is missing from the official accounts, the facts *Outside History* (as she titled her Selected Poems, 1980–1990), the stories passed down orally from the losers and victims in power struggles great and small. Poetry, she has said, is a way to "fathom silences, follow the outsider's trail."

Noting the difference "between the past and history," between the "articulate" and the "silent and fugitive," Boland has been drawn to women's "secret" history. But while her poems are often concerned with women's issues, she is quick to make a further distinction: "I'm a feminist. I'm not a feminist poet." Feminism is a powerful ethic, she points out, but it is not an aesthetic. When she was asked by a reporter whether she believed poetry could change the world, she replied: "No, but it can change people. And that's enough."

Eavan Boland was born on September 24, 1944, in Dublin, where she lived until she was six. Her mother Frances Kelly was a painter, her father a diplomat. His postings took them to London (he was the Irish ambassador) and to New York (representative at the United Nations) in the fifties, a period Boland has termed her "exile." She returned to Ireland to study English and Latin at Trinity College, Dublin, took first-class honors, and became, at twenty-three, one of the youngest lecturers there ever. She also began writing for the *Irish Times*. Following a self-published book, her first professional collection, *New Territory*, appeared in 1967. In 1969 she married the novelist Kevin Casey, and they have two grown daughters.

In 1979 the family moved to the United States, where Boland's poetry became influenced by the women's movement. (She also credits Emily Dickinson, Adrienne Rich, and particularly Elizabeth Bishop for helping shape her character as a poet.) Boland taught at University College Dublin, Bowdoin College, and the University of Iowa's International Writing Program, and since 1995 has been a professor of English at Stanford, where she directs the creative writing program. The others of her eleven poetry collections are: *In Her Own Image* (1980), *Night Feed* (1982), *The Journey and Other Poems* (1986), *In a Time of Violence* (1994), *An Origin Like Water: Collected Poems 1967–1987* (1996), *The Lost Land* (1998), *Against Love Poetry* (2001, named a Notable Book of the Year by the *New York Times*), and *Domestic Violence* (2007). Boland has written *Object Lessons: The Life of the Woman and the Poet in Our Time* (1995) and co-edited with Mark Strand *The Making of a Poem: A Norton Anthology of Poetic Forms* (2000). She has also published a volume of translations, *After Every War: Twentieth-Century Women Poets* (2004), from the German of Nelly Sachs, Ingeborg Bachmann, Else Lasker-Schüler, and six others. Boland's *New Collected Poems* appeared in 2008.

THE POMEGRANATE

The only legend I have ever loved is
the story of a daughter lost in hell.
And found and rescued there.
Love and blackmail are the gist of it.
Ceres and Persephone the names.
And the best thing about the legend is
I can enter it anywhere. And have.
As a child in exile in
a city of fogs and strange consonants,
I read it first and at first I was
an exiled child in the crackling dusk of
the underworld, the stars blighted. Later
I walked out in a summer twilight
searching for my daughter at bed-time.
When she came running I was ready
to make any bargain to keep her.
I carried her back past whitebeams
and wasps and honey-scented buddleias.
But I was Ceres then and I knew
winter was in store for every leaf
on every tree on that road.
Was inescapable for each one we passed.
And for me.
                    It is winter
and the stars are hidden.
I climb the stairs and stand where I can see
my child asleep beside her teen magazines,
her can of Coke, her plate of uncut fruit.
The pomegranate! How did I forget it?
She could have come home and been safe
and ended the story and all
our heart-broken searching but she reached
out a hand and plucked a pomegranate.
She put out her hand and pulled down
the French sound for apple and
the noise of stone and the proof
that even in the place of death,
at the heart of legend, in the midst

of rocks full of unshed tears
ready to be diamonds by the time
the story was told, a child can be
hungry. I could warn her. There is still a chance.
The rain is cold. The road is flint-coloured.
The suburb has cars and cable television.
The veiled stars are above ground.
It is another world. But what else
can a mother give her daughter but such
beautiful rifts in time?
If I defer the grief I will diminish the gift.
The legend will be hers as well as mine.
She will enter it. As I have.
She will wake up. She will hold
the papery flushed skin in her hand.
And to her lips. I will say nothing.

KAY RYAN

▣ Very few poets can say so much in so little space as Kay Ryan. Seldom more than twenty lines long (and those lines rarely exceeding six syllables), Ryan's witty poems are bracing distillations of her precise observations of the world and the vagaries of humankind. Aside from the shardlike fragments of Sappho or the sharpest haiku, it is unusual to find such compression of thought and deftness of touch as are typical in her minimalist art. Whatever she fixes in her sights is viewed with extreme clarity but slightly askew too, the better to discern those aspects largely overlooked or unseen entirely by the casual passerby.

For her wry, idiosyncratic take on life and use of compact, seemingly simple forms, Ryan is often compared with Emily Dickinson; in her fine craftsmanship and didactic yet subtly subversive tendencies, she is also likened to Marianne Moore. But those forebears are regular chatterboxes compared to Ryan—though noisy pomposity and foolish pretension are things up with which all three will not put. In "Blandeur" (as opposed to Grandeur), for example, she slyly advocates a democratic leveling of Earth's extremities. And in "Blunt" she suggests: "If we could love / the blunt / and not / the point / we would / almost constantly / have what we want." Combining clever rhymes, artful wordplay, and striking images, Ryan's cunning verses are both amusing and wise. In her epigrammatic efficiency, Ryan resembles those unsentimental moralists, the Augustan satirists. She gently prods and provokes from slightly off-kilter angles, then pounces with her dead-on accurate insights.

Kay Ryan was born in San Jose, California, September 21, 1945. Her father was a well-driller, and she grew up in the Mojave Desert and small, working-class towns in the San Joaquin Valley. She received her B.A. and M.A. from the University of California at Los Angeles but never took a poetry-writing course. In fact she was not allowed to join the poetry club at UCLA, she told the *Christian Science Monitor*, because she was considered "too much of an outsider." (She almost took a Ph.D. in literary criticism but, she said in *Salon*, "I couldn't bear the idea of being a doctor of something I couldn't fix.") For over thirty years Ryan has taught remedial English (not creative writing) at the College of Marin in Kentfield, California, and says that she deliberately has tried to live "very quietly, so I could be happy."

Ryan's first book, *Dragon Acts to Dragon Ends*, was privately printed in 1983 with underwriting from friends. Her second, *Strangely Marked Metal*, was issued by a small literary press in 1985. Both books were ignored. In the face of silence, the reaction so many poets regularly face, she persisted. Many years later, when she finally became well known, she commented on readership—or its absence—and playing on the original meaning of *stanza* (room), reflected on the true nature of appreciation in her poem "Ideal Audience":

> Not scattered legions,
> not a dozen from
> a single region
> for whom accent
> matters, not a seven-
> member coven,
> not five shirttail
> cousins; just
> one free citizen—
> maybe not alive
> now even—who
> will know with

exquisite gloom
that only we two
ever found this room.

It was almost a decade before she published another collection, *Flamingo Watching* (1994), which was followed by *Elephant Rocks* (1996) and then *Say Uncle* (2002), her first book from a commercial New York publisher. Readers of little magazines had discovered her twenty years earlier, and she had a small but devoted group of fans. But each of the three books garnered larger attention and identified Ryan as one of the truly distinctive American poets, a writer with a style and a voice unmistakably her own. In 2004 she published *The Niagara River* to wide praise.

Besides early recognition in the form of foundation grants, in more recent years she has received major prizes and publication in large journals. As people have discovered her considerable wit and charm as a reader, particularly through radio programs such as Garrison Keillor's "Prairie Home Companion," demand for her public appearances has grown. She now travels widely around the country giving readings, including at such prestigious venues as the 92nd Street Y in New York and the Library of Congress. But most of the time she lives quietly, with her life partner Carol, in the San Francisco Bay area. Ryan's philosophy, like her writing, is straightforward. "Poems should leave you feeling freer and not more burdened," she told the *Monitor* reporter. "I like to think of all good poetry as providing more oxygen into the atmosphere; it just makes it easier to breathe."

REPULSIVE THEORY

Little has been made
of the soft skirting action
of magnets reversed,
while much has been
made of attraction.
But is it not this pillowy
principle of repulsion
that produces the
doily edges of oceans
or the arabesques of thought?

And do these cutout coasts
and in-curved rhetorical beaches
not baffle the onslaught
of the sea or objectionable people
and give private life
what small protection it's got?
Praise then the oiled motions
of avoidance, the pearly
convolutions of all that
slides off or takes a
wide berth; praise every
eddying vacancy of Earth,
all the dimpled depths
of pooling space, the whole
swirl set up by fending off—
extending far beyond the personal,
I'm convinced—
immense and good
in a cosmological sense:
unpressing us against
each other, lending
the necessary *never*
to never-ending.

THE WELL OR THE CUP

How can
you tell
at the start
what you
can give away
and what
you must hold
to your heart.
What is
the well
and what is
a cup. Some
people get
drunk up.

JANE KENYON

◲ In her unfortunately abbreviated and often difficult life, Jane Kenyon wrote clear-sighted and luminous poems that accept and celebrate the imperfect world by embracing its beauty while coming to terms with its bitterness. Laboring frequently under debilitating depression, the poet articulated painful truths yet maintained a sense of equilibrium that arose from her deep reserves of courage, confidence, and generosity. In an interview with Bill Moyers near the end of her life, Kenyon recalled an epiphany she experienced as a young woman, a spiritual awakening in which she "relaxed into existence" and assumed her place amid the mysteries of realities seen and unseen. From this revelation she approached poetry with a sense of vocation and, as she told her literary biographer, a consciousness of the power of the art to name, to tell the truth, to articulate feelings difficult to describe, and to offer compassion in the face of suffering, loss, and the inevitability of death. "We have the consolation of beauty," she added, "of one soul extending to another soul and saying, 'I've been there too.'"

Jane Kenyon was born May 23, 1947, in Ann Arbor, Michigan, home of the University of Michigan, where she took her B.A. in literature in 1970 and an M.A. in 1972. While a student she met the poet Donald Hall, a professor in the English Department since 1957 and nineteen years her senior; they were married in 1972. In 1975 Hall resigned to devote himself entirely to writing, and the couple moved permanently to New Hampshire and Eagle Pond Farm, the family home built by Hall's great-grandfather in 1865. A prolific author and anthologist, Hall continued to work as a freelancer, and both poets produced several collections at the farm. They frequently gave poetry readings together around the United States and abroad.

Kenyon published four admirably crafted books: *From Room to Room* (1978), *The Boat of Quiet Hours* (1986), *Let Evening Come* (1990), and *Constance* (1993), which attracted devoted and steadily growing audiences with each new volume. Her translations from Russian of *Twenty Poems of Anna Akhmatova* appeared in 1985. Her gifts for metaphor and striking images were immediately apparent in her first collection, as when she described the movement of box elder leaves, "turning all at once / like a school of fish." Pithy and graceful, the poems rewarded with their revelations of beauty among commonplace objects. In *The Boat of Quiet Hours* Kenyon found her true voice while her vision turned darker in scenes of deaths and departures. Some of the poems depict low spirits that plagued the author, with the enervation and sense of alienation that accompanied them, as in "Rain in January": "When my arm slipped / from the arm of the chair / I let it hang beside me, pale, / useless, and strange."

In the last two volumes published in her lifetime, the mood is often somber as well. Deaths and illnesses, particularly her husband's recent diagnosis of cancer, preoccupy the poet but seem to elicit also an ever greater clarity of thought along with further depths of feeling in the empathetic author-observer. A great number of readers particularly identified with and found solace in her brilliant meditation on clinical depression, the sequence "Having It Out with Melancholy." Based on her own long experience, Kenyon's lines brought a wealth of subtle understanding to this all-too-common condition and to a range of psychological states associated with it. She does not indulge in self-pity or in self-deception. Rather, in giving voice to vague disquiets and inarticulate feelings, she offers clarity amid confusion and warm but unsentimental compassion to spirits in distress: gifts that distinguished Kenyon's work and lift it to a level not usually associated with contemporary poetry, with its distancing ironies and sophisticated formal evasions. Her special qualities of mind and heart made the loss of the artist—still young and just reaching the height of her powers—all the more lamentable.

In January 1994, shortly after the publication of *Constance*, Kenyon was diagnosed with cancer, a particularly virulent strain of leukemia. During treatment, and compounding the struggle, her mother died. For a time it appeared that complex advanced methods, including a bone-marrow transplant, might arrest the disease. But despite heroic measures, after fifteen months she succumbed, at home on the farm, the morning of April 22, 1995.

Kenyon managed to complete work on another substantial volume, which she arranged in final form for the press just before her death, and *Otherwise: New and Selected Poems* was released posthumously in 1996. That year her publisher also issued *A Hundred White Daffodils: Essays, Interviews, the Akhmatova Translations, Newspaper Columns, and One Poem*. In 2004 Ausable Press published *Letters to Jane*, an edition of correspondence from the poet Hayden Carruth during the year before her death. Donald Hall reflected on her life and remarkable spirit, and attempted to assuage his grief at her loss after twenty-three years of marriage, in his moving, book-length elegy, *Without* (1998). He also composed a prose memoir, *The Best Day the Worst Day: Life with Jane Kenyon* (2005). John H. Timmerman's *Jane Kenyon: A Literary Life* appeared in 2002. The *Collected Poems*, comprising the contents of all her books and the Akhmatova translations, was published in 2007.

HAPPINESS

There's just no accounting for happiness,
or the way it turns up like a prodigal
who comes back to the dust at your feet
having squandered a fortune far away.

And how can you not forgive?
You make a feast in honor of what
was lost, and take from its place the finest
garment, which you saved for an occasion
you could not imagine, and you weep night and day
to know that you were not abandoned,
that happiness saved its most extreme form
for you alone.

No, happiness is the uncle you never
knew about, who flies a single-engine plane
onto the grassy landing strip, hitchhikes
into town, and inquires at every door
until he finds you asleep midafternoon
as you so often are during the unmerciful
hours of your despair.

It comes to the monk in his cell.
It comes to the woman sweeping the street
with a birch broom, to the child
whose mother has passed out from drink.
It comes to the lover, to the dog chewing
a sock, to the pusher, to the basket maker,
and to the clerk stacking cans of carrots
in the night.
It even comes to the boulder

in the perpetual shade of pine barrens,
to rain falling on the open sea,
to the wineglass, weary of holding wine.

OTHERWISE

I got out of bed
on two strong legs.
It might have been
otherwise. I ate
cereal, sweet
milk, ripe, flawless
peach. It might
have been otherwise.
I took the dog uphill
to the birch wood.
All morning I did
the work I love.

At noon I lay down
with my mate. It might
have been otherwise.
We ate dinner together
at a table with silver
candlesticks. It might
have been otherwise.
I slept in a bed
in a room with paintings
on the walls, and
planned another day
just like this day.
But one day, I know,
it will be otherwise.

HEATHER McHUGH

Wit, outrageous wordplay, a wry attitude toward humankind, and
a robust sense of fun—a quality now sparse in poetry—distinguish the

lively and illuminating lines of Heather McHugh. "My whole work is to catch the word by surprise, sneaking up on language, sneaking up on the world as it lurks in words," she has said. "I love the recesses of reason." McHugh delights in words and their individual provenances and power, and demonstrates how in their etymologies and frequent ambiguities they contain dense cultural history, and how idioms and clichés reveal deep-set habits of mind, not least our complicated means of dealing with, or avoiding, reality. As a philologist, the poet is perforce a philosopher and a psychologist as well.

Throughout her career McHugh has displayed a refreshing irreverence toward received pieties, exposing with verbal sleights of hand how unwise conventional wisdom so often is. Her sly jabs at folly and her sassy flair in dissecting the human condition generally are expressed through language that is itself minutely examined, parsed, deconstructed, and ingeniously recombined. But behind McHugh's linguistic high jinks and abundant humor there lies serious purpose. For all her *esprit*, within the laughing poet there breathes the soul of a moralist and a Metaphysical that John Donne could appreciate.

Heather McHugh was born in San Diego to Canadian parents August 20, 1948, and grew up in rural Virginia. At age sixteen she entered Harvard, where she took one of Robert Lowell's famous poetry classes, and received her B.A. in English in 1970. She earned her M.A. at the University of Denver in 1972. For a decade she taught at the State University of New York at Binghamton, occasionally directing the writing program, and in 1983 joined the faculty at the University of Washington, where she is now Milliman Distinguished Writer-in-Residence and professor of English. Since 1976 she has also been a member of the core faculty of the M.F.A. Program for Writers at Warren Wilson College. Over the years she has been a visiting professor at the Writers' Workshop at the University of Iowa, the University of Texas, Columbia, Syracuse, North Carolina, and Cincinnati, as well as the University of California at Berkeley, Los Angeles, and Irvine.

Dangers, McHugh's first collection, was published in 1976, followed by *A World of Difference* in 1981. Both won praise from readers and reviewers of every stripe for their originality, intelligence, brash energy, and amusing approach to matters both intimate and grand. Mostly short and always sprightly, the poems provide sharp, usually unexpected observations on the world of nature and the ways, often wayward, of women and men. Here as in her later work, McHugh focuses particularly on the singular detail, the exception to the rule, the odd angle that reveals the core of the objects she surveys. But the center of attention is often language itself, as her lines play out in an often quirky vocabulary and sinuous phrasing whose syntactical turns mirror the action under consideration. Even the puns, which the exuberant author can never resist, "work," sometimes even better on rereading: unlike the groan-inducing jokesters who annoy with their jejune utterances, McHugh finds in superficial word resemblances significances and odd connections that are curiously apropos for the occasions of her pieces. The poet has acknowledged her debt to Beckett, and the terse, enigmatic aura of his dramas hovers in some of her more ironic scenarios. There is a touch of Magritte, too, in the surreal atmosphere that tints several poems.

In 1987, McHugh published *To the Quick*, and *Shades* the following year. These and her earlier work, including many fine previously uncollected pieces, were reprinted in *Hinge & Sign: Poems 1968–1993*, which was nominated for the National Book Award. This very substantial and consistently engaging collection opens with an almost too clever preface, in which the author notes: "I suppose I have a gift for listening to the language before I make it listen to me; it's a habit of resisting habit, and keeps me (as I grow older and more patient) from some of the more presumptuous familiarities." She continues, "The main discipline is to keep finding life strange (this is the extent, and intent, of spirituality in me)." The first of the new poems is "What He Thought," a remarkable narrative of a dinner conversation in Rome that produces a startling answer to the question "What's poetry?" Referring to the nearby statue of Giordano Bruno, the sixteenth-century humanist scholar who was burned at the stake on that spot for his heretical view of an infinite cosmos, an old Italian poet relates:

> And so his captors
> placed upon his face
> an iron mask, in which
>
> he could not speak. That's
> how they burned him. That is how
> he died: without a word, in front
> of everyone.
> And poetry—

> (we'd all
> put down our forks by now, to listen to
> the man in grey; he went on
> softly)—
> > poetry is what
>
> he thought, but did not say.

The poem is uncharacteristically long, its "plot" atypically straight-forward for McHugh, but its conclusion, broaching the nature of poetry, is a preoccupation in much of her work. In many variations, McHugh's poems ponder and illustrate the larger philosophical is-sue: the relation between words and the world—how words both connect us to and divide us from reality—the ways in which lan-guage shapes perception and thus in a true sense makes or *is* our re-ality. The other major preoccupations of the poems are love, sex, sickness and death, consciousness, the nature of God or belief, and the role of the imagination with regard to all these things.

The Father of the Predicaments came out in 1999 and takes its ti-tle from a saying of Aristotle, that "the father of the predicaments is being." Although McHugh's subjects here are, as in her earlier vol-umes, matters of life and death, she does not treat them solemnly: the verbal pyrotechnics, comic riffs, teasing conundrums, paradoxes, puns, and other pleasures in playing with words are all present in profusion. Yet there is greater intensity in this volume as well as a somberness that rises from the author's heightened sense of mortal-ity, particularly as articulated in the opening poem of the book. In her preface to *Hinge & Sign*, McHugh confessed, "Writing has always been in me the site, not of an intention, but of an intensity." Here the author at times defuses or deflects the tension by self-reflexive com-ments and chiding, as when she mockingly declares: "McHugh, you'll be the death of me." In any case, the metaphysician-poet makes the most of the mind-body split and provides her own bitter-sweet answer to the query, What is poetry?, through the continuing experimental process of creating poems themselves, most recently a new collection, *Eyeshot* (2003).

McHugh has published a volume of prose, *Broken English: Po-etry and Partiality* (1993, reissued 1999), with essays on Rilke, Celan, Gertrude Stein, Dickinson, ancient Greek poets, and Yoruba poets of Nigeria. She has also produced books of translations, including

D'Après Tout: Poems of Jean Follain (1981), *Because the Sea Is Black: Poems by Blaga Dimitrova* (rendered from the Bulgarian with her husband, Nikolai Popov, 1989), *Glottal Stop: 101 Poems of Paul Celan* (from the German, also with Popov, 2000), and *Cyclops*, an adaptation of Euripides (2000). She has edited an issue of *Ploughshares* (Spring 2001) and *The Best American Poetry 2007*, and served as a judge for many prizes. McHugh herself has received dozens of accolades, chief among them election as a member of the American Academy of Arts and Sciences and as a chancellor of the Academy of American Poets, the O. B. Hardison Prize from the Folger Shakespeare Library, a Lila Wallace–Reader's Digest Writing Award, fellowships from the National Endowment for the Arts and the Guggenheim Foundation, and several Pushcart Prizes.

OUTCRY

She rides the last few minutes
hard, pressing her heels
in the stirrups, keeping what she can
concealed, a stone mid-fist.

But now she's grown too big, the room
too lit with wet. A man
has got a hand in her again, he wants
to pick her pocket, leave her flat.
The room begins to heave,
the white elastic walls of senses
wow, the words well up, the skin
must give and give until the sheet-

rock splits, the syllable comes
leaking from her lips:
her body breaks

in two. Spectators
grin. The sex
is speakable.
The secret's out.

A PHYSICS

When you get down to it, Earth
has our own great ranges
of feeling—Rocky, Smoky, Blue—
and a heart that can melt stones.

The still pools fill with sky,
as if aloof, and we have eyes
for all of this—and more, for Earth's
reminding moon. We too are ruled

by such attractions—spun and swaddled,
rocked and lent a light. We run
our clocks on wheels, our trains
on time. But all the while we want

to love each other endlessly—not only for
a hundred years, not only six feet up and down.
We want the suns and moons of silver
in ourselves, not only counted coins in a cup. The whole

idea of love was not to fall. And neither was
the whole idea of God. We put him well
above ourselves, because we meant,
in time, to measure up.

CAROLYN FORCHÉ

Carolyn Forché's most famous collection almost did not get published. When it did appear, controversy ensued. The book was *The Country Between Us*, based on Forché's experiences in 1979–1980 in El Salvador, where with Archbishop Oscar Humberto Romero she worked to locate people who had "disappeared" early in the twelve-year dirty war waged through death squads run by the right wing and military forces. For his outspokenness against violence and the government's civil rights offenses, Romero himself was murdered on March 24, 1980, while saying Mass. During her efforts tracing and reporting the whereabouts of victims to Amnesty International, Forché learned of numerous atrocities, particularly against helpless peasants. Seared into memory or reconstructed, horrific images of the outrages formed the graphic contents of the volume. All the publishers Forché approached turned it down, though one expressed interest—provided she "balanced" the collection with lighter, more standard pieces. She refused. Finally she sent the manuscript to Margaret Atwood, and with her aid *The Country Between Us* was accepted by Harper & Row and published in 1981.

Although conflicts over eight decades of the century had already produced savagery on a colossal scale, and while numerous poets in Eastern Europe and Latin America had treated war, state-sponsored terror, and political oppression in their work, often at great personal cost, in the United States it was still considered inappropriate, almost taboo, to depict those harsh realities in poetry. Critics took Forché to task for violating decorum in speaking up about such things as torture in verse. Commenting on these initial negative reactions, Forché remarked that they denied a North American author's right even "to contemplate such issues in her work" and argued "against any mixing of what they saw as the mutually exclusive realms of the personal and the political." (Similar objections were also raised against the explicit political poetry that issued from the various civil rights movements.) Ordinary readers ignored the supposed rules about what was "proper" in poetry: *The Country Between Us* attracted a large audience and had several printings.

Carolyn Louise Forché was born April 28, 1950, in Detroit, where her father worked as a tool and die maker. Her mother was of Czech descent and raised their seven children according to church teaching. Forché has termed herself a "junkheap Catholic," drawn early to issues of social justice and impressed as a child by pictures in *Look* magazine of a Nazi concentration camp. With her mother's encouragement, she began writing poems when she was nine. She studied at Michigan State University for her B.A. (1972) and at Bowling Green for the M.F.A. (1976). Eventually she took a series of teaching positions, at the University of Arkansas, Columbia, Vassar, Skidmore, and other institutions, before joining the fine arts faculty at George Mason University in 1994.

Forché's first collection, *Gathering the Tribes* (1976), was chosen by Stanley Kunitz for the Yale Younger Poet Series. The work was highly praised, especially by the old-time rebel Kenneth Rexroth,

who somewhat inaccurately identified the author as a "genuine pro-
letarian poet." In the well-crafted book Forché did include working-
class people, including her immigrant grandmother, but she focused
on the strong bonds within the family and her experiences growing
up: topics typical of first books of poetry then (as now and earlier),
with no overtly political slant. She then began translating the exiled
El Salvadoran poet Claribel Alegria, and on a Guggenheim fellow-
ship visited her in Majorca to work on *Flowers from the Volcano*
(1983). Alegria's nephew, Leonel Gomez Vides, urged her to see
their homeland, where he predicted war would break out in a few
years. She recalls him inquiring bluntly: "[D]o you want to write po-
etry about yourself for the rest of your life?" So instead of staying in
Europe, she decided to use the fellowship to go to El Salvador, ar-
riving in 1978 and, as it happened, only months before the violence
erupted.

Forché's work for Amnesty International brought her in fre-
quent contact with Romero, who was under serious threat. As the
situation worsened, he advised her to return home, to tell the Amer-
ican people what was happening and urge them to stop U.S. military
aid, which was being used for repressive purposes. In her investiga-
tions she also met sinister figures on the other side, including "The
Colonel," who became the subject of the most disturbing item in
The Country Between Us. Deliberately avoiding "poetic" effects,
Forché presented the macabre story without emotion. "What you
have heard is true," it begins. "I was in his house. His wife carried a
tray of coffee and sugar." After an ordinary visit with the family, the
Colonel produces a grocery sack and spills on the table the contents:
many human ears removed from people he has tortured. The poet
records that they looked like "dried peach halves." The Colonel
asks, "Something for your poetry, no?" The flat exposition and doc-
umentary manner here and elsewhere are unnerving, and the style is
what Forché came to call her "poetry of witness."

Although only one part of her book treated explicitly her expe-
riences in El Salvador, it was the most quoted and hotly debated sec-
tion of *The Country Between Us*, and propelled Forché into celebrity
status beyond the poetry community, especially among activists
against U.S. policy in Latin America. The animosity it generated
she suspects was responsible for the thirteen-year interval before her
next volume was published. Meanwhile Forché taught, and in 1983
she was a correspondent for National Public Radio in Beirut during

the civil war in Lebanon, including the bombing of the barracks housing U.S. and French troops.

By the time *The Angel of History* came out in 1994, the world had seen and was on the brink of several even greater atrocities in internecine warfare, including the massacres in Bosnia and the genocide in Rwanda. Now Forché's once-controversial position on poetry as witness to contemporary history seemed no longer questionable but commendable. The new volume itself was stronger, subtler, and more various that its predecessor, qualities recognized by the *Los Angeles Times* Book Award. Beyond her eyewitness observations of the destruction in El Salvador and Beirut, Forché treats the Chernobyl nuclear disaster and reimagines the major atrocities of World War II and the Nazi Holocaust, as well as the devastation inflicted by the atomic bombs in Japan. The several sections form a multifaceted depiction of catastrophe and a powerful commentary on the inhumanity during and the torment following warfare. Among the voices heard are those of a suicidal survivor of the Nazis in a Paris hospital, the poet's Czech grandmother, and Miklós Radnóti, the Hungarian poet whose final work was found on his body in a concentration camp mass grave. The sequence is represented here by "The Garden Shukkei-en," in which a Hiroshima survivor, now a tour guide in the Garden, speaks for those who lived but still suffer in memory and bewilderment at what befell the city.

In 1993, Forché published *Blue Hour*, returning to such personal topics as family history and motherhood, but in an even more stripped-down, almost impersonal style. Her tone is elusive but strangely intriguing, like the "blue hour" between darkness and dawn of the title, the moment of possible awakening into new understanding. The greater part of the book is made up of a forty-six-page sequence, "On Earth," organized in an abecedarian format (each section formed by words and concepts arranged by a different letter, through the alphabet), which is both connected (or at least associative) and random. The volume received the National Book Critics Circle Award.

Forché has also received prizes from the Academy of American Poets (the Lamont Selection, for *Country*) and the Poetry Society of America, and fellowships from the National Endowment for the Arts and the Guggenheim and Lannan foundations, as well as the Edita and Ira Morris Hiroshima Foundation Award for Peace and Culture. In 1993 she edited the anthology *Against Forgetting: Twentieth-Century*

Poetry of Witness, and in 2001 she published, with Philip Gerard, *Writing Creative Non-Fiction*. Her other translations include works by the Palestinian Mahmoud Darwish, *Unfortunately, It Was Paradise: Selected Poems* (with Munir Akash, 2003), and the Holocaust victim Robert Desnos's *Selected Poetry* (with William Kulik, 1991). With her husband, the photographer Harry Mattison, she also collaborated on *El Salvador: Work of Thirty Photographers* (1983). She lives in Maryland with him and their son, Sean Christophe Mattison, a filmmaker.

THE GARDEN SHUKKEI-EN

By way of a vanished bridge we cross this river
as a cloud of lifted snow would ascend a mountain.

She has always been afraid to come here.

It is the river she most
remembers, the living
and the dead both crying for help.

A world that allowed neither tears nor lamentation.

The *matsu* trees brush her hair as she passes
beneath them, as do the shining strands of barbed wire.

Where this lake is, there was a lake,
where these black pine grow, there grew black pine.

Where there is no teahouse I see a wooden teahouse
and the corpses of those who slept in it.

On the opposite bank of the Ota, a weeping willow
etches its memory of their faces into the water.

Where light touches the face, the character for heart is written.

She strokes a burnt trunk wrapped in straw:
I was weak and my skin hung from my fingertips like cloth.

Do you think for a moment we were human beings to them?

She comes to the stone angel holding paper cranes.
Not an angel, but a woman where she once had been,

who walks through the garden Shukkei-en
calling the carp to the surface by clapping her hands.

Do Americans think of us?

So she began as we squatted over the toilets:
If you want, I'll tell you, but nothing I say will be enough.

We tried to dress our burns with vegetable oil.

Her hair is the white froth of rice rising up kettlesides, her mind
    also.
In the postwar years she thought deeply about how to live.

The common greeting *dozo-yiroshku* is please take care of me.
All *hibakusha* still alive were children then.

A cemetery seen from the air is a child's city.

I don't like this particular red flower because
it reminds me of a woman's brain crushed under a roof.

Perhaps my language is too precise, and therefore difficult to
    understand?

We have not, all these years, felt what you call happiness.
But at times, with good fortune, we experience something close.
As our life resembles life, and this garden the garden.
And in the silence surrounding what happened to us

it is the bell to awaken God that we've heard ringing.

RITA DOVE

Rita Dove was the youngest person ever to win the Pulitzer Prize
and only the second African American, after Gwendolyn Brooks,
when in 1985, at age thirty-two, she received the award for *Thomas*

and Beulah, a cinematic sequence based on her maternal grandparents' youth, courtship, and long marriage. The twice-told story, from the alternating viewpoints of each protagonist, was the first long poem devoted to the migration of millions of blacks from the rural South to the urban North, one of the most significant social movements in twentieth-century America. History is a major preoccupation in Dove's poetry, particularly events that are underreported or disregarded and lives of people who are ignored in official accounts. The poet revives great issues of the past, not by editorializing but through specific, identifiable instances.

Rita Dove was born August 28, 1952, in Akron, Ohio, where her father, a research chemist, was the first black scientist to be employed in the rubber industry, at Goodyear Tire. Ray Dove was a stern disciplinarian and teacher who drilled his offspring the old-fashioned way, by rote—a trying experience his daughter later depicted with mixed feelings in her poem "Flash Cards":

> . . . *What you don't understand,*
> *master*, my father said; the faster
> I answered, the faster they came.

Having suffered discrimination himself, her father took pains to protect his children from it, the poet has said. But he could not shield her from every indignity, as she discovered at the age of ten on a visit to a segregated "forbidden beach" in Florida, described in "Crab-Boil," a short and very subtle exposition of a sensitive young girl's reasoning as she is confronted by a moral dilemma. In the intense drama of the poem, the conflict between the child's delicate conscience and the forces of conformity demonstrates, and quietly comments on, larger questions of justice and compromise in society. These and other memorable poems about childhood were gathered in *Grace Notes*, published in 1989.

Like her older brother and two younger sisters, the future poet made frequent trips to the public library. As a child Dove became intrigued by the German books in her father's home library, and studied the language in high school. A very conscientious student, she was named a Presidential Scholar in 1970, as one of the one hundred most outstanding graduates in the nation that year. She then attended Miami University, in Oxford, Ohio, where she won a scholarship, graduated summa cum laude, and was elected to Phi Beta Kappa in 1973.

She received a Fulbright fellowship for 1974–1975, which she used to study European literature at the University of Tübingen, in Germany. On her return from Europe she entered the Iowa Writers' Workshop where she received her M.F.A. in 1977. While at Iowa she met and translated work by the German-born novelist and poet Fred Viebahn, who was in the International Writing Program. They married two years later and have a grown daughter, Aviva, born in 1983.

Dove's first book, *The Yellow House on the Corner*, was published to good reviews in 1980. The collection is wide-ranging, containing both slave narratives and biographies of noted composers, as well as three affecting reminiscences of "Adolescence." *Museum* (1984) reveals a more diverse range of historical subjects, from fossils to the life of Catherine of Siena. Tales from Boccaccio mingle with the life of the black abolitionist David Walker and "Parsley," Dove's striking account of the bizarre but true story of the massacre of twenty thousand Haitian laborers in the Dominican Republic by the dictator Rafael Trujillo. Because they could not trill the *r* in the Spanish word for parsley, *perejil*, he found a method to distinguish them from the Dominican workers and thus mark them for death. The poem unfolds with a tone of eerie calm that heightens the horror it reveals while affirming what Hannah Arendt termed "the banality of evil."

In 1993 Dove's *Selected Poems* appeared, with an introduction by the author. It was followed in 1995 by an impressive new volume, *Mother Love,* an intricately constructed series of sonnets in which Dove ingeniously reworks the myth of Demeter and Persephone in contemporary settings, to depict the complex relationship between parent and daughter and the rites of her passage to adulthood. *On the Bus with Rosa Parks* (2000) was named a *New York Times* Notable Book of the Year as well as a finalist for the National Book Critics Circle Award. It was followed by *American Smooth* (2004), which includes an ambitious historical sequence about black American soldiers in World War I.

Dove has also published a book of short stories, *Fifth Sunday* (1985); a novel, *Through the Ivory Gate* (1992); and a collection of essays, *The Poet's World* (1995). Her verse drama *The Darker Face of the Earth* (1994) was produced in a revised stage version at the 1996 Oregon Shakespeare Festival in Ashland and then at the Kennedy Center in 1997, and was presented at the Royal National Theatre in

London in 1999. Her song cycle "Seven for Love" was set to music by John Williams and premiered at Tanglewood in 1998 in a performance by the Boston Symphony conducted by the composer.

Dove began her teaching career in 1981 at Arizona State University in Tempe, and in 1989 joined the faculty at the University of Virginia, where she is now Commonwealth Professor of English. From 1993 to 1995 she served as Poet Laureate of the United States, in which position she directed imaginative programs to encourage the appreciation of poetry. She also advised Mrs. Clinton on poetry as part of the "America's Millennium" celebrations at the White House in 2000. She was appointed poet laureate of Virginia for 2004–2006. Besides the Pulitzer, Dove has received numerous awards, including more than twenty honorary doctorates, the 1996 National Humanities Medal/Charles Frankel prize, and the 1996 Heinz Award in the Arts and Humanities. Besides serving on the boards of several organizations, she was a senator of Phi Beta Kappa (1994–2000) and president of the Associated Writing Programs (1986–1987). She was elected a chancellor of the Academy of American Poets for the term 2006–2012, and is a member of P.E.N. American Center, the American Philosophical Society, and the American Academy of Arts and Sciences.

CRAB-BOIL

(Ft. Myers, 1962)

Why do I remember the sky
above the forbidden beach,
why only blue and the scratch,
shell on tin, of their distress?
The rest

imagination supplies:
bucket and angry pink beseeching
claws. Why does Aunt Helen
laugh before saying "Look at that—

a bunch of niggers, not
a-one get out 'fore the others pull him
back." I don't believe her—

just as I don't believe *they* won't come
and chase us back to the colored-only shore
crisp with litter and broken glass.

"When do we kill them?"
"Kill 'em? Hell, the water does *that*.
They don't feel a thing . . . no nervous system."

I decide to believe this: I'm hungry.
Dismantled, they're merely exotic,
a blushing meat. After all, she *has*
grown old in the South. If
we're kicked out now, I'm ready.

LOUISE ERDRICH

Louise Erdrich is best known now for her novels, but she began as a poet and has remained one. Her poetic output has been relatively small, but the work has been consistently fresh in its inventions and unflinching in its accounts of history. In each genre Erdrich composes in a conversational but heightened tone, with a keen ear for the nuances of speech that convey the essence of personalities. Just as her fiction has a lyrical cast, her poetry has strong narrative content and flow. Her stories in verse are artfully constructed to seem almost without artifice, and make their points with dry irony, sly humor, and sharp satire. But whether in the comic or the serious mode, the poet shows how, for better or (usually) worse, the past is always present.

First of seven children, Karen Louise Erdrich was born June 7, 1954. She was raised in Wahpeton, North Dakota, and is enrolled as a member of the Turtle Mountain Band of Chippewa, where her grandfather was tribal chair of the reservation. Her mother was French Ojibwe, her father of German descent; both worked at the Bureau of Indian Affairs school. Erdrich's father encouraged her childhood efforts, giving her a nickel for every story she wrote. She entered Dartmouth in the first class after the college went coeducational in 1972. That year too the Native American Studies Department opened, and Erdrich began to study her own background in a class taught by the chair, Michael Dorris, an anthropologist who later became her collaborator, then her husband.

After graduating she returned home to teach poetry writing to young people through a program of the North Dakota State Arts Council. She also took a succession of jobs—waitress, construction job flag signaler, lifeguard: useful experiences for her later work— and became an editor of *The Circle*, a Boston Indian Council newspaper. On a fellowship in 1978 she enrolled in the writing program at Johns Hopkins and began making poems and stories based on her Indian heritage. Most were rejected by publishers to whom she first submitted them but later appeared in her novels.

After earning her master's, Erdrich returned to Dartmouth as a writer-in-residence. Michael Dorris was impressed with her poetry, and the two exchanged work while he did research in New Zealand and she completed a textbook (*Imagination*, 1980). On his return they began collaborating on short fiction, and their story "The World's Greatest Fisherman" won the Nelson Algren competition. They married in 1981. They later expanded the story into the novel *Love Medicine*, published to great popular and critical acclaim in 1984. (It won the National Book Critics Circle Award and has never gone out of print.) It was followed by *The Beet Queen* (1986), *Tracks* (1988), *Bingo Palace* (1994), and *Tales of Burning Love* (1997). The five volumes, composed of interconnected short stories told by various narrators, track three generations of immigrant and Anishinaabe families in North Dakota from World War I to the present.

Erdrich also published her first poetry collection, *Jacklight*, in 1984, and followed that success with *Baptism of Desire* in 1989. Fourteen years later she reconfigured the best lyrics and sequences from these books, joining them with new, very touching autobiographical pieces and bold nature poems into *Original Fire*. Most of the work, early and more recent, centers on Native American culture and communal life, set against the ever-looming background of white encroachment on and final conquest of their land, and the ensuing, relentless destruction of traditional Indian ways of living.

This dark chronicle and its grim social and spiritual consequences Erdrich depicts memorably through a variety of representative and deeply resonant scenes: views of the mindless slaughter of the buffalo, the experiences of hapless runaways from an Indian boarding school, a dramatic monologue by a white woman in the seventeenth century describing her captivity with the Wampanoag and her ambivalence after her rescue, the reactions of Indian teenagers at a drive-in theater watching a John Wayne western's (per)version of their warrior ancestors' history, an account of an alcoholic uncle's boisterous, bittersweet family reunion. In the telling, Erdrich does not preach or moralize (readers can draw their own conclusions from the evidence), though a few late satirical pieces form scathing commentaries. Rather, she portrays people within their distinctive environments, from the legendary past to the often problematic present, not merely as historical examples but as individual human beings: shrewd, flawed, bold, damaged, determined, disappointed, and, despite all, *enduring*.

Other sections have a more direct narrative format, especially the poems that treat or retell various Native American myths. Erdrich adds her own comic (and bawdy) contribution to the Chippewa tradition of trickster fables in a series of "Potchikoo Stories," prose-poem tall tales about a "potato boy" born of a Chippewa girl after she was overwhelmed in a potato field. Although he lives to old age, he finally is undone when his daughters appear, block out the sun, and crush him. But after many misadventures, including visits to the placid Indian heaven and the white man's hell (where Erdrich posits a singularly modern torture), "Saint Potchikoo" still survives: "With his old body burnt, Potchikoo existed in his spiritual flesh. Yet having been to the other side of life and back, he wasn't sure where he belonged." Another large group, "The Butcher's Wife," is a loosely linked sequence that tells the far less humorous story of Mary Kröger, the title character's marriage, and her uneasy but eventful life after her husband's death. (The characters return and are given fuller treatment in Erdrich's novel *The Master Butchers Singing Club*, 2003.)

As the fourth section of *Original Fire*, "The Seven Sleepers" comprises highly irreverent poems based on the lives of the Savior, Mary Magdalene, and noted Roman Catholic saints, as well as decidedly irreligious and somewhat surreal takes on the Seven Sacraments. Erdrich's animus here rises from righteous anger at the harsh treatment, particularly the victimization of Indian children, at the hands of the "Holy Colonial Church." The vitriol builds to a corrosive climax in "The Buffalo Prayer" and "Rez Litany." The "Prayer" begins: "Our Lady of the Buffalo Bones, pray for us. / Our Lady of the bales of skins and rotting hulks / from which our tongues alone were taken, / pray for us. . . ." The "Litany" is a long recitation—and savage indictment—of the multiple malfeasances from which Native Americans have suffered, on or off the reservation, and of the systematic destruction of their culture, "beginning with Saint Assimilus, / patron of residential and of government / boarding schools." Perhaps more successful as polemic than satisfying as poetry, the bill of particulars scores the Indian Health Service for its "mistaken blood tests and botched / surgeries" and "the twin saints of commodity food" as well as the "triplicate documents and directives" demanded by the Bureau of Indian Affairs and "Saint Quantum, Martyr of Blood / and Holy Protector of the Tribal Rolls," and above all the scourge of alcoholism stemming from the days of the "trader's rum."

In "Original Fire," the concluding section of the book, Erdrich returns to her more characteristic poise in a series of piquant reflections on the experiences of childbearing, birth, and young motherhood. Besides memoirs from her childhood, the poet offers profound meditations on the natural world and the realm of the spirit that in tone and imagination reflect ancient Native American wisdom, most notably in the final sequence, "Asiniig."

Erdrich and Dorris also collaborated on *The Crown of Columbus* (1991). The only novel on which they publicly shared credit, it was not a great success, and their joint ventures ended. But they later completed a series of interviews collected in *Conversations with Louise Erdrich and Michael Dorris* (1994). The couple raised six children, three of them adopted. One son was killed by a car, another was involved in an unfortunate court case in 1995, after he accused them of child abuse. They divorced soon after. Dorris, who had long suffered from depression, committed suicide in 1997. Erdrich has since published several more novels. She also operates Birchbark Books in Minneapolis.

ASINIIG

The Ojibwe word for stone, asin, is animate. Stones are alive. They are addressed as grandmothers and grandfathers. The Universe began with a conversation between stones.

I

A thousand generations of you live and die
in the space of a single one of our thoughts.
A complete thought is a mountain.
We don't have very many ideas.

When the original fire which formed us
subsided,
we thought of you.
We allowed you to occur.
We are still deciding whether that was
wise.

2 CHILDREN

We have never denied you anything
you truly wanted
no matter how foolish
no matter how destructive
but you never seem to learn.

That which you cry for,
this wish to be like us,
we have tried to give it to you
in small doses, like a medicine, every day
so you will not be frightened.
Still, when death comes
you weep,
you do not recognize it
as the immortality you crave.

3 THE SWEAT LODGE

We love it when you sing to us,
and speak to us,
and lift us from the heart of the fire
with the deer's antlers, and place us
in the center of the lodge.
Then we are at our most beautiful.
Powerful red blossoms,
we are breathing.
We can reach through your bones
to where you hurt.
You call us grandfather, grandmother.
You scatter bits of cedar, sage, wikenh, tobacco
and bear root over us,
and then the water
which cracks us to the core.

When we break ourselves open—
that is when the healing starts.
When you break yourselves open—
that is how the healing continues.

4 LOVE

If only you could be more like us
when it comes to the affections.
Have you ever seen a stone
throw itself?
On the other hand
whose idea do you think it is
to fly through the air?
Mystery is not a passive condition.
To see a thing so perfectly what it is—
doesn't it make you
want to hold it,
to marvel, to touch
its answered question?

5 GRATITUDE

You have no call to treat us this way.
We allow you to put us to every use.
Yet, when have you ever
stopped in the street to lay your forehead
against the cool, black granite facade
of some building, and ask the stone
to bless you?
We are not impartial.
We acknowledge some forms
of consideration.
We open for those
who adhere to our one rule
endure.

6 INFINITE THOUGHT

Listen, there is no consciousness
before birth or
after death
except the one you share

with us.
So you had best learn
how to speak to us now
without the use of signs.
Remember, there will be no hands,
except remembered hands.
No lips, no face,
except remembered face.
No legs and in fact no
appendages, except
the remembered ones,
which always hurt
as consciousness hurts.
Now do you understand what it is?
Your consciousness
is the itch, the ghost of consciousness,
remembered
from how it felt
to be one of us.

ADVICE TO MYSELF

Leave the dishes.
Let the celery rot in the bottom drawer of the refrigerator
and an earthen scum harden on the kitchen floor.
Leave the black crumbs in the bottom of the toaster.
Throw the cracked bowl out and don't patch the cup.
Don't patch anything. Don't mend. Buy safety pins.
Don't even sew on a button.
Let the wind have its way, then the earth
that invades as dust and then the dead
foaming up in gray rolls underneath the couch.
Talk to them. Tell them they are welcome.
Don't keep all the pieces of the puzzles
or the doll's tiny shoes in pairs, don't worry
who uses whose toothbrush or if anything
matches, at all.
Except one word to another. Or a thought.
Pursue the authentic—decide first

what is authentic,
then go after it with all your heart.
Your heart, that place
you don't even think of cleaning out.
That closet stuffed with savage mementos.
Don't sort the paper clips from screws from saved baby teeth
or worry if we're all eating cereal for dinner
again. Don't answer the telephone, ever,
or weep over anything at all that breaks.
Pink molds will grow within those sealed cartons
in the refrigerator. Accept new forms of life
and talk to the dead
who drift in though the screened windows, who collect
patiently on the tops of food jars and books.
Recycle the mail, don't read it, don't read anything
except what destroys
the insulation between yourself and your experience
or what pulls down or what strikes at or what shatters
this ruse you call necessity.

NOTES TO THE POEMS

EMILY DICKINSON

Introduction
plush: soft cushion, stuffed animal.
ignis fatuus: literally, foolish fire (Lat.). A phenomenon, also known as will-o'-the wisp, in which flickering lights appear over marshland, caused by ignition of gases from disintegrating organic matter. By extension, an illusion, something that deludes or misleads.

[I'm Nobody! Who are you?]
In the fascicle manuscript (there is no fair copy), Dickinson left an alternate version that substitutes the underscored words "*advertise*" for "banish us" and "*one's*" for "your." See Franklin's introduction to his reading edition, p. 8.

[I can wade Grief—]
"Give Himmaleh—": the Himalayas.

[I dwell in Possibility—]
Gambrels: sloping sides of a gable roof.
Tippet: long shoulder covering or stole (when a vestment worn by the Anglican clergy).
Tulle: fine mesh fabric made of silk; named after the French city.

MINA LOY

Gertrude Stein
Curie: Madame Maria Sk?odowska-Curie (1867–1934), Polish-French physicist and chemist who was the first woman to win the Nobel Prize and the only person to win it in both fields. She was also the first woman to be awarded a doctor's degree in France and the first female professor at the Sorbonne in Paris. With her husband Pierre, she discovered the elements radium and polonium; she coined the word *radioactivity*.

From *Songs to Joannes*
Joannes: Giovanni Papini (1881–1956), poet, critic, and journalist; a founder of the Futurist movement.
mezzanino: mezzanine (It.).
mucous-membrane: Loy's neologism, playing on "mucous membrane."
porte-enfant: baby carriage (Fr.).
sarsenet: fine silk cloth.
Shuttle-cock and battle-door: battledore: wooden paddle used in the game of badminton.

ELINOR WYLIE

Parting Gift
Metropolitan Tower: built in 1909 as the headquarters of the Metropolitan Life Insurance Company at Twenty-third Street and Madison Avenue in New York City. Clad in white marble and fifty-one stories (seven hundred feet) high, it was the world's tallest building until 1913.
Cluny Museum: Musée de Cluny in Paris, built on the site of the former Roman baths, originally a residence established by the abbots of Cluny. Besides the nine original gold crowns of the Visigoth kings (seventh-century Spain), it contains numerous artworks and artifacts (tapestries, jewelry, clothing, tools) from the Middle Ages and Renaissance.

H.D.

Birds in Snow
flags: flagstones.

From The Walls Do Not Fall
Luxor: site of the ancient Egyptian city of Thebes, where the ruins of the temple complexes of Luxor and Karnac are located. H.D. contrasts the "immortality" of Egyptian culture, despite the ravages of the ages, with the current destruction of London. On the raids, see note to Sitwell's "Still Falls the Rain," below.
Samuel: Old Testament judge and prophet, and the priest who anointed Saul and David, the first kings of Israel.
Pythian: the priestess in charge of the oracle at the shrine of Apollo at Delphi in Greece. While seated on a tripod above the fumes issuing from a fissure in the earth, the sibyl issued prophecies, apparently clearly; at other shrines the sibyls usually spoke unintelligibly or ambiguously, and their messages were interpreted by temple priests. The name itself is taken from Pytho, in legend the original name for Delphi.
Pompeii: an ancient Roman luxury resort town on the bay across from present-day Naples. It was buried by ash from an eruption of the volcano Vesuvius in August of 79 A.D., which preserved the city until it was rediscovered and first excavations began in 1748.

EDITH SITWELL

Sir Beelzebub

Beelzebub: the devil or chief spirit of evil, literally, "lord of the flies" (Hebrew); the name was first used for a Philistine god. In the Gospels of Mark and Luke it means Prince of Devils; in *Paradise Lost* Milton gives the name to Satan's right-hand fallen angel, and the term is sometimes used as synonymous with Satan.

syllabub: dessert made of whipped cream and liquor (usually brandy) or wine (sherry).

Proserpine: called Persephone in Greek myth, she was abducted from her mother Demeter (Ceres to the Romans), goddess of the Earth, by Hades (Pluto or Dis), king of the Underworld. As a result of her captivity underground, the land became barren, and the starving people beseeched Zeus, her father, that she be released to her mother; they were reunited and fertility returned. But Hades tricked Persephone into eating the seeds of a pomegranate (four or six, in different versions), and for each one she consumed she had to return for a month to the Underworld: thus the origin of the seasons of winter and summer.

gendarmerie: French police. Their uniforms are dark blue.

Tennyson: Alfred, Lord Tennyson (1809–1892) was given the title after he was named Poet Laureate, following Wordsworth (1770–1850); two of his most famous poems are "Crossing the Bar" (a bar is a sandy ridge in a harbor) and *In Memoriam A.H.H.*, a long elegy to his friend Arthur Henry Hallam (1811–1833), also a poet, whom he met when they were students at Cambridge.

Balaclava: site of a major battle in 1854 during the Crimean War, described in Tennyson's *The Charge of the Light Brigade*.

Still Falls the Rain

The Raids: during the Battle of Britain, beginning August 13, 1940, the Germans sent waves of bombing raids on England, and London was targeted repeatedly over a period of eight months. Originally Hitler planned only to destroy the Royal Air Force, and succeeded in taking out a quarter of the aircraft. But on August 24, 1940, a German plane bombed London accidentally; Britain retaliated by bombing Berlin. Furious, Hitler ordered the Luftwaffe to bomb London exclusively thereafter. On the first night alone, six hundred German bombers passed over, dropping explosives and incendiaries on East London, where factories and the docks were located. During the onslaught, the English tried to carry on life as normally as possible. But eventually more than 100,000 buildings were destroyed and 30,000 Londoners were killed by the bombs and the fires that ensued.

Potter's Field: cemetery reserved for strangers and indigents outside ancient Jerusalem. When Judas threw away the thirty pieces of silver he was paid to betray Jesus, the money was used to purchase the land; for that reason it was also called the Field of Blood.

Dives and Lazarus: in the parable by Jesus related in the Gospel of Luke (16:19–31), Dives the rich man goes to hell, but Lazarus, a beggar and leper, is sent to heaven.

baited bear: as a popular entertainment in the Middle Ages and later, chained bears were made to defend themselves while being set upon by dogs.

O Ile leape . . .: Faustus's cry of despair at the conclusion of Christopher Marlowe's play *The Tragical History of Dr. Faustus* (1604), when he realizes he has lost his soul and is condemned to hell by the bargain he made with Mephistopheles.

Caesar's laurel crown: compared by Sitwell with the crown of thorns placed on Christ's head in mockery as "King of the Jews." The laurels were a sign of victory, worn by Julius Caesar in triumphal procession; but here, "dark-smirched with pain," the crown's ironic significance is emphasized: after he assumed dictatorial powers, Caesar was stabbed to death on the floor of the Roman Senate chamber, March 15 (the Ides), 44 B.C.

MARIANNE MOORE

No Swan So Fine

Moore's note: "A pair of Louis XV candelabra with Dresden figures of swans belonging to Lord Balfour. 'There is no water so still as in the dead fountains of Versailles.' Percy Phillip, *New York Times Magazine*, May 19, 1931."

Versailles: huge palace and gardens outside Paris. Begun by Louis XIII in 1624 as a hunting lodge, it was enlarged to giant proportions and furnished in lavish style by succeeding monarchs, especially Louis XIV, who made it the seat of power. The dynasty ended with the execution of Louis XVI and his queen, Marie-Antoinette, in 1793. Unlike the dead royalty who possessed them, the porcelain candelabra, like other fine works of art, "live" on.

The Past Is the Present

Habakkuk: Old Testament prophet. The Book of Habakkuk, attributed to him, is the eighth of the twelve named after the minor prophets in the Hebrew Bible.

Silence

Longfellow's grave: Henry Wadsworth Longfellow (1807–1882) was the most popular American poet of his time. A Harvard professor for twenty years, he lived almost half a century in Cambridge, Massachusetts, and is buried in the city's Mount Auburn Cemetery, the first "garden cemetery" in the United States.

glass flowers at Harvard: in the University's Museum of Natural History, the collection of some 4,000 exquisitely detailed botanical models in colored glass representing almost 850 species. Originally commissioned in 1886 by Professor George Lincoln Goodale, the pieces were created by the German artisans Leopold Blaschka and his son Rudolph, working until

1936. A massive conservation project was begun in 1998 to preserve the fragile collection, which is still consulted by students.

PHYLLIS McGINLEY

Public Journal
Isherwood, Spender, et al.: all longtime friends from their Oxford days or earlier. Christopher Isherwood (1904–1986), fiction writer, playwright, author of *Berlin Stories, I Am a Camera,* and many other works, collaborated with Auden on the plays *The Dog Beneath the Skin, The Ascent of F6,* and *On the Frontier.* In the twenties the two spent time together in Berlin with Stephen Spender (1909–1995), poet, literary biographer, and critic; during the Spanish Civil War, Auden and Spender went to Spain with the International Brigade fighting Franco's fascists, and Spender reported on the conflict for the British Communist party. W. H. Auden (1907–1973), greatest and best-known poet of the group, was also a noted critic, librettist, and anthologist; in 1936 he traveled to Iceland with L(ouis) MacNeice (1907–1963), poet and longtime broadcaster with the BBC, and together they wrote *Letters from Iceland* (1937). Auden also traveled to China with Isherwood during the Sino-Japanese War in 1938, and together they wrote *Journey to a War* (1939). Unlike his friends, MacNeice never joined a political party and was always skeptical of what he called "the armchair reformist." McGinley's poem was originally published in the *Atlantic Monthly* in July 1940, several months after Isherwood and Auden immigrated to the States in 1939, when England was on the brink of war, which created controversy and much criticism against the two. Both eventually became U.S. citizens.
Czecho-Slovakia and the invaded border: in the fall of 1938 Nazi Germany took over the country on the pretext of protecting ethnic Germans living in the Sudetenland, the region along the northern and western borders of Czechoslovakia. It did so with impunity, after British Prime Minister Neville Chamberlain signed an agreement in Munich on September 29, 1938, and with the complicity of other Western European countries offered up the country to appease Hitler. Waving the papers on his return to England, Chamberlain uttered words that came back to haunt him: "I believe it is peace for our time." Hitler soon violated the agreement, and World War II broke out about eleven months later.
Anthony Eden: Eden (1897–1977), a longtime English diplomat noted for his elegant manners and attire, frequently wore a style of Homburg (bowler) hat that became known as an "Anthony Eden." British foreign secretary 1935–1938, he was opposed to appeasement and resigned in February 1938 when Chamberlain began negotiations with Mussolini's fascist government (Italy being Hitler's closest ally).
stormy petrol: *petrol*: English term for gasoline; a play on the term (*stormy*) *petrel*, a small sea bird of the North Atlantic and Mediterranean with sooty-colored plumage.

Austin: small, relatively inexpensive automobile manufactured in England by the Austin Motor Car Company.
like Poland: Germany invaded Poland on September 1, 1939, and ruthlessly conquered the unprepared country. McGinley's catalogue, mixing the monumentally catastrophic with the trivial, mocks the mentioned poets using a device typical of Alexander Pope (cf. *The Rape of the Lock*).

JUDITH WRIGHT

Bora Ring
Title: circular platform of beaten earth used by Australian Aborigines for ceremonies, particularly initiation rites.
corroboree: Aboriginal dance ceremony held at night with songs and rhythmic musical accompaniment to celebrate sacred or nonsacred events such as tribal victories.

Ishtar
Title: Ishtar was the Babylonian and Assyrian goddess of love and fertility, as well as war; in Semitic cultures she was called Astarte. Known as the "courtesan of the gods" and as a cruel and fickle lover, she was associated with sexuality in general, and her cult practiced sacred prostitution.

AMY CLAMPITT

Nothing Stays Put
Dedication: James Harold Flye was an Episcopal priest who taught history for many years at St. Andrew's School in Sewanee, Tennessee, and is best known for his friendship with James Agee, the author of *A Death in the Family* and *Let Us Now Praise Famous Men*. They met when Agee was ten years old, and Fr. Flye became a mentor, confidant, and almost a foster father to him. They corresponded until Agee's death, from a heart attack, in 1955. *Letters of James Agee to Father Flye* was published in 1962, with later editions. Fr. Flye retired in 1954 and moved to New York City in 1959, where until the early seventies he assisted at the Church of St. Luke in Greenwich Village.
protea: flowering plants, also called sugarbushes; the genus was given the name by Linnaeus in 1735, after the Greek god Proteus, who could change shape at will, since proteas also have many different forms. Botanists discovered a species of the plant in South Africa ("the antipodes") in the seventeenth century.
alstroemerias: brightly colored flowers with little or no scent, originally native to South America, mostly Chile and Brazil. There are some fifty species, all members of the Amaryllis family.
freesia: fragrant flowering plant native to Africa, named after the German physician Friedrich Heinrich Theodor Freese (1795–1876).
cannas: canna lilies.

CAROLYN KIZER

From Pro Femina

Sappho: ancient Greek lyric poet, born on the island of Lesbos between 630 and 612 B.C., died c. 570 B.C. Widely known and praised in antiquity, most of Sappho's poetry is now lost or exists only in fragments.

Juvenal: Roman satiric poet of the late first century–early second century A.D. His verses, much admired and imitated over the centuries, contain severe critiques of the pagan world and are noted for their misogynistic remarks.

Strindberg: August Strindberg (1849–1912), Swedish painter and playwright, and one of the fathers of naturalistic modern theater. He was considered a misogynist, perhaps unfairly; in any case, each of his three marriages ended in acrimonious divorce. His plays include *Miss Julie* and *The Dance of Death*. One of his oft-quoted remarks: "Only men can love, and it blinds them."

Nietzsche: Friedrich Nietzsche (1844–1900), highly influential German philosopher, debunked the core beliefs of Western civilization, religion, and morality; noted for his concept of the *Übermensch* (Superman or overman) in *Thus Spake Zarathustra* (*Also Sprach Zarathustra*, 1883–1885) and his declaration that "God is dead" in *The Gay Science* (*Die fröhliche Wissenschaft*, 1882).

Defarges: after Madame Thérèse Defarge, the great villainess of Charles Dickens's novel *A Tale of Two Cities* (1859), in which she sits quietly knitting while plotting ruthless revenge on aristocrats in the aftermath of the French Revolution. Their names were secretly stitched into her needlework.

pomegranate . . . dead: see note on Proserpine for Sitwell's "Sir Beelzebub" above.

Athena: the Greek goddess of wisdom and protector of heroes, she sprang fully grown from the forehead of her father, Zeus, king of the gods. The patron of weaving, she is most often portrayed in her role as a warrior deity wearing a helmet and breastplate (the aegis) and carrying a shield decorated with the head of the Gorgon Medusa.

MAXINE KUMIN

The Envelope

Martin Heidegger: German philosopher (1889–1976), author of *Being and Time* (1927). He wrote a great deal on the fear of dying, and believed Western philosophical investigations into the question of being itself were fundamentally flawed. His ideas and approach influenced the work of many modern and contemporary thinkers, including Jean-Paul Sartre, Karl Jaspers, Leo Strauss, and Michel Foucault, and his students Herbert Marcuse and Hannah Arendt.

A Calling
Georgia O'Keeffe: American artist (1887–1986) famed for her somewhat abstract paintings of flowers, natural objects, and scenes of the southwest United States, where she spent many summers and settled (in New Mexico) in her later life.

ANNE SEXTON

Housewife
Jonah: Hebrew prophet. In the Book of Jonah he is commanded by God to prophesy in Nineveh, but does not wish to go and instead sails to Joppa and Tarshish. When a great storm arises, he admits to the sailors that he is the reason, and asks to be thrown overboard. He is swallowed by a whale, which saves him from drowning; and when he prays for forgiveness, God answers his plea and has the whale vomit him up onto dry land.

ADRIENNE RICH

"I am in Danger—Sir—"
Higginson: Rich's note: "See *The Letters of Emily Dickinson*, Thomas Johnson and Theodora Ward, eds., Vol. 2 (Cambridge: Harvard University Press, 1958), p. 409." In one of her letters to the editor Thomas Wentworth Higginson, who considered her poems faulty, Dickinson wrote: "You think my gait 'spasmodic'—I am in danger—Sir—you think me 'uncontrolled'— I have no Tribunal." He described her as "my partially cracked poetess at Amherst." Concerning Higginson, see the introduction to Dickinson above.
snood: head-covering, hairnet.
at Harvard: the Rare Book Library holds Dickinson manuscripts, personal items, and memorabilia; the sheets were the basis for Thomas H. Johnson's three-volume variorum edition of the poems (1955), listing variant readings of the texts, and the later, definitive edition by R. W. Franklin (Harvard University Press, 1998, 1999).

SYLVIA PLATH

Daddy
In a BBC broadcast, Plath explained that the persona in the poem was "a girl with an Electra complex," complicated by the fact that "her father was also a Nazi and her mother very possibly part Jewish." The two "strains" combine in the daughter "and paralyse each other—she has to act out the awful little allegory once over before she is free of it." (Note to the poem in Diane Wood Middlebrook's edition of Plath's poems for Everyman's Library Pocket Poets, 1998.) In his edition of *The Collected Poems* (1981), Ted Hughes omitted the poem.

Ghastly statue . . . gray toe: alluding to the giant figure of Otto Plath as represented in "The Colossus" and to the gangrene that resulted from his diabetes.

Nauset: beach near Boston.

Ach, du: Ah, you (German).

Polish town: Grabow, Dr. Plath's birthplace.

Dachau, Auschwitz, Belsen: Nazi concentration camps in Poland (Auschwitz) and Germany (Dachau, Bergen-Belsen) where Jews, Gypsies, homosexuals, and other "undesirables" were exterminated during World War II.

Tyrol: Austrian alps.

Taroc: Tarot cards.

Luftwaffe: German air force.

Meinkampf: referring to Hitler and his autobiography *Mein Kampf* (My Struggle, first published in 1925).

MARGE PIERCY

For strong women
Boris Godunov: long Russian opera by Modest Mussorgsky (1839–1881).

For the young who want to
phlogiston: a term formerly used for a hypothetical substance believed to be a constituent of all combustible substances. It was thought to be released as a flame in combustion.

EAVAN BOLAND

The Pomegranate
legend: for a summary of the story of Proserpine and Demeter, see note to Sitwell's "Sir Beelzebub" above.

CAROLYN FORCHÉ

The Garden Shukkei-en
Forché's note: "Shukkei-en is an ornamental garden in Hiroshima. It has been restored. The Ota is one of the rivers of Hiroshima." The first (and only) use of nuclear weapons in war occurred in Japan. On August 6, 1945, the so-called "Little Boy" bomb was dropped by the U.S. B-29 Super-fortress *Enola Gay* on Hiroshima, a target of some military and industrial importance with a population of about 250,000 at that time. An estimated 70,000 people, most of them civilians, were killed outright by the blast, many more soon after, bringing the toll in 1945 to perhaps 140,000. Many others died of radiation poisoning in the decades that followed. On August 9, 1945, the "Fat Man" bomb was dropped on Nagasaki; an estimated

74,000 were killed there. Japan surrendered to the Allied Powers on August 15, 1945; the formal instrument was signed on September 2, officially ending World War II.

hibakusha: survivors of the bombings; the Japanese word means literally "explosion-affected people." In 2005 there were about 266,000 *hibakusha* living in the country.

CREDITS

EVERY EFFORT has been made to identify, locate, and secure permission wherever necessary from those who hold rights to the poems in this anthology. Any omitted acknowledgments brought to the editors' attention will be added to future editions.

Fleur Adcock: "Advice to a Discarded Lover" and "Poem Ended by Death" from *Poems 1960–2000* by Fleur Adcock. Copyright © 2000 by Fleur Adcock. Reprinted by permission of Bloodaxe Books, 2005. Margaret Atwood: "Carrying Food Home in Winter," "Crow Song," "Habitation," "Pig Song," "Rat Song," "The Animals in that Country," and excerpt from "You Fit into Me" from *Selected Poems, 1965–1975* by Margaret Atwood. Copyright © 1976 by Margaret Atwood. Reprinted by permission of Houghton Mifflin Company. All rights reserved. "Carrying Food Home in Winter," "Habitation," and "The Animals in that Country" from *Selected Poems 1966–1984* by Margaret Atwood. Copyright © 1990 by Oxford University Press Canada. Reprinted by permission of the publisher.

Louise Bogan: "Women" from *The Blue Estuaries* by Louise Bogan. Copyright © 1968 by Louise Bogan. Copyright © renewed 1996 by Ruth Limmer. Reprinted by permission of Farrar, Straus and Giroux, LLC. Eavan Boland: "The Pomegranate" from *In a Time of Violence* by Eavan Boland. Copyright © 1994 by Eavan Boland. Used by permission of W.W. Norton & Company, Inc. Gwendolyn Brooks: "kitchenette building" and "We Real Cool" from *Selected Poems* by Gwendolyn Brooks. Copyright © 1944, 1945, 1949, 1959, 1960, 1963 by Gwendolyn Brooks Blakely. Reprinted by consent of Brooks Permissions.

Amy Clampitt: "Nothing Stays Put" from *Collected Poems of Amy Clampitt* by Amy Clampitt. Copyright © 1997 by the Estate of Amy Clampitt. Used by permission of Alfred A. Knopf, a division of Random House, Inc. Lucille Clifton: "the lost baby poem" and excerpt from "in the inner city" from *Good Woman: Poems and a Memoir 1969–1980* by Lucille Clifton. Copyright © 1987 by Lucille Clifton. Reprinted with the permission of BOA Editions Ltd., www.boaeditions.org.

Emily Dickinson: Poems reprinted by permission of the publishers and the Trustees of Amherst College from *The Poems of Emily Dickinson: Reading Edition*, Ralph W. Franklin, ed., Cambridge, Mass.: The Belknap Press of Harvard University Press, Copyright © 1998, 1999 by the President and Fellows of Harvard College. Copyright © 1951, 1955, 1979, 1983 by the President and Fellows of Harvard College. H.D. (Hilda Doolittle): "Birds in Snow" from *Collected Poems, 1912–1944* by H.D. (Hilda Doolittle). Copyright © 1982 by The Estate of Hilda Doolittle. "The Walls Do Not Fall [I, VI]" from *Trilogy*. Copyright © 1944, 1945, 1946 by Oxford University Press, renewed 1973 by Norman Holmes Pearson. Reprinted by permission of New Directions Publishing Corp. Rita Dove: "Crab-Boil" and excerpt from "Flash Cards" from *Grace Notes* by Rita Dove. Copyright © 1989 by Rita Dove. Used by permission of the author and W.W. Norton & Company, Inc.

Louise Erdrich: "Advice to Myself," "Asiniig," and excerpts from "Rez Litany" and "The Buffalo Prayer" from *Original Fire: Selected and New Poems* by Louise Erdrich. Copyright © 2003 by Louise Erdrich. Reprinted by permission of HarperCollins Publishers.

Carolyn Forché: "The Garden Shukkei-en" from *The Angel of History* by Carolyn Forché. Copyright © 1994 by Carolyn Forché. Reprinted by permission of Harper-Collins Publishers.

Nikki Giovanni: "Legacies" and excerpt from "My House" from *My House* by Nikki Giovanni. Copyright © 1972 by Nikki Giovanni. Excerpt from "Woman Poem" from *Black Feeling, Black Talk, Black Judgment* by Nikki Giovanni. Copyright © 1968, 1970 by Nikki Giovanni. Reprinted by permission of HarperCollins Publishers. Louise Glück: "A Fable" from *Ararat* by Louise Glück. Copyright © 1990 by Louise Glück. Reprinted by permission of HarperCollins Publishers. "Eros" from *The Seven Ages* by Louise Glück. Copyright © 2001 by Louise Glück. Reprinted by permission of HarperCollins Publishers. Excerpt from "Witchgrass" from *The Wild Iris* by Louise Glück. Copyright © 1992 by Louise Glück. Reprinted by permission of HarperCollins Publishers.

Marilyn Hacker: "Invocation" from *Squares and Courtyards* by Marilyn Hacker. Copyright © 2000 by Marilyn Hacker. "Morning News" from *Desesperanto: Poems 1999–2002* by Marilyn Hacker. Copyright © 2003 by Marilyn Hacker. Used by permission of W.W. Norton & Company, Inc. Excerpt from "Occasional Verses" from *Separations* by Marilyn Hacker. Copyright © 1972, 1973, 1974, 1975, 1976 by Marilyn Hacker. Reprinted by permission of Frances Collin, Literary Agent.

Jane Kenyon: "Happiness," "Otherwise," and excerpt from "Rain in January" from *Collected Poems* by Jane Kenyon. Copyright © 2005 by The Estate of Jane Kenyon. Reprinted by permission of Graywolf Press, Saint Paul, Minnesota. Carolyn Kizer: "Children" from *Yin* by Carolyn Kizer. Copyright © 1984 by Carolyn Kizer. Reprinted with the permission of BOA Editions, Ltd., www.boaeditions.org. "Pro Femina I" and "Pro Femina II" from *Cool, Calm and Collected: Poems 1960–2000* by Carolyn Kizer. Copyright © 2001 by Carolyn Kizer. Reprinted with the permission of Copper Canyon Press, www.coppercanyonpress.org. Maxine Kumin: "A Calling" and excerpt from "Nurture" copyright © 1989, 1997 by Maxine Kumin; "The Envelope" copyright © 1978, 1997 by Maxine Kumin; excerpt from "Woodchucks" copyright © 1972, 1997 by Maxine Kumin from *Selected Poems 1960–1990* by Maxine Kumin. Used by permission of W.W. Norton & Company, Inc.

Denise Levertov: "Divorcing" from *The Freeing of the Dust* by Denise Levertov. Copyright © 1975 by Denise Levertov. "The Ache of Marriage" from *Poems 1960–1967* by Denise Levertov. Copyright © 1966 by Denise Levertov. Reprinted by permission of New Directions Publishing Corp. Audre Lorde: "Now That I Am Forever with Child" from *The Collected Poems of Audre Lorde* by Audre Lorde. Copyright © 1976, 1982, 1992 by Audre Lorde. Copyright © 1997 by the Estate of Audre Lorde. Used by permission of W.W. Norton & Company, Inc. Amy Lowell: "Katydids" from *What's O'Clock* by Amy Lowell. Copyright © 1925 by Houghton Mifflin Company, copyright © renewed 1953 by Harvey H. Bundy and G. d'Andelot Belin, Jr., Trustees of the Estate of Amy Lowell. All rights reserved. Reprinted by permission of Houghton Mifflin Company. Mina Loy: "Gertrude Stein" and excerpts from "Songs to Joannes" from *The Lost Lunar Baedeker* by Mina Loy. Works of Mina Loy copyright © 1996 by the Estate of Mina Loy. Introduction and edition copyright © 1996 by Roger L. Conover. Reprinted by permission of Farrar, Straus and Giroux, LLC.

Phyllis McGinley: "Public Journal" from *Times Three* by Phyllis McGinley. Copyright © 1940 by Phyllis McGinley, renewed from *Times Three* by Phyllis McGinley. Used by permission of Viking Penguin, a division of Penguin Group (USA) Inc. Heather McHugh: "A Physics," "Outcry," and excerpt from "What He Thought" from *Hinge & Sign: Poems, 1968–1993* by Heather McHugh. Copyright © 1994 by Heather McHugh. Reprinted by permission of Wesleyan University Press. Marianne Moore: "No Swan So Fine," "Poetry," and "Silence," from *The Collected Poems of Marianne Moore* by Marianne Moore. Copyright © 1935 by Marianne Moore; copyright renewed © 1963 by Marianne Moore & T.S. Eliot. Reprinted by permission of Scribner, an imprint of Simon & Schuster Adult Publishing Group and the Literary Executor for the Moore Estate, Marianne Craig Moore. All rights reserved. "The Past Is the Present" from *The Poems of Marianne*

Moore, edited by Grace Schulman. Copyright © 2005 by Marianne Craig Moore. Reprinted by permission of the Literary Executor for the Moore Estate, Marianne Craig Moore. Lisel Mueller: Excerpt from "In Passing" from *Alive Together* by Lisel Mueller. Copyright © 1996 by Lisel Mueller. "Necessities" and excerpt from "Voyager" from *Second Language: Poems* by Lisel Mueller. Copyright © 1986 by Lisel Mueller. Reprinted by permission of Louisiana State University Press.

Sharon Olds: "The Language of the Brag" from *Satan Says* by Sharon Olds. Copyright © 1980 by Sharon Olds. Reprinted by permission of the University of Pittsburgh Press. "Topography" from *The Gold Cell* by Sharon Olds. Copyright © 1987 by Sharon Olds. Reprinted by permission of Alfred A. Knopf, a division of Random House, Inc. Mary Oliver: "Roses, Late Summer," excerpt from "Some Questions You Might Ask," and excerpt from "The Summer Day" from *House of Light* by Mary Oliver. Copyright © 1990 by Mary Oliver. Excerpts from "A Certain Sharpness in the Morning Air," "Gannets," and "October" from *New and Selected Poems Volume One* by Mary Oliver. Copyright © 1992 by Mary Oliver. Excerpt from "Poppies" from *Blue Iris* by Mary Oliver. Copyright © 2004 by Mary Oliver. Excerpt from "In the Storm," excerpt from "On Thy Wondrous Works I Will Meditate," and "The Place I Want to Get Back To" from *Thirst* by Mary Oliver. Copyright © 2006 by Mary Oliver. Reprinted by permission of Beacon Press, Boston. Excerpt from "Entering the Kingdom" from *Twelve Moons* by Mary Oliver. Copyright © 1972, 1973, 1974, 1976, 1977, 1978, 1979 by Mary Oliver. Excerpt from "Skunk Cabbage" from *American Primitive* by Mary Oliver. Copyright © 1978, 1979, 1980, 1981, 1982, 1983 by Mary Oliver. Reprinted by permission of Little, Brown & Company.

Dorothy Parker: "One Perfect Rose" copyright 1926, copyright renewed © 1954 by Dorothy Parker; "Résumé" copyright 1926, 1928, copyright renewed © 1954, 1956 by Dorothy Parker; "Symptom Recital" copyright 1926, copyright renewed © 1954 by Dorothy Parker from *The Portable Dorothy Parker* by Dorothy Parker, edited by Marion Meade. Used by permission of Viking Penguin, a division of Penguin Group (USA) Inc. Linda Pastan: "25th High School Reunion" copyright 1978, 1998 by Linda Pastan; "Prosody 101" copyright © 1985, 1998 by Linda Pastan; "The Obligation to Be Happy" copyright © 1998 by Linda Pastan; "What We Want" copyright © 1981, 1998 by Linda Pastan from *Carnival Evening: New and Selected Poems 1968–1998* by Linda Pastan. Used by permission of W.W. Norton & Company, Inc. Marge Piercy: Excerpt from "Cats like angels," "For strong women," "For the young who want to," "My mother's novel," and excerpt from "Right to life" from *The Moon Is Always Female* by Marge Piercy. Copyright © 1980 by Marge Piercy. Reprinted by permission of Alfred A. Knopf, a division of Random House, Inc. Excerpt from "Family values" from *Colors Passing Through Us: Poems* by Marge Piercy. Copyright © 2003 by Middlemarsh, Inc. Reprinted by permission of Alfred A. Knopf, a division of Random House, Inc. Excerpt from "The art of blessing the day" from *The Art of Blessing the Day* by Marge Piercy. Copyright ©1999 by Middlemarsh, Inc. Reprinted by permission of Alfred A. Knopf, a division of Random House, Inc. Sylvia Plath: "Daddy" and "Edge" from *Ariel* by Sylvia Plath. Copyright © 1963 by Ted Hughes. "Morning Song" from *Ariel* by Sylvia Plath. Copyright © 1961 by Ted Hughes. Reprinted by permission of HarperCollins Publishers.

Adrienne Rich: "I Am in Danger—Sir—." Copyright © 2002 by Adrienne Rich. Copyright © 1966 by W.W. Norton & Company, Inc.; Poem III of "Twenty-One Love Poems." Copyright © 2002 by Adrienne Rich. Copyright © 1978 by W.W. Norton & Company, Inc.; Poem XI of "Twenty-One Love Poems." Copyright © 2002 by Adrienne Rich. Copyright © 1978 by W.W. Norton & Company, Inc.; "For the Record." Copyright © 2002, 1986 by Adrienne Rich from *The Fact of a Doorframe: Selected Poems 1950–2001* by Adrienne Rich. Used by permission of the author and W.W. Norton & Company, Inc. Kay Ryan: "Ideal Audience," "Repulsive Theory," and "The Well or the Cup" from *The Niagara River* by Kay Ryan. Copyright © 2005 by Kay Ryan. Excerpt from "Blunt" from *Say Uncle* by Kay Ryan. Copyright © 2000 by Kay Ryan. Used by permission of Grove/Atlantic, Inc. Muriel Rukeyser: "More of a Corpse Than a Woman," "Myth," "Waiting for Icarus," and "What They Said" from *The Collected Poems of Muriel Rukeyser*, Edited by Janet E. Kaufman & Anne F. Herzog, University of Pittsburgh Press. Copyright © 2005 by Muriel Rukeyser. Reprinted by permission of International Creative Management, Inc.

Anne Sexton: "Housewife" and "The Truth the Dead Know" from *All My Pretty Ones* by Anne Sexton. Copyright © 1962 by Anne Sexton, renewed 1990 by Linda G. Sexton. Reprinted by permission of Houghton Mifflin Company. All rights reserved. Edith Sitwell: "Sir Beelzebub" and "Still Falls the Rain" from *Collected Poems* by Edith Sitwell. Copyright © 1930, 1957, 1993, 2006 by the Executors of FTS Sitwell. Reprinted by permission of David Higham Associates Limited. Stevie Smith: "Not Waving But Drowning" and "The Queen and the Young Princess," from *Collected Poems of Stevie Smith* by Stevie Smith. Copyright © 1972 by Stevie Smith. Reprinted by permission of New Directions Publishing Corp. Ruth Stone: "Getting to Know You" and "Train Ride" from *In the Next Galaxy* by Ruth Stone. Copyright © 2002 by Ruth Stone. Excerpt from "What Is a Poem?" from *In the Dark* by Ruth Stone. Copyright © 2004 by Ruth Stone. Reprinted with the permission of Copper Canyon Press, www.coppercanyonpress.org. Edna St. Vincent Millay: "First Fig," "I, being born a woman and distressed," and "What lips my lips have kissed" from *Collected Poems* by Edna St. Vincent Millay. Copyright © 1922, 1923, 1950, 1951 by Edna St. Vincent Millay and Norma Millay Ellis. Reprinted by permission of Elizabeth Barnett, Literary Executor, The Millay Society. May Swenson: "Neither Wanting More" from *The Complete Love Poems of May Swenson* by May Swenson. Copyright © 1991, 2003 by The Literary Estate of May Swenson. "Staring at the Sea on the Day of the Death of Another" from *Nature: Poems Old and New* by May Swenson. Copyright © 1994 by The Literary Estate of May Swenson. Reprinted by permission of Houghton Mifflin Company. All rights reserved. "Unconscious Came a Beauty" from *New and Selected Things Taking Place* by May Swenson. Copyright © 1978 by May Swenson. Reprinted with permission of The Literary Estate of May Swenson.

Mona Van Duyn: "In Bed with a Book," from *Near Changes* by Mona Van Duyn. Copyright © 1990 by Mona Van Duyn. Used by permission of Alfred A. Knopf, a division of Random House, Inc. "The Stream" and excerpt from "Toward a Definition of Marriage" from *Selected Poems* by Mona Van Duyn. Copyright © 2002 by Mona Van Duyn. Used by permission of Alfred A. Knopf, a division of Random House, Inc. Ellen Bryant Voigt: "Amaryllis" copyright © 1987, 2007 by Ellen Bryant Voigt; "Lesson," copyright © 2002, 2007 by Ellen Bryant Voigt and excerpt from "The Photograph" copyright © 1987, 2007 by Ellen Bryant Voigt from *Messenger: New and Selected Poems 1976–2006* by Ellen Bryant Voigt. Used by permission of W.W. Norton & Company, Inc.

Elinor Wylie: "Parting Gift" and "The Eagle and the Mole" by Elinor Wylie from *Selected Works of Elinor Wylie* edited by Evelyn Helmick Hively. Copyright © 2005 by The Kent State University Press. Reprinted with permission of The Kent State University Press. Judith Wright: "Bora Ring," "Five Senses," and "Woman to Child" from *A Human Pattern: Selected Poems* by Judith Wright. Copyright © 1996 by The Estate of Judith Wright. Reprinted by permission of ETT Imprint, Sydney. "Ishtar" from *Collected Poems* by Judith Wright. Copyright © 1971. Reprinted by permission of HarperCollins Publishers Australia.

INDEX OF AUTHORS AND TITLES

(bold figures indicate principal introductions to the authors' work)

INDEX OF TITLES

A NOTE ON THE EDITORS

Joseph Parisi joined *Poetry* magazine in 1976 and was its editor from 1983 to 2003, the longest tenure after that of the magazine's founder, Harriet Monroe. He also served as executive director of *Poetry*'s parent organization, the Modern Poetry Association (now the Poetry Foundation). His most recent books are *100 Essential Modern Poems* and, co-edited with Stephen Young, *Dear Editor: A History of* Poetry *in Letters*, *Between the Lines*, and *The* Poetry *Anthology, 1912–2002*. Mr. Parisi was born in Duluth, Minnesota, and received a Ph.D. in English from the University of Chicago. He was awarded a Guggenheim fellowship in 2000 and was elected a by-fellow of Churchill College, Cambridge, in 2002. He lives in Chicago.

Kathleen Welton is a thirty-year veteran of the publishing industry and is a member of the Academy of American Poets and the Poetry Society of America. Born in Santa Monica, California, she studied at Stanford University. She is director of Book Publishing at the American Bar Association and has also served as publisher of IDG Books and Dearborn Trade. She lives in Chicago.